GW00383374

Company Law

Seventh Edition

J. D. De Freitas LLB, LLM, MA, FABE, Solicitor
Senior Lecturer in Law
London South Bank University

Castlevale Limited, London

First Published by Castlevale Ltd., 1982
Second Edition 1989
Third Edition 1996
Fourth Edition 2004
Fifth Edition 2006
Sixth Edition 2009
Seventh Edition 2011

2 Saint Crispin House
2 Barclay Road
Croydon
Surrey CRO 1JN

Copyright by J.D. De Freitas 2011

ISBN 0 907235 01 8

This book is copyright and may not be reproduced in whole or in part (except for purposes of review) without the express permission in writing of the author.

To the memory of P.H. Daly

Contents

Preface

This book is intended as a concise but comprehensive textbook for students preparing for professional and other examinations in Company Law. The examination courses which include Company Law are too numerous to list, but this book will have relevance for all of them. In particular it will be useful to students preparing for the professional examinations of the Association of Chartered Certified Accountants, the Chartered Institute of Management Accountants, the Institute of Chartered Secretaries and Administrators; and to students preparing for law degrees.

The text is self-contained and although students should read as widely as they can (in particular the law periodicals such British Company Cases) to keep abreast with the changing nature of the subject, the student who masters it should have no difficulty in passing the examination.

Students should read each chapter once through, and then go over it again, this time making notes in a file or notebook. Research suggests that the act of writing and collating notes aids learning and recall. To assist students with examination preparation, the book includes a chapter on 'Examination Technique' and a selection of examination questions with suggested answers from professional examinations.

The author would like to thank the following professional bodies for permission to use their past examination questions:

> Association of Chartered Certified Accountants
> Chartered Institute of Management Accountants
> Institute of Chartered Secretaries and Administrators

In addition, thanks are due to Altan Kemal, senior partner of Alton & Co., for the chapters on 'Auditor' and 'Accounts'; to

Michelle Ramsammy, Alan Moore and John Sewter for their valuable contributions and comments on this edition; and to Bob Grewal, a former examiner in law with the Association of Chartered Certified Accountants, for the chapter on 'Examination Technique'. Finally, the author wishes to record his gratitude to London South Bank University for making available its research facilities for the production of this edition.

Jerry De Freitas
London South Bank University
January 2011

Chapter 1

Registered Companies

Introduction
The principal statute under which newly-formed companies are registered is the **Companies Act 2006**. This Act is supplemented by the **Companies Act 1985** under which most old companies are registered, and the **Companies (Audit, Investigations and Community Enterprise) Act 2004** which deals with auditing issues and introduces a new type of commercial company, the community interest company (**CIC**). These Acts collectively are referred to as the 'Companies Acts'. Other important pieces of legislation affecting registered companies are the **Insolvency Acts 1986 – 2000** which deal with corporate insolvency, the **Financial Services and Markets Act 2000** which regulates the raising of corporate finance, and the **Enterprise Act 2002**. Unless otherwise stated, references to sections in the text will be to the **Companies Act 2006**. The provisions of the Companies Acts are administered by the Department for Business, Innovation and Skills (BIS).

Nature of a Company
A company is an association of persons incorporated under the Companies Act. 'Incorporated' means that the association becomes a legal entity, or person, distinct from its owners. Frequently, the purpose of the company will be to trade at a gain for its owners (as with companies limited by shares); but occasionally, the purpose will be educational, charitable, or some other non-profit making purpose (as with companies limited by guarantee). A company's constitution is contained in

articles of association and resolutions and agreements affecting the company's constitution; but there are also certain other documents of constitutional importance such as the company's certificate of incorporation which indicates whether the company is a public or a private company, and a statement of capital (or statement of guarantee for a company limited by guarantee).

A company has two controlling elements: members and directors. The members (also called shareholders, if the company has a share capital) own the company and take decisions by passing resolutions. The Companies Act identifies two types of resolution which members may pass. There is the **ordinary resolution**, which is a resolution passed by a simple majority (50% +1) of the votes cast by members entitled to vote. Then, there is the **special resolution**, which requires a seventy five per cent majority of the votes cast. If company legislation does not state which type of resolution members may use to perform an act, members may perform that act by passing an ordinary resolution, unless the Act permits the company's own articles to require the company to obtain a higher majority for taking decisions. Resolutions are passed at general meetings; but if the company is a private company it may pass resolutions outside the framework of a general meeting by using a written resolution, whereby members can take decisions, such as from their homes, by signing a written resolution sent to them by the directors. The Companies Act specifically reserves certain matters which can only be dealt with by decisions of the members such as alteration of the company's capital, alteration of the company's constitution and decisions to wind up the company voluntarily. The directors are appointed by the members and are given the task and powers to carry on the day to day administration of the company. The directors take notice and act on resolutions passed by the members **(art.3)**. However, they need not comply with any resolution if it involves them doing something which is unlawful or contrary to their general duties of directors to the company.

Doctrine of Incorporation

Section 7 of the Companies Act provides that any one or more persons associated for a lawful purpose may, by subscribing their names to a memorandum of association and complying with the requirements of the Companies Act in respect of registration, form an incorporated company. A company is incorporated at the time of registration **(s.16)**; and on incorporation, it becomes a legal entity distinct from its members and directors, enjoying all the attributes of corporate status. This is so even if the company is 100% owned and managed by one member. This concept of corporate personality is referred to as the **Doctrine of Incorporation.** The company will have a name; it may own and dispose of its property and may enter into contracts with anyone including any of its members or its directors. In relation to such activities, the company itself is primarily liable; not its members or its directors. The company may have a common seal with its name engraved on it so that legal documents such as written contracts may be signed on its behalf. However, there is no legal requirement to have a common seal since documents signed by a director and the secretary or by two directors and expressed (no particular form of words is necessary) to be executed by the company will have the same effect as if they were under the company's common seal. A company which has a common seal also may have an official seal to enter into transactions outside the United Kingdom and for sealing securities (e.g., share certificates) issued by the company. Where the official seal is intended for use abroad, the company may, by writing under its common seal, authorise any person to affix the

official seal to any deed or other document to which the
company is a party **(s. 49)**.

Illustrations of the Doctrine

In **Salomon v Salomon & Co. Ltd. (1897)**, S, a sole trader for
some 30 years, decided in 1892 to convert his boot business
into a limited company. He formed a company and transferred
the business as a going concern to it. He minimised the risks to
the assets transferred to the company by requiring the company
to give him, as the price for the assets, fully paid shares and a
debenture secured by a floating charge on the company's
assets. By having shares **S** owned the company with other
shareholders; and by having a secured debenture (a debenture
is a document evidencing a loan and if it is secured it has to be
repaid before unsecured debts) he was also a creditor of the
company. Thus, if the company should fail he would only lose
his share capital since debentures have to be repaid before
shareholders' capital. **S** held all of the company's 20,007
shares except for 6 shares which were held by his wife and five
children; and he appointed himself managing director. Thirteen
months later the company went into insolvent liquidation and it
was discovered that the assets were only sufficient to discharge
S's debenture and that there was nothing left for the unsecured
creditors. The unsecured creditors challenged the validity of
S's debenture on grounds that (i) the company was acting as an
agent or alias of **S** and that **S** as principal had to indemnify the
company's creditors personally and (ii) **S** had overvalued his
business intentionally when he sold it to the company. The
House of Lords rejected both arguments and laid down the
following principles: (a) once a company is incorporated
legally it has to be treated like any other independent person,
with rights and liabilities appropriate to itself (*per* Lord
Halsbury LC); (b) though it may be that after incorporation the

business is precisely the same as it was before, the same persons are managers and the same hands receive the profits, a company is not in law the agent of its subscribers or trustee for them (*per* Lord Macnaghten); (c) where a promoter sells property to a company he has set up no one can complain that the price is extravagant if there is a full and frank disclosure of the transaction to the members of the company.

In **Macaura v Northern Assurance Co. (1952)**, **M**, the owner of a timber estate, insured against fire and later assigned the whole of the timber to a one-man company owned by him and his nominees. He forgot to assign the insurance policy to the company and to obtain the necessary consent of the insurers. When the timber was destroyed by fire the insurers refused to pay, on the ground that **M** did not have an insurable interest in the timber (as insurance law requires). The House of Lords held that even though **M** owned the company by virtue of his shareholding, the company was in law a separate person from its members and owned the timber in its own right. So **M** had no insurable interest in the timber.

In **Foss v Harbottle (1843)**, two shareholders brought an action on behalf of a company against its directors who, as promoters, had sold property to the company at an undisclosed profit. The action was dismissed by Vice Chancellor Wigram, who refused to depart from the rule that required that 'the corporation should sue in its own name and its corporate character.' Here, the action should have been brought by the general meeting, not by individual shareholders.

Lifting the Veil
The principles applied in **Salomon** and the other foregoing cases show the reluctance of the courts to ignore the separate

personality of a company from its members. In this way, there is a '*veil*' (i.e., an imaginary curtain) shielding the people who own the company (i.e., the members) and the people who manage the company (i.e., the directors) from the company. Thus, when members of the public deal with the business they are dealing with the company as a separate person, and not with its members or its directors. Exceptions are made where the law will 'lift' the corporate veil by "piercing" it (i.e., disregarding the corporate status in the sense of treating the rights or liabilities or activities of the company as the rights or liabilities or activities of its members or directors), by "peeking" it (i.e., lifting and looking behind the corporate veil for limited purposes and then replacing it), or by "extending" it (i.e., treating a number of companies as a single unit).

Company legislation has laid down instances where the corporate veil will be lifted and the courts have occasionally done the same; but with the latter a clear policy for intervention is not easily discernible.

Veil lifting by company legislation includes:

(a) **Fraudulent Trading:** Where in the course of winding up an insolvent company, it appears that the company's business was being carried on with the intention of defrauding its creditors, or for any fraudulent purpose, then any person who knew of this and was a party to the fraud may be made personally liable by the courts for all or any of the company's debts and liabilities **(s. 213 IA)**. For a person to be made liable for fraudulent trading there must be 'actual dishonesty' (per Maugham J in **Re Patrick and Lyon Ltd. (1933)**); and this is often difficult to prove because the courts have always insisted on a strict standard of proof.

(b) Wrongful Trading: Where in the course of winding up an insolvent company, the liquidator finds that a director (including a former director) or shadow director has been guilty of wrongful trading he may apply to the courts for an order that the wrongdoer should contribute towards the company's assets **(s.214 IA)**. Wrongful trading occurs where a director continues to trade on behalf of the company beyond a period when a reasonable person would have reached the conclusion that there was no possibility of the company surviving. This section catches the 'honest but incompetent director'. Therefore if a director is reckless as to the company's financial position or holds an unreasonable belief that 'things could only get better' and the company subsequently goes into insolvent liquidation, he would incur liability under the section. (see Chapter 17).
Unlike fraudulent trading, wrongful trading does not impose liability on shareholders unless they are shadow directors.

(c) Group Accounts: Where a company has subsidiaries, then for accounting purposes, the veil is extended to conceal the separate identity of the subsidiaries; and the parent or holding company will have to prepare group accounts (in addition to individual accounts) to reflect the financial position of the group **(s. 399)**. Group accounts normally take the form of a consolidated balance sheet and a consolidated profit and loss account. In general, these combine the information contained the separate balance sheet and profit and loss accounts of the holding company and the subsidiaries, but with any adjustments which the directors of the holding company think necessary (e.g., writing off inter-company debts). Group Accounts are dealt with more fully in Chapter 14.

(d) Trading without a certificate to trade: Where a public company commences to trade or exercises any of its borrowing powers without first obtaining a trading certificate, and fails to meet its obligations under the transaction within twenty one days from being called to do so, the directors of the company will be jointly and severally liable to indemnify the third party **(s. 767)**.

Veil lifting by the courts includes:
 (e) Fraud: Where the company is a 'sham' (i.e., it was set up by a person to avoid an existing legal obligation imposed on him or to avoid such rights of relief against him as a third party already has), the courts will pierce the veil of incorporation, thus ignoring the company's corporate identity, and make orders against the company for the actions of its shareholders. In **Gildford Motors Ltd v Horne (1933)**, a former director of the claimant company had bound himself by a restraint of trade clause preventing him from competing with the company after his employment with the company terminated. He wanted to start up his own business; so he left the claimant company and formed a new company (of which his wife and an employee were the sole directors and shareholders) for the purpose of enabling him to get round the restraint of trade. He then purported to work for the new company. The court granted an injunction against the company he formed from carrying on the business because the company was 'a mere cloak or sham' in an attempt to enable the former director to evade limitations imposed on his conduct by law.

Similarly, in **Re Bugle Press Ltd (1960)**, two persons holding 90% of the shares in their company wanted to purchase the remaining shares held by the minority shareholder. The minority shareholder refused to sell. The majority shareholders then formed a new company which then attempted to invoke what is now section 979 of the Companies Act 2006 to purchase the shares compulsorily. Under this section if a company makes an offer to members of another company to purchase their shares, then if the offer is accepted by the holders of not less that 90% of the shares in the offeree company, the offeror company may purchase compulsorily the remaining shares. Not surprisingly, the court refused to treat the new company as a separate legal entity, holding that it was in fact the majority shareholders attempting to commit a fraud on the minority shareholder.

In **Re H (Restraint Order: Realisable Property) (1996)**, the defendants involved in an alleged exercise fraud, transferred assets to two companies which they controlled. The Court of Appeal rejected the argument that the assets of the companies and those of the defendants were separate and upheld an order made against the assets of the two companies.

The courts will not pierce the veil of incorporation where the obligation is imposed on the company in the first place or where the company is liable on a judgement and its assets are dissipated by its controllers in order to prevent the company from having to pay any damages which may be awarded against it. In **Ord v Belhaven Pubs Ltd (1998)**, Ord took a lease of a pub from the defendant company as a result of untrue statements by the latter as to the pub's profitability. By the time the falsity came to light, the defendant company had ceased trading and most of its assets had been transferred by its holding company to other members of the group in a group reconstruction. Ord applied for leave to transfer the action from the defendant company to its holding company. However, the Court of Appeal refused and upheld the principle of separate personality of a company from its members and directors. In **Yukong Line Ltd v Rendsburg Investments Corp (1998)**, the company was in breach of a charterparty which its controller had signed on its behalf. In order to avoid a possible judgement which might be made against it, the company's controller transferred the company's assets to a second company which he also controlled. The judge refused to regard the controller and the company as one and the same person or to make the second company liable. The judge concluded that in such cases, the liquidator of the company should take action under the Insolvency Acts against the controller for misuse of the company's assets.

(f) Enemy Character: Where the personal qualities of a company's shareholders or those controlling it are crucial to determine its character, then public interest may require the courts to peek the veil of incorporation (e.g., to see whether the company is under the control of alien enemies in war time, as in **Daimler Co. Ltd. v Continental Tyre & Rubber Co. Ltd. (1916)**).

(g) Group Enterprise: As seen earlier, section 399 treats a group as a single unit for accounting purposes; but it gives no lead to the courts about when they are to do the same. Nevertheless, the courts have used the same notion in certain cases. In **Smith, Stone and Knight Ltd. v Birmingham Corp (1939)**, the courts held that a subsidiary carrying on a waste paper business was not carrying on the business on its own account but as agent of its holding company because the legal ownership of the business as well as the premises on which the business was carried on was not transferred to the subsidiary. The finding was important because it enabled the holding company to obtain compensation under what is now the Land Compensation Act 1961 for injury to business when the land on which business was carried on was subject to a compulsory purchase order. Compensation for disturbance of business was only available if the site was owner/occupied. If the **Salomon** principle was to apply, the holding company would not have been able to claim compensation because, although it owned the business and the land, the business was being carried on by another company, albeit its subsidiary; and the subsidiary company could not claim the compensation since it did not own the land. In **DHN Food Distributors Ltd v Tower Hamlet London Borough Council (1976)**, the Court of Appeal treated two companies in a group as a single unit (even though there was no agency relationship between them) because they were involved in carrying on what amounted to a single business, rather than separate businesses. In the **DHN** case, a holding company carried on business from premises owned by a subsidiary. The subsidiary did not carry on any business and the two companies had the same directors. The court held the two companies to be a single 'economic unit' so that when the local council compulsorily purchases the premises, it had to pay compensation for both the site and for disturbance of the business (the council had argued that because the subsidiary carried on no business on the site the council was not obliged to pay compensation for disturbance of a business).

The **DHN** case was not followed in **Woolfson v Strathclyde Regional Council (1978)** where, on similar facts, the House of Lords upheld a decision of the Scottish judges who refused to lift the veil of incorporation. The Court of Appeal in **Adams v Cape Industries plc (1900)** endorsed the **Woolfson**'s case reluctance to follow **DHN**. In **Adams**, the US courts awarded judgement against a US subsidiary of an English holding company; with the result that the subsidiary was forced into insolvent liquidation. The beneficiaries of the judgement tried to enforce the judgement in the English courts against the English holding company by arguing that the English holding company was 'present' in the United States through its local subsidiary and was therefore liable on the US judgement. The English courts refused to treat the English holding company and its wholly owned US subsidiary as a single 'economic entity', and repeated that the veil of incorporation was sacrosanct and should only be lifted in very exceptional circumstances and that this was not one of those circumstances.

Current judicial attitude to dismiss the 'economic entity' approach as a means of lifting the veil of incorporation, suggests that with group enterprise, the courts will only extend the veil and treat the group (or individual members of the group) as a single unit if an agency relationship is established or if subjective fraud by its controllers is proved.

(h) Quasi-partnership: Where a director has shares in the company and he is removed from office by the members before his term of office expires he may apply to the courts for a winding up order of the company on the 'just and equitable' ground under section 122(1)(g) of the Insolvency Act. The courts will then peek the veil of incorporation to see whether the company is in essence a quasi-partnership (**Ebrahimi v Westbourne Galleries Ltd (1973)**).

Advantages of Incorporation

To appreciate the benefits of running a new business through a company or converting an existing business into a company, a company should be contrasted with an unincorporated association such as an unlimited liability partnership firm which is regulated by the Partnership Act 1890 (partnership firms (LLPs) which are incorporated under the Limited Liability Partnership Act 2000 are legal persons and are similar to private limited companies in most respects except that their profits are subject to income tax rather than corporation tax provisions; and they cannot be formed for a non-commercial purpose). Some of these benefits have already been mentioned. Thus, a company may own and dispose of it assets, it may enter into contracts on its own behalf and is liable for its own debts. Among other benefits are:

(a) Management: The management of a company is vested in a board of directors, but the management of a partnership firm (including a LLP) is vested in the partners. A company's structure is therefore particularly useful to persons who want to invest in a business venture without having to bother too much about its day-to-day activities.

(b) Transfer of Interest: A member may transfer his shares in his company freely unless the articles state other. A partner (including a member of a LLP) needs the consent of his fellow partners before he can transfer his interest with a view to introducing a new partner into the firm.

(c) Raising Finance: Subject to section 755 which prohibits public offers by private companies limited by shares, it is easier for a company than for a partnership to raise capital. A company may invite a wider range of investors to subscribe or purchase its shares and debentures. A company can also borrow money through a provision called a floating charge. A floating charge is a charge on a *class* of assets (as opposed to specific assets) including present and future stock-in-trade, and is a form of security peculiar to companies. Partnership firms which are not legal persons are unable to use this form of security because of the Bills of Sale Acts 1878 and 1882. These Acts require the registration of charges of chattels with a detailed description of the chattels concerned where an attempt is made to transfer a proprietary interest in them, though retaining their possession. As a floating charge covers future assets, an unlimited liability partnership firm will be unable to describe the chattels with sufficient certainty for registration purposes. Charges created by companies are excluded from the Bills of Sale Acts **(s. 17 Bills of Sale Act 1882)**.

(d) Perpetual Existence: Even though the membership of a company may change from time to time, the company's identity as a separate person is not affected. Thus, if the only two members of the company are killed in a road accident and their personal representatives fail to register themselves as members, the company continues to exist even though it has no member left **(Re Tedman (Noel) Holdings Property Ltd. (1967))**. An unlimited liability partnership firm is automatically dissolved when the existing partners change.

(e) Taxation: A company is subject to a standard rate of corporation tax. Moreover, corporation tax rules regarding expenses are more generous to the taxpayer. For example, directors' salary may be deducted from gross profits before such profits are taxed. All partnership firms (whether they are legal persons or not) are subject to income tax at a progressively increasing rate, and any deduction of partnership salary from gross profits is treated as an appropriation of profits.

(f) Limited Liability: The liability of a member of a company may be limited to any amount unpaid on the nominal value of his shares or the amount guaranteed by him in the registration documents. The liability of a partner of an unlimited liability partnership firm is unlimited; so he runs the risk of losing his personal assets.

Disadvantages of Incorporation
The main disadvantages are formalities, expense, and publicity. Apart from the documents to be filed at Companies Registry before the Registrar will register a business as a company, a company is subject to statutory regulation on the way it is run. Its accounts have to be audited by a statutory auditor (unless it

is an audit exempt private company). As the price of conferring the privilege of limited liability on its members, the law requires all major company documents including its annual financial statements to be filed at the Registry and open to public inspection for a fee. In addition, a company suffers from the following drawbacks:

(a) Distributions: A limited company cannot make a distribution to its members unless there are profits available for distribution **(s.830)**. The effect of this provision is that a company must make good its accumulated realised losses before it can pay a dividend to its members. A partnership firm does not suffer from such restriction.

(b) Agency: Being an artificial person, a company needs human agents to act on its behalf. There are complex rules governing the liability of a company for the acts of its agents. Normally, a company will be liable in contract and tort on the basis of agency and vicarious liability. Also, as documents which require authentication by a company can become authenticated if signed by an authorised officer of the company or if stamped with the company's common seal **(s.43)**, the company can also become liable in this way. However, where the law requires that personal fault (and knowledge of the company) be present (as would be the case in criminal law and tort), the courts sometimes treat the directors as organs of the company managing the enterprise. They then become the company's motive force, its *alter ego* (second self), and not just its delegates. Their action will be the company's action, and their fault will be the company's fault **(Lennards Carrying Co. v Asiatic Petroleum Co. Ltd. (1915)**. Where the directors delegate control and management of some part of the business to others, with discretionary powers, the latter will also be the company's *alter ego*. A person identified as the directing mind of the company, who is guilty of manslaughter as a result of an act arising out of the business' activities, will make the company itself guilty of corporate manslaughter **(Corporate Manslaughter and Corporate Homicide Act 2007)**.

(c) Taxation: If a company's proprietor pays himself a salary, Class 1 National Insurance contributions are payable both by the proprietor as employee and by the company as employer. This is in contrast to a partnership business where only the proprietor is liable to pay National Insurance contributions.

Classification of Registered Companies

The principal classification of registered companies is between public and private companies. A secondary classification is between limited and unlimited. A public company must always have a share capital and be limited. A private company can be limited by shares or by guarantee, or it can be unlimited.

Public Companies
Section 4 defines a public company as a company limited by shares whose certificate of incorporation states that it is a public company. To obtain this certificate the company must be properly registered or re-registered as a public company.
The main features of a public company are that its name ends with the words '*public limited company*' or the abbreviation '*plc*' or the Welsh equivalent '*cc*' rather than just the word '*limited*', its issued capital is not less than the statutory minimum (currently set at £50,000 or 65,600 in euros), and its certificate of incorporation (i.e., registration) states that it is a public company. The principal inducement for registering (or re-registering) as a public company is that it alone can issue its

securities (shares and debentures) to the public and obtain a stock exchange listing for the securities.

Private Companies

Section 4 states that a private company is 'any company which is not a public company'. This type of company is most suitable for small businesses. The statutory provisions regulating private companies are not as stringent as those affecting a public company, especially those provisions relating to capital, payment for shares and dividend.

A practical advantage of running a business through a private company rather than a public company is that the company, and thus the business, remains under the control of the family or 'partners'. This is usually achieved by restricting the right of shareholders to transfer their shares in the company to outsiders; and it may be done by one of two methods:

(a) **Pre-emption clause**: this is a clause inserted in the articles requiring a member who wishes to sell his shares to offer the shares first to the existing members or to the company at a fair price determined in accordance with the articles (e.g., by valuation of the directors or auditors) before they can be passed on to outsiders. The company can purchase the shares as long as its articles do not prohibit it from doing so and it satisfies the requirements in section 690 (see Chapter 8).

A member who transfers his share in breach of a pre-emption clause is not entitled to have the transfer registered in the register of members, and the company can make an application to the courts to have the transfer set aside. In **Lyle & Scott v Scott's Trustees (1959)**, the court set aside a contract by the defendants, who in breach of a pre-emption clause, had transferred their shares to an outsider with the intention that he should delay applying for registration and giving him their proxies so that he could obtain control of the company.

(b) **Directors Discretion clause**: this is a clause inserted in the articles giving the directors discretion to refuse to register a transfer. The discretion may be *absolute* where the directors may refuse to register a transfer for whatever reason or it may be *qualified* where the directors can only refuse to register a transfer on certain grounds specified in the articles. In either case the discretion against registration of a transfer must be exercised formally and not later than two months after an application is made for registration (see Chapter 7).

Differences between a Public and a Private Company
(1) A public company may raise finance by inviting the public to subscribe for its shares and debentures.
A private company is prohibited from offering its securities with a view to their ultimate distribution to the public **(s.755)**.

(2) A public company cannot commence business or exercise any of its borrowing powers without first obtaining a certificate (commonly called '**trading certificate**') from the Registrar of Companies permitting it to trade **(s.761)**. An application for a certificate must state that the nominal value of the company's allotted share capital is not less than the authorised minimum, £50,000 or 65,600 in euros, (shares allotted under an employee share scheme cannot be counted towards this minimum capital unless at least one quarter of the nominal value and the whole of any premium payable on the shares is paid up); specify the amount or estimated amount of the company's preliminary expenses; and any amount or benefit paid or given to the promoter and the consideration he has paid for it. The application must be accompanied by a statement of compliance signed by a director or the company secretary indicating that the company has met the requirements for a certificate under section 761. The trading certificate is conclusive evidence that the company is entitled to do business and exercise its

borrowing powers from the date specified in the certificate **(s.761 (4))**.

For failure to obtain a trading certificate two consequences may result. First, both the company and any officer in default will be guilty of a criminal offence **(s.767 (1))**, although the validity of any transaction entered into by the company with a third party is not affected. Secondly, the company may be wound up compulsorily by the courts if a trading certificate is not obtained within one year of its incorporation **(s.122 (1) (b) Insolvency Act 1986)**.

A private company does not have to obtain a trading certificate and may commence trading as soon as it is incorporated.

(3) A public company cannot allot its shares for services **(s. 585)**; and it can only allot shares for assets (e.g., a van) if there is a proper valuation of the assets by an independent expert qualified to be the company's auditor and a valuation report is made to the company within six months prior to the allotment **(s. 593)**.

A private company is not affected by such rules.

(4) A public company must satisfy both the *realised profits test* and the *net assets test* before it can distribute its profits to its members **(ss. 830 and 831)**. The combined effect of these tests means that a public company must make good both its accumulated realised and unrealised losses before it can use its realised profits to pay a dividend to its shareholders.

A private company need only satisfy the *realised profits test* (see Chapter 8).

(5) A public company must convene an extraordinary general meeting for the members to consider its future in the event of it suffering a serious loss of capital **(s. 656)**. Serious capital loss

occurs where the company's net assets fall to half or less of its called up share capital.

A private company, in similar circumstances, does not have to do the same.

(6) A public company must prepare for its members full accounts which comply with prescribed formats set out in the Companies Act; and it must file a copy of those accounts at Companies Registry. Moreover, its accounts must be audited by accountants recognised by the Department for Business, Innovation and Skills (**BIS**) for this purpose.

A private company, if qualified by its size, need only prepare and file a modified version of those accounts and may be exempted from having its accounts audited (see Chapter 14).

(7) A public company must have at least two directors **(s.154 (2))**, and their appointments must be voted on separately **(s.160)**.

A private company needs only one director **(s. 154 (1))**; and even if it wishes to have two or more directors their appointments may be made *en bloc* by a single resolution.

(8) An individual can only be appointed secretary of a public company if he is suitably qualified (e.g., an accountant from one of the chartered bodies, a lawyer or a chartered secretary) and has the necessary knowledge and experience **(s.273)**.

A private company is not required by law to have a company secretary; but if it chooses to have one, any individual can be appointed company secretary (see Chapter 12).

(9) Members of a public company take decisions by resolution passed only at a properly constituted general meeting of members (or by unanimous consent at common law).

Members of a private company can take decisions by resolution passed either at a meeting of the members or by *written resolution*

Companies Limited by Shares

These are by far the largest number of registered companies. Section 545 provides, in effect, that a company limited by shares is a company whose constitution provides it with power to raise share capital. With such companies, the potential liability of each member, in the event of the company being unable to pay its debts, is limited to any amount unpaid on his shares. Thus, the company's share capital must always be broken down into shares of a fixed amount (called *nominal* or *par* value of the shares); and subject to section 213 of the Insolvency Act, this amount will determine the maximum statutory liability of each member to the company **(Hansraj Gupta v Asthana (1932))**. Where the shares are issued for a sum in excess of their nominal value (a premium), the member incurs a contractual liability to pay the excess sum as well **(Niemann v Smedley (1973))**. The privilege of limited liability is a main reason for running a business as a limited company.

This type of company enables its corporators to raise initial working capital through shares taken up by the subscribers to its memorandum and through shares allotted to others for cash or non-cash assets.

Companies Limited by Guarantee

Here, the liability of members is limited not by reference to shares, since the company has no share capital, but by the amount guaranteed in the statement of guarantee filed with the application for registration of the company. The liability will attach to members only in the event of a winding up of the company. A member is liable only to contribute to the assets of the company if the company is wound up during the time he is a member or within one year of him ceasing to the a member.

This type of company is particularly useful where initial working capital is insignificant and can be raised from fees and donations, such as when the company is formed for an educational purpose (e.g., publicly-funded universities). The Companies Act 2006 provides exemption to charities from having to use 'limited' after their name; and it allows old companies which were exempted under the Companies Act 1985 to keep their exemption as long as they satisfy certain conditions under sections 61 and 62 of the 2006 Act. The Companies Registrar also has power under section 60 to exempt other new companies limited by guarantee from displaying 'limited' in their name. New companies limited by guarantee can distribute their profits to members, but not to other persons **(s.37)**; although they will then lose their exemption from the Registrar to dispense with 'limited' in their name. Since a company limited by guarantee is formed for a charitable or other non-commercial purpose, it will obtain useful tax concessions. Only private companies may be limited by guarantee. The Secretary of State has provided model articles for private companies limited by guarantee which do not register their own articles.

Listed Companies

These are public companies whose securities are quoted on a regulated exchange. As public companies require a higher level of capital than private companies, a listed company is provided with facilities in a designated market to raise its long-term finance.

Like all other registered companies which are regulated by statute, a listed company is also subject to statutory regulation; but in addition, it is subject to extra-legal structural controls on the board of directors to ensure transparency and accountability by the directors to the shareholders. The system by which listed companies are directed and controlled is called 'corporate Governance'. The current extra-legal rules on corporate governance are contained in the Revised Combined Code of Corporate Governance 2003 which is the responsibility of the Financial Reporting Council. The revised Code sets out principles of good corporate governance and provisions of good practice to ensure that these principles are achieved. These principles of good practice will be dealt in Chapter 16. A listed company must disclose in its annual report and accounts how it is complying (or explain why it is not complying) with the Code. A listed company must ensure that its articles comply with the relevant listing requirements and best practice.

Single-Member Companies.
A limited company (public or private) can be registered as a single-member company by one person stating his name and address in, and subscribing the memorandum. In such a case, the register of members must state the name and address of the sole member and include a statement that the company has only one member **(s.123)**. A company which is registered with at least two members will also become a single-member company if the number of its members falls to one; but where this happens, it must be recorded in the register of members at the side of the name and address of the remaining member and the date when the reduction occurred. If the membership of the company is increased from one to two or more members, the register of members must state, with the name and address of the person who was formerly the sole member, when this event occurred. For breach of this section, there will be a default fine on the company and its officers.

The sole member can act as the company's director and as its secretary; but if the company is a public company any provision which requires or authorises a matter to be done by both a director and secretary of the company cannot be satisfied if done by the same person in both capacity **(s.28)**. Where a single member is the company's sole director and he enters into an unwritten contract (other than a contract in the ordinary course of the company's business) with the company, the contract must be recorded in writing otherwise there will be a default fine on the company's officers **(s.231)**. The single member can exercise all the powers of the general meeting; but if he makes a decision which may be taken only in general meeting (e.g., the removal of the auditor before his term of office expires) that decision must be recorded in writing. Records of decisions of a sole member must be kept for a minimum of 10 years; otherwise there is a penalty on every officer for non-compliance.

Unlimited Companies
This type of company is not popular, since members will be personally liable to the creditors for the company's unsatisfied debts. However, the company enjoys all the other privileges of incorporation. In addition, if it has a share capital (necessary for dividends and voting rights) the shares may be issued at no par value, and no capital duty is payable. Moreover, there is no need to annexe to its annual returns certified copies of the company's balance sheet and profit and loss account, or copies of its directors' and auditors' reports. The company's affairs are therefore kept secret from the public. However, it still has to prepare audited accounts; and the accounts must still be approved by the members. An unlimited company does not have to hold an Annual General Meeting and may transact business by use of the written resolution procedure. An unlimited company must file its own articles on registration.
This type of company is particularly useful for an investment company, since capital may be returned to members without any legal restrictions.

Overseas Companies. This type of company is incorporated abroad but it has an establishment (a place of business or a branch) in the United Kingdom. Within one month of having an establishment in the United Kingdom, it must register with the Registrar of Companies. It must file a copy of its constitution, particulars of its directors and secretary, and the name and address of every person resident in the United Kingdom who is authorised to accept service of legal documents and communications on its behalf. These documents must be kept up to date. Moreover, its name and country of incorporation must be stated on its business premises and stationeries, and copies of its accounts prepared in accordance with the law governing its parent company must be filed at Companies Registry.

English company legislation restricts the use of company names by overseas companies; and where such companies issue a prospectus they must comply with the provisions of the Financial Services and Markets Act 2000.

Communities Interest Companies (CICs). This type of commercial company was introduced by the Companies (Audit, Investigations and Community Enterprise) Act 2004 and the Community Interest Company Regulations 2005 for persons wanting to establish social enterprises for the purpose of benefiting the community as a whole or a section of the community. It can be run with a view to make a profit (contrast a charity which is not able to generate profits); but its assets cannot be distributed to directors or members and must be used for the community purposes for which it was formed or must be transferred to another similar company or a charity. A community interest company can be a public company (CIPLC) or a private company limited by shares or by guarantee (CIC). It is subject to the same provisions of the Companies Acts as other registered companies; but, in addition, it has to comply with the CICs' provisions of the Enterprise Act such as having to file at Companies Registry an annual community interest report with its accounts. The report will show how the objects of the company are being achieved. The Office of the Regulator of Community Interest Companies which is located at Companies Registry oversees community interest companies.

Old Companies. This type of company comes within the category of companies which were registered under previous Companies Acts (Companies Acts 1948 and 1985). Such companies were required to provide a lot more information in their memorandum of association than is required for new companies registered under the Companies Act 2006. For example, their memorandum had to state what activities (objects) they intended to pursue, and they were confined to those activities; and if they intended to raise money by selling 'shares' in the business, the maximum amount of capital which they were authorised to issue (the authorised capital). The authorised capital acted as a ceiling on the number of shares the company could issue. The Companies Act 2006 provides that such information will now be treated as if they were in the articles of old companies; so that such companies will continue to be bound by such provisions until they amend their articles. Moreover, old companies which used the model statutory articles (amended Table A articles) will continue to be bound by them until they alter their articles by special resolution.

Chapter 2

Company Formation

Registration of New Companies

In order to bring a company into existence it is necessary to comply with the procedure which has been established by BIS under the Companies Act 2006. This procedure is outlined below and is broadly applicable to both public and private companies. Any differences are made clear by the text. While considerable changes have been enacted to differentiate between them, the normal form of registration continues to be that of a private company.

The documents to be signed and filed at Companies Registry (a company can also be formed on-line), together with the registration fees, in order to register a company are:

(1) Memorandum of Association
(2) An application for registration
(3) Articles of Association, if necessary
(4) Statement of capital and initial shareholdings, if relevant
(5) Statement of guarantee, if relevant
(6) Statement of officers
(7) Statement of compliance

(1) Memorandum of Association. The individuals (it could be one individual only) who wish to form the company must subscribe (write) their names to this document to show that they wish to form a company and that they agree to become its members and, if the company is to be limited by shares, they must indicate that they are willing to take at least one share each in the company. The subscribers become members when the company is registered, and not when their names are entered in the register of members. The memorandum cannot be altered once it is registered.

(2) An Application for Registration. This document must state (a) the company's proposed name; (b) whether the company's registered office will be located in England and Wales (or Wales), Scotland or Northern Ireland; (c) whether the liability of the company's members will be limited, and if so, whether it will be limited by shares or by guarantee; and (d) whether the company is to be a private or a public company.

(a) The Company's Name
A company is an artificial person created by law and so it has to be identified and distinguished from other companies. This purpose is satisfied by the requirement that the company should have a name. The name will be chosen by the person setting up the company (i.e., the company's promoter); but his freedom of choice is limited by three factors, namely, the Registrar's sanction, the company names adjudicators' sanction and a passing-off action.

(i) **Registrar's sanction**. The Registrar of Companies is under a statutory duty to refuse to register the company in the following cases: if the last word of the name does not end in '*limited*', or '*public limited company*' or '*unlimited*' (or their abbreviations) to indicate to the public the type of company they are dealing with **(ss.58, 59 CA** and the **(Companies (Company and Business Names) (Miscellaneous Provisions)**

Regulations 2009); or if the name is offensive to the public or is a criminal offence **(s.53)**; or if the name gives the impression that the company is connected in any way with Her Majesty's Government or any local authority **(s.54)**; or if the name is specified by the Secretary of State as requiring approval from him before it can be used and such permission has not been obtained **(s.55)**; or if the name includes symbols prohibited by the Secretary of State **(s.57)**; or if the name is the same as one appearing in an index of names kept at Companies Registry **(s.66 CA)**.

(ii) **Company names adjudicators' sanction**. If the new company's registered name interferes with a name in which a person has goodwill ('goodwill' includes reputation of any description), or is so similar to such a name that its use in the UK would be likely to mislead the public in believing a connection between the company and that person, that person may lodge an objection with a company names adjudicator (also known as 'Company Names Tribunal' and based at the UK Intellectual Property Office) to prevent the new company from using the name **(s.69)**. Independent company names adjudicators are appointed by the Secretary of State under a power given to him by the Companies Act to deal with complaints that a company's registered name is similar to a name in which another person has goodwill **(s.70)**. There is a presumption that the new company's name was adopted lawfully if (i) the name was registered before the start of the activities on which the objector relies to show goodwill; or (ii) the company is operating under the name, or is proposing to do so and has already incurred substantial start-up costs in preparation, or was formerly operating under the name and is now dormant; or (iii) the company's business is to set up off-the-shelf companies for sale and it had given the offending name to an off-the-shelf company which is available for sale to the objector on standard terms of its business. The presumption is rebutted if the objector can show that the respondent company had chosen the offending name with the principal intention of seeking money (or other value) from the objector or to prevent him from registering the name. An objection will also be dismissed if (iv) the name was adopted in good faith; or (v) the interests of the objector are not adversely affected to any significant extent **(s.69)**.

The company names adjudicator may dismiss an objection or uphold it. If the objection is upheld, the adjudicator will make an order requiring the respondent company to change its name by a specific date (unless an appeal is made to the High Court to overturn the adjudicator's decision); and if the company fails to comply, the adjudicator can choose a new name for the company **(s.74)**.

(iii) **Passing-off action**. If the name is so similar to that of an established business as to impinge on its goodwill and connections, that business may apply to the courts in a passing-off action at common law for an injunction (and damages) to restrain the new company from carrying on business under that name.

A passing-off action will succeed only if the name is similar, the business is similar, and the name is not in common use but rather, it is recognised by the public as distinctive specifically to the complainant company's goods or services. In **North Cheshire & Manchester Brewery Co v Manchester Brewery Co (1899)**, the appellants set up the same business as the respondents under a similar name. An injunction was granted restraining the appellants from using the name, because it was calculated to deceive and cause confusion to the public.

Other rules relating to a company's name are:

Power to dispense with *'limited'*. Sections 60 allows a private company limited by guarantee which is currently exempted under the Companies Act 1985 from having to display '*limited*' in its name where it satisfies certain conditions (e.g., the company is formed for a non-trading purpose such as to promote art, education, or charity and its constitution requires it to use all its income in promoting its objects, and prohibits its from paying dividends and distributing its assets to members in a winding up) to keep its exemption as long as it continues to meet those conditions and until it changes its registered name. A new private company registered under the Companies Act 2006 can only obtain such exemption if it is a charity or if it is exempted by regulations made by the Secretary of State under section 60. The Companies (Company and Business Names) (Miscellaneous Provisions) Regulations 2009 now exempt a private company limited by guarantee from displaying 'limited' as part of its name if (a) the objects of the company are to promote or regulate commerce, art, science, education, religion, charity or any profession and (b) its articles require the company to apply its income to promote its objects and prohibits the payment of dividends, or any return of capital to its members, and on its winding up, require the company to transfer all its assets which would otherwise be available to its members, to another company with similar objects .

Publication of name. A company must publish its name in letters easily legible outside all its places of business including its registered office, and in all business communications such as on its common seal (if it has one), all business letters, invoices, order forms, cheques etc., and all its websites **(s.82)**. In addition, the company's business letters, order forms and websites must state its place of registration, its registered number, and the postal address of its registered office. Such information must also be provided on electronic documents such as e-mails **(The Companies Act 2006 Registrar, Languages and Trading disclosures Regulations 2006)**. There is a fine for non-compliance. In addition, the company will not be able to enforce any right arising out of a contract made in the course of business at a time when the company was in breach of the trading disclosure requirements if the defendant shows that the breach had caused him to suffer financial loss **(s.83)**. Where the company is the subject of an insolvency procedure, such as liquidation, administration or receivership, this fact must also be disclosed on company documents and its websites.

Business name. A company can carry on business under a name other than its registered name. Such name is known as a 'trading name' or a 'business name'. The statutory restrictions which apply to registered names also apply to business names. Thus, sensitive words or expressions which require prior approval before they can be used as part of a registered name cannot be used in a business name **(s.1193)**; and business names which give misleading indication of the company's activities are prohibited **(s.1198)**. A company which carries on business under a lawful business name must include in legible characters its corporate (registered) name as well as the address of its registered office whenever the business name appears on any business premises or business documents. The civil consequences under section 83 for breach of the disclosure requirements equally apply to business names.

Change of name

A company may change its name on its own initiative; or it may be compelled to do so by the courts (e.g., as a result of a passing-off action) or by the company names adjudicators or by the Secretary of State. In either case, the change of name may be effected by special resolution; or if there is a procedure in the company's articles for changing its name that procedure may be used instead **(s.77)**. The rules governing the choosing of registered names must also be complied with. Where the company *proposes* to change its name by special resolution, the company must notify the Registrar of the change in name **(s.78)**. This requirement is in addition to the obligation under section 30 to file a copy of the special resolution at Companies Registry within 15 days after it is passed. Where the change of name is made in accordance of a provision in the company's articles, the company must inform the Registrar of the name change and state that the change is made in accordance with the articles **(s.79)**. The Secretary of State's power to require the company to change its name is statutorily regulated. If the name is the same as, or in the opinion of the Secretary of State, too like a name which appears or should have appeared in the Registrar's index of names at the time of registration, the Secretary of State can only require the company to change its name within one year of incorporation, and must specify the period within which the company has to change its name **(s.68 (2))**. If misleading information was provided by the company in order to register a name or if the company had given undertakings to enable the use of a name and it has not fulfilled these undertakings the Secretary of State may require the company to change its name within five years of incorporation **(s.75)**. If the name gives a misleading indication of the company's activities and is likely to cause harm to the pubic, the Secretary of State may require the company to change of name at any time **(s.76)** and, unless an appeal is lodged with the courts within three weeks, the company must change its name within six weeks of receiving instructions to change the name. A fine is imposed on the company for non-compliance. On a change of name, the new name is entered in the register and an amended certificate of incorporation is issued by the Registrar **(s.80)**. The change takes effect from the date specified in the new certificate **(s.81)**. The change does not affect any rights or obligations of the company or render defective any legal proceedings by or against the company.

(b) The Registered Office.

The part of the United Kingdom and Northern Ireland where the registered office will be located will determine the domicile of the company. Thus, the company will be an English company and English law will govern the company (e.g., to decide whether it is validly incorporated and on its ability to contract) if the application states that the company's registered office will be situated in England and Wales. If the application states that the registered office will be only in Wales (as with Welsh companies), the company has a choice of delivering for registration its documents in Welsh **(s.1104)**. If it states Scotland or Northern Ireland, then Scottish or Northern Ireland laws and the court system of Scotland or Northern Ireland will govern the company. There are separate registries for companies to be registered in England and Wales, Scotland and Northern Ireland. The application will also state the intended address of the company's registered office. This address is the official address of the company.

Companies cannot change later the part of the United Kingdom and Northern Ireland where their registered office is located; except that if the registered office is actually situated in Wales but the company is registered as having its registered office in England and Wales, the company may by special resolution require the register to be amended so that it states that the company's registered office is to be situated in Wales and vice versa **(s.88)**. Where the special resolution is passed (so that the company can become or cease to be Welsh) the Registrar will amend the register and will issue a new certificate of incorporation.

The postal address of the registered office may be changed freely within the country of domicile by the company giving notice to the Registrar. The new address takes effect only when the Registrar registers it, but there is a 14 days overlap between the old and the new address; so that service of legal documents at either address will be effective service on the company **(s.87)**. In **Re Baby Moon (UK) Ltd. (1984)**, the courts held that it was unlawful for a company registered in England to have the address of its registered office in Scotland.

English law requires all companies to have a registered office at all times **(s.86)**. The registered office enables members of the public to know where the company can be found and to which communications and legal notices can be sent (e.g., a winding up petition can only be served at the company's registered office). Section 1139 provides that service of a document at the company's registered office is service on the company. The registered office is also the place where certain statutory books and registers can be inspected. The following statutory books and registers are kept at the registered office (unless the Secretary of State by statutory order under section 1136 specifies elsewhere): a minutes book of members' general meetings **(s.358)**; for single-member companies, a book of written resolutions **(s.358)**; a minutes book of the directors' meeting **(s.248)**; a register of charges **(s.877)**; a register of directors **(s.162)**; a register of directors' residential address **(s.165)**; for public companies, a register of secretaries **(s.275)**; a register of members **(s.114)**; a register of debenture holders **(s.743)**; for public companies, a register of interests disclosed **(s.808)**; and accounting records (i.e. the day-to-day entries of monies received and expended, record of assets and liabilities and statements of stocktaking) **(s.388).** Members are entitled to inspect all the above books, except the minutes book of directors' meetings and the accounting records, free of charge during business hours for at least two hours a day. Creditors may examine the register of charges also without a fee. The general public is entitled to view all the above-mentioned books and registers, except the register of directors' residential address, the minutes books and the accounting records, on payment of a fee. The company must state the postal address of its registered office, as well as its registered number, on all business letters and order forms **(s.87 (3))**.

(3) Articles of Association (unless the company relies on default model articles prescribed by the Secretary of State). This document is considered in Chapter 3.

(4) Statement of capital and initial shareholdings. This statement is only required if the company will have a share capital **(s.10)**. It must state the total number of shares of the company to be taken on formation by the subscribers to the memorandum, the aggregate nominal value of those shares, (for each class of shares) prescribed particulars of the rights attached to the shares and the total number of shares of that class and the nominal value of shares of that class, the number of shares taken by each subscriber and the amount to be paid up immediately and the amount (if any) to be unpaid on each share (whether on account of the nominal value of the share or by way of premium). The subscribers' name and address must also be disclosed. The statement of capital will have to be updated whenever there is an alteration of share capital, such as when new shares are issued.

(5) Statement of guarantee. This statement is only required if the company will be limited by guarantee **(s.11)**. It must state that each member undertakes that, if the company is wound up while he is a member, or within one year after he ceases to be a member, he will contribute to the assets of the company such amount as may be required for payment of the debts and liabilities contracted before he ceases to be a member, and payment of the costs of winding up, not exceeding a specified amount.

(6) Statement of the company's proposed officers. It must contain the name and particulars of the first directors and, where relevant, secretary together with their written consent to act. The statement must be signed by the subscribers of the memorandum of association **(s.12)**. The proposed officers take up their appointment on the date of registration of the company **(s.16)**.

(7) A Statement of Compliance (known as **Form 13**) signed by a solicitor engaged in the formation of the company, or a person named as a director or secretary of the company. This statement will specify that all the requirements of the Companies Act with regard to registration have been complied with.

If the Registrar is satisfied that the documents mentioned above are in order, he will register the company **(s.14)**, give the company a registered number **(s.1066)**, issue a certificate of incorporation **(s.15)**, and publish this in the Gazette or by some other specified means **(s.1077)**.

The certificate of incorporation will state the name and registered number of the company; the date of incorporation; whether the company is limited or unlimited, and if limited, whether it is limited by shares or guarantee; whether it is a private company or a public company; and that part of the UK where the registered office will be located (England and Wales, Wales, Scotland or Northern Ireland). The certificate of incorporation is *conclusive* evidence that the requirements in respect of registration have been complied with, and that the company is duly registered under the Act **(s.15 (4))**. Thus, the accuracy of the certificate cannot be challenged. In **Jubilee Cotton Mills Ltd. v Lewis (1924)**, the necessary documents of a company were delivered to and accepted by the Registrar on 6 January. A certificate of incorporation was signed and issued by the Registrar on 8 January but was dated 6 January, the date on which the directors allotted shares. The allottee later refused to pay the amount due on the shares, by arguing that the company did not exist on the date the shares were allotted to him. The court held the certificate of incorporation to be conclusive as to the date on which the company was incorporated, so that the allottee had to pay for the shares.

The certificate of incorporation is not conclusive evidence as to the legality of the company's objects. Thus, where the Registrar registers a company which sets out its objects in its articles and those objects are unlawful, an application can be made to the courts to cancel the registration. In **R v Registrar of Companies, Ex Parte Attorney General (1991)**, the Registrar registered a company whose object was to promote prostitution. On application by the Attorney General to the courts for cancellation of the registration, the judge cancelled the registration even though the profits of trading as a prostitute were subject to taxation.

Companies off the shelf. These are ready-made companies which are freely available from firms of law stationers at a price. They dispense with the need for the promoter having to set up the company himself by using the procedures outlined above. When a customer buys a ready-made company, he gets a share transfer form signed by the existing shareholders (the law stationers) to make out in his own name. The customer becomes the new owner of the company as soon as the transfer is completed.

Shelf companies are cheap to purchase and they save time. Moreover, the promoter's liability under section 51 for pre-incorporation contracts (see Chapter 4) will not arise, even if the contract was made before the shelf company was bought by the promoter as long as he made it clear that he was only acting as agent for that particular company. This is so even if the shelf company did not have the right name when the contract was made **(Oshkosh B'Gosh Inc. Ltd. v Dan Marbel Inc. Ltd. (1988))**. It also enables the company to ratify the contract and thus enforce it against the third party, after the promoter purchases it. The main disadvantage with shelf companies is that some provisions in their constitution (such as the company's name) may not be suitable to meet the buyer's needs; so that additional expenses may be incurred by the purchaser to make the necessary changes.

Conversion of Registered companies

Re-registration of Public companies as Private

In the normal way, a public company may wish to be converted into a private limited company where it decides to reduce its activities and to carry on business as a domestic concern. In other cases, company legislation requires a public company to re-register as private when its issued share capital falls below the statutory minimum.

The procedure for re-registration is set out in section 97. A special resolution is required so that the company can re-register as a private company. It must then make changes to its name and articles as are necessary in connection with it becoming a private company limited by share or, as the case may be, by guarantee. An application for re-registration in the prescribed form (the application must contain a statement of the company's proposed name on re-registration), together with accompanying documents (i.e., a copy of the resolution to re-register as a private limited, a copy of the company's amended articles company, and a statement of compliance), is then made to the Registrar by a director or the secretary for a new certificate of incorporation appropriate to a private company.

The Registrar will issue a new certificate of incorporation (which must state that it is being issued on the re-registration of the company) unless an objection is lodged with the courts under section 98 to cancel the resolution to re-register by the holders of at least 5 per cent in nominal value of the company's issued shares (or any class thereof) or by any 50 members. The company has a duty to inform the Registrar immediately on learning that an application has been made to the courts to cancel the resolution for re-registration as a private company. The objection must be lodged within 28 days after the passing of the special resolution. The courts may then make any order they think fit. They can confirm or set aside the resolution; they can require the company to purchase the shares of the dissentient members while upholding the resolution where, for example, the company had also altered its articles depriving members of their right to transfer their shares freely; or can include any provision in the articles, such as one requiring existing members to purchase the shares of the objectors should they at some future time decide to sell them, thus giving the objectors a ready-made market for their shares. The company must give a copy of any court order made under section 98 within 15 days (or such longer time as the court may direct), or else it will be subject to a fine.

Re-registration of Private Companies as Public

Section 90 prescribes detailed and complex rules for the conversion of a private limited company into a public limited company. Basically a special resolution is required to alter the company's name and articles in order to meet the requirements of public companies. Thus the name will have to be amended to include '*public limited company*', and a statement of capital **(s.91)** must indicate that the company's issued share capital is not less than the authorised minimum, and that each of the company's allotted shares has been paid up to at least a quarter of the nominal value of the share together with any premium payable on the share. If the articles contain a clause restricting the transferability of the company's shares, it will have to be removed in order that the shares may be dealt with or quoted on the Stock Exchange.

An application to the Registrar for re-registration is then made and it must be supported by the following documents:

  (a) a printed copy of the amended articles (unless statutory articles are to apply).

  (b) a written statement by the company's auditors to the effect that at the relevant balance sheet date the amount of the company's net assets was not less than the aggregate of its called-up share capital and its undistributable reserves.

  (c) a copy of the relevant balance sheet made up to not later than seven months before the application for re-registration together with an auditors' unqualified report.

  (d) a copy of an expert's report on the value of non-cash assets given for shares, if an allotment was made between the date of the balance sheet and the passing of the special resolution.

(e) a statement of the company's proposed secretary.

(f) a statement of compliance by a director that (i) the special resolution was passed, (ii) the nominal value of the company's allotted capital is not less than the authorised minimum, (iii) not less than one quarter of the nominal value of each of the allotted shares, together with any premium, has been paid up, (iv) where shares have been allotted for an undertaking to do work or perform services, the undertaking has been performed or otherwise discharged, (v) where shares have been allotted for the transfer of assets, then either the assets have been transferred at the date the special resolution was passed or there is a contract obliging transfer within five years, and (vi) since the date to which the relevant balance sheet was made up, the company's financial position has remained stable and its net assets have not been reduced to less than the aggregate of its called-up capital and undistributable reserves.

Once the above requirements are satisfied, the Registrar will issue a new certificate of incorporation (which must make it clear that it is being issued on the re-registration of the company); and this certificate will be conclusive evidence that the requirements of the Companies Act have been complied with and that the company is a public company. A private company cannot re-register as a public company if it had previously re-registered as an unlimited company **(s.90 (2) (e))**.

Re-registration of Unlimited Companies as Public

As was explained earlier, an unlimited company must necessarily be a private company. If it wishes to alter its status to that of a public company, the procedure is the same as under section 90 except that the special resolution to be passed by members must state that the liability of the members will be limited by shares. The liability of members for the company's debts incurred prior to re-registration is not affected by the conversion.

Chapter 3

The Articles of Association

The articles of association (and resolutions and agreements relating to the articles) make up the constitution of the company. They will specify the manner in which the business of the company is to be conducted, and will regulate the rights of the members among themselves. If the members want to limit the objects (activities) of the company, as would be necessary under the Charities Act 1993 where the company is a charity, the articles will state what the objects of the company are. The articles have to be in a single document and divided into numbered paragraphs.

All registered companies must have articles. If a company does not register its own articles, default model articles will apply to the company. 'Default' model articles are articles created by the Secretary of State for various types of companies which do not register their own articles. Even where a company registers its own articles, the default model articles will still apply to those matters not specifically dealt with in the company's own articles, unless the company has expressly excluded the default model articles altogether on incorporation. The Secretary of State has introduced new default model articles for three types of companies registered under the Companies Act 2006: private companies limited by shares, public companies, and companies limited by guarantee. Companies registered under the 1985 Companies Act will still be subject to the model articles which were in force at the time they were registered (e.g., Table A); but they may choose to adopt the new model articles by their members passing a special resolution.

Amendment of Articles

A company can amend its articles at common law informally (i.e., without the need for any resolution to be passed) if it obtains the unanimous consent of its members, or under the Companies Act formally by passing a special resolution. The resolution must be passed at a general meeting; but if the company is a private company, it can pass the resolution outside the framework of a formal general meeting by using a written resolution.

(a) Informal amendment. In **Cane v Jones (1980)**, the company's shares were held by two factions within the same family. The articles provided the chairman with a casting vote at general meetings. It was subsequently agreed that this should no longer be the case, but instead that an independent chairman should be appointed in the event of an equality of votes. No formal meeting was held, but each member had signed separate papers to this effect. The court held that the agreement was valid. The fact that no meeting was convened and no resolution passed to amend the articles was irrelevant. The judge said that it was a basic principle of company law that all the corporators, acting together, could do anything that was not *ultra vires* the company.

The articles cannot be amended by unanimous consent if the matter to be amended was inserted by the courts (e.g., under section 994) without the courts' consent.

(b) Formal amendment. Section 21(1) permits a company to amend its articles by special resolution (this is subject to section 64 of the Charities Act 1993, where the company is a charity). However, an ordinary resolution may be used if the provision to be amended relates to the directors' powers to issue shares **(s.551(8))**.

The restriction which applies to amendment by unanimous consent also applies to section 21; but in addition there are further restrictions. The articles cannot be amended if the effect is to increase a member's liability to the company or to require him to take more shares in the company without his consent **(s.25)**. Also, any special right given to a class of shareholders and contained in the articles cannot be varied without the consent of the class concerned. Normally, class consent is given by special resolution **(s.630)**. In **Cumbrian Newspapers Group Ltd. v Cumberland & Westmorland v Herald Newspaper Ltd. (1986)**, the articles of the defendant company included a provision giving the claimant company rights of pre-emption over ordinary shares and the right to appoint a director. These rights were given to the claimant company in its capacity as shareholder to induce it to join the company and to enable it to prevent any take-over of the defendant company. Subsequently, the directors of the defendant company proposed to hold an extraordinary general meeting and to pass a special resolution to vary these rights. The claimant company successfully applied for an injunction to prevent the variation of its rights in the articles without its consent. Entrenched provisions in the articles cannot be amended by special resolution **(s.22)**. An entrenched provision is some matter which is included in the articles with a view that it cannot be changed at all (such a provision can be altered now by unanimous consent of the members or by the courts) or else it can only be changed if certain conditions are met, or procedures are complied with, that are more restrictive than by passing a special resolution. Entrenched provisions can be included in the articles on formation of the company, or later by unanimous consent of all the members of the company. The Registrar must be notified when a company includes entrenched provisions in its articles, whether on formation or subsequently, or amends such provisions **(s. 23)**. Finally, an amendment of the articles under section 21 must be made in good faith and for the benefit of the company; otherwise it might be set aside by the courts at common law on the ground that it amounts to fraud on the minority. In **Allen v Gold Reefs of West Africa Ltd. (1900)**, Lindley MR said:

"the power...must be exercised not only in the manner required by law, but also *bona fide* for the benefit of the company as a whole, and it must not be exceeded".

In **Allen v Gold Reefs of West Africa Ltd.**, the deceased owed the company money and was the only holder of fully paid shares in the company. In order to enforce the loan against his estate, the company amended its articles to extend its lien on partly paid shares to cover fully paid shares which could then be sold if money owing to the company had not been paid at the date of repayment. It was held that this was not fraud on the minority because the amendment affected all the company's issued shares and not merely the deceased's shares.

The test whether an amendment is 'bona fide for the company as a whole' is a subjective test. It is whether the majority shareholders honestly believe that their action will benefit the general membership of the company. If their belief is honest then the amendment will be valid even though it prejudices the minority of members. In **Rights & Issues Trust Ltd. v Stylo Shoes Ltd. (1965)**, on the issue of new shares to another company, the ordinary shareholders amended the company's articles doubling the voting rights of its management shares in order that the existing managers might retain control over the company. The courts accepted the amendment because the holders of the management shares did not vote on the resolution; and by their act *all* the ordinary shareholders (and not just those who objected) had suffered the same dilution of their voting strength. In **Citco Banking Corp. NV v Pusser's Ltd (2007)**, the Privy Council stated that where an amendment of the articles will benefit a particular member, as well as the company as a whole, this does not prevent the member from voting on the resolution to amend the articles. If no reasonable shareholders could consider the amendment could be for the benefit of the company, then this may be evidence of bad faith (Scrutton LJ in **Shuttleworth v Cox Bros. & Co (1927)**). The burden of proof is on the person who challenges the validity of the amendment.

The requirement that an amendment of the articles must be 'bona fide for the benefit of the company as a whole' raises a problem with *expropriation clauses*. These are clauses which enable the majority to compulsorily purchase the shares of the minority. If such a clause was in the original articles, then it will bind the minority; but if it is inserted in the articles, subsequent to incorporation, it will only be valid if it provides for fair compensation and is needed to protect the interests of the company as a corporate entity or was for the company's benefit.

In **Brown v Br. Abrasive Wheel Co. (1919)**, the company wanted more money. The majority of members agreed to provide more, but the minority did not want to contribute. The majority decided to alter the articles giving them power to purchase compulsorily the minority shares. The court decided that it was fraud on the minority. However in **Sidebottom v Kershaw, Leese & Co. Ltd. (1920)**, where a similar expropriation clause was included in the articles to prevent members from competing with the company, the clause was upheld by the courts on the ground that it was inserted to protect the company's trade secrets from its competitors.

Effect of Amendments

An amendment properly made is as valid as if it had been originally in the articles **(s.25)**. Moreover, the courts will not grant an injunction to prevent the company from lawfully amending its articles simply because it is done to facilitate a breach of contract **(Punt v Symons (1903))**. Such a situation can arise where a person has a separate contract with the company, some terms of which are contained in the articles. If those terms in the articles are amended, the contract becomes ineffectual. Thus, the company will be liable in damages for breach of contract; but it cannot be restrained by injunction from amending those terms. In **Southern Foundries Ltd. v Shirlaw (1940)**, Shirlaw had a separate contract to manage the company for ten years. The articles provided that if the managing director ceases to be a director he would lose his appointment as managing director. The company amended its articles permitting it to remove a director on notice. Shirlaw was subsequently removed, and so lost his appointment. Lord Porter held that although the courts could not prevent the company from amending its articles when it could lawfully do so, Shirlaw was entitled to damages for breach of contract.

A member is not bound by an amendment made to the articles after he becomes a member if the alteration has the effect of requiring him to take up more shares in the company or in any other way increases his liability to the company without his written consent **(s. 25)**.

Where the articles are altered by unanimous agreement or by special resolution under section 21, or by ordinary resolution under section 551(8) (variation of directors' power to issue shares), a copy of the resolution (or agreement) and the amended articles must be filed at Companies Registry within 15 days of the alteration **(s.26)**. Failure to comply is not only a criminal offence but the Companies Act 2006 also creates a new civil penalty of £200. However, the civil penalty will only apply if the Registrar requires the company to deliver a copy of the amended articles and the company does not comply with his request within 28 days.

The Articles as the Statutory Contract

When a person becomes a member of a company, the company's articles (and resolutions and agreements affecting the articles) regulate his relationship with the company and with his fellow members and have contractual effect. This is the result of section 33 (1) which provides "The provisions of a company's constitution bind the company and its members to the same extent as if there were covenants on the part of the company and of each member to observe those provisions."

The statutory contract is in no sense a 'normal' contract whereby rights and obligations can be expected to flow from the law of contract. Thus, where the articles confer rights on a member as member, that member cannot complain if those rights are taken away from him by a valid amendment of the articles. Nor can the courts rectify the articles where they do not accord with the true intention of the signatories of the memorandum. However, in order to make the articles work, the courts may *construe* them in such a way as to give them reasonable business efficacy **(A-G of Belize v Belize Telecom Ltd. (2009))**.

In **Bratton Seymour Services Co. Ltd. v Oxborough (1992)**, Steyn LJ identified the distinguishing features of the statutory contract as follows: (a) Its force is derived not from a bargain struck between the parties but by statute; (b) It can be altered by special resolution which of course does not require the consent of all the contracting parties; (c) It is not liable to be set aside on the grounds of misrepresentation, mistake, duress or undue influence; and (d) The remedy of rectification is not available.

The statutory contract only applies to membership matters. 'Membership matters' include membership rights as well as membership obligations.

Accordingly:

(a) Each member is bound to the company and *vice versa*. Therefore if a member breaks the contract the company can sue him in its own name. In **Hickman v Kent and Bromney Sheepbreeders Association (1915)**, the articles provided that if a member had a dispute with the company over his membership, the matter should go to arbitration. Hickman, a member, brought a court action against his company in connection with his expulsion therefrom. On the company's application to have the action set aside, the court stayed the action since the member had agreed by the statutory contract that all disputes would go to arbitration. Conversely, the member can sue the company for breach of any right given to him as member. In **Pender v Lushington (1877)**, the articles provided that each member should be entitled to one vote for every 10 shares, but that no member would be entitled to more than 100 votes. One member had more than 1000 shares and to avoid that limit he transferred some shares to a nominee, who was then registered as owner of the shares. Subsequently, the chairman at a general meeting improperly rejected the votes cast by the nominee on the ground that the transfer was merely a device to avoid the provision in the articles. The court held that the articles bound the company to the shareholder, whose votes must therefore be counted.

The company is bound to the member only in respect of membership rights. 'Membership rights' are rights which affect a member in his capacity as a member such as the right to be paid a dividend in accordance with the terms of the articles once the company has declared a dividend **(Wood v Odessa Waterworks Co. (1889))**; the right to a return of capital in a winding up, once creditors have been repaid **(Griffith v Paget (1877))**; and the right to be registered in the register of members on a valid transfer of shares **(Re British Sugar Refining Co. (1857))**. Outsider rights contained in the articles and held by members are not normally enforceable against the company. 'Outsider rights' are rights which affect a member in some other capacity, such as a director, or promoter or secretary. Such rights are usually concerned with the general administration of the company. In **Eley v Positive Life Assurance Co. Ltd. (1876)**, the articles provided that Eley would be the solicitor of the company for life. When Eley was dismissed as solicitor of the company, he claimed damages for breach of contract, relying on the statutory contract. However, the Court of Appeal held that Eley could not enforce the right, even though he was a member, because the relevant provision in the articles related to him as a solicitor rather than as a member.

On certain occasions a member has been able to enforce his outsider right in the articles by suing (as member) the directors to comply with their obligation to observe the articles and all their provisions, whatever those provisions might be. Such a claim succeeded in the House of Lords in **Salmon v Quinn & Axten (1909)**, where a member and managing director of the company successfully enforced a provision in the articles which provided the managing director with a veto in certain circumstances over decisions of the board of directors. In this case, the board ignored the veto when the claimant exercised it under the articles; so the claimant commenced court proceedings. Current judicial attitude, however, has not been in favour of enforcing outsider rights in this way. As Steyn LJ said in the Court of Appeal in **Bratton Seymour Services Co. Ltd. v Oxborough** when reviewing the binding nature of the statutory contract "If it contains provisions conferring rights and obligations on outsiders, then those provisions do not bite as part of the contract between the company and the members, even if the outsider is coincidentally a member."

(b) Every member is bound to the other members. Therefore if the articles give a member some personal right, then the contract is directly enforceable by that member against the other members without making the company a party to the action. In **Borland's Trustee v Steel Bros. & Co. (1901)** the articles stated that, in the event of a member becoming bankrupt, his shares had to be sold to certain other members. The court held that a trustee of a bankrupt member had to comply with the terms of the articles. Similarly, in **Rayfield v Hands (1960)**, paragraph II of the company's articles provided that 'Every member who intends to transfer his shares should inform the directors, who will take the said shares equally between them at a fair value'. The court held that the directors, as members, were bound by the statutory contract to take up the shares of a member who wished to sell. The legal principle laid down in this case can bind only a director who has shares in the company. A director who holds no shares in the company cannot be bound by the statutory contract.

Articles as an Implied Contract

Although it may not be possible to rely on the statutory contract under section 33 because, for example, the person is an outsider, he may be able to claim an implied contract as evidenced by the articles. Thus in **Re New British Iron Co., ex parte Beckwith (1898)**, where the directors took up their appointment on the basis of a provision in the articles which provided remuneration at an annual sum of £1000 for the company's directors, the courts allowed them to claim the arrears of remuneration when the company went into liquidation.

For the courts to imply a contract the relevant provision must have been in the articles when the outsider took up his appointment in the company, and not inserted subsequently. Moreover, the courts will imply the contract only on the basis that the articles can be altered from time to time. Accordingly, a director cannot complain if the articles and his implied contract are altered to his detriment **(Browne v La Trinidad (1887))**.

An implied contract is therefore less advantageous than an express contract in that it only allows the outsider to claim what is already due to him (e.g., arrears of remuneration) and not damages for future losses.

Shareholder Agreements

In addition to the articles of association, the contents of which are largely determined by statute and by choice of the founders of the company, the shareholders may supplement this document, with an independent shareholder agreement to regulate their relationship with one another, such as how the company is to be run, or how to vote on an issue covered by the agreement, or how a quorum of a meeting will be determined. In **Harman and another v BML Group Ltd.**

(1994), a company had five members, four (the majority) held 'A' shares and the fifth (the minority) held 'B' shares.. A shareholder agreement between the five members provided, *inter alia*, that a shareholders' meeting would not have a quorum unless the 'B' shareholder or his proxy was present. The majority applied to the courts for an order under what is now section 306 authorising them to call a meeting of the company, whether or not the 'B' shareholder was present. The Court of Appeal held that the provision of the shareholder agreement was equivalent to an entrenched class right, and that the courts could not exercise their power under section 306 to override the 'B' shareholder's class right.

The effectiveness of a shareholder agreement will depend on the number of persons bound by it. It may involve some or all of the members and the company, and it has contractual force; so if it is broken injunctive proceedings may be instituted by any aggrieved party to the agreement. As a result of the Court of Appeal's decision in **Fulham Football Club v Cabra Estates plc (1994)**, a shareholder agreement may be entered into by some of the members and the directors of the company as to the future exercise of the directors' powers; and the courts will enforce the agreement as long as the directors honestly believe, at the time the agreement is made, that the agreement is in the company's interest. However, the company as a signatory to the agreement cannot be bound by any provision in the agreement restricting its right to exercise any of its statutory powers (e.g. the power to alter its articles by special resolution). In **Russell v Northern Bank Development Corp. Ltd. (1992)**, an agreement was entered into by a holding company and all five members of the company, where the parties agreed that the capital of the holding company could only be increased if all the parties to the agreement give their written consent. When, subsequently, the board of the company proposed a motion to increase the share capital, the claimant sought an injunction to restrain th $\imath$ company from doing so on grounds that this was in breach of the shareholder agreement. The House of Lords held that the agreement was a shareholder agreement on how to vote and as such was valid. However, it was also an agreement between the holding company and its shareholders that the holding company would not, without all the shareholders' consent, increase its capital (a statutory power) and that this part of the agreement was void as being contrary to the Companies Act. Nevertheless, as the objectionable part was severable, the House of Lords ruled that the pure shareholder agreement was binding.

A shareholder agreement entered into by all or some (the majority) of the members is useful in that all aspects of the agreement (apart from restrictions imposed on the company in the exercise of its statutory powers) are enforceable and not just membership matters (as with the articles).

Chapter 4

Promoters

Definition

The term 'promoter' is not statutorily defined; so it is necessary to look at case law for a judicial definition. In **Twycross v Grant (1877)**, Cockburn CJ defined a promoter as any person who 'undertakes to form a company with reference to a given project and to set it going and …takes the necessary steps to accomplish that purpose'.

The range of persons covered by this definition is wide and includes persons who set up a company whether to run it personally or to sell it (i.e. its shares) to third parties, persons who give instructions for the preparations and registration of the documents necessary to create a company, and persons who take an active part to raise the initial capital to set a company going soon after its incorporation. It excludes persons who act in a professional capacity for persons engaged in the formation of a company. However if, apart from acting in a purely professional capacity, such persons help to arrange the 'floating off' of the company's initial capital, they may be considered as promoters (**Lagunas Nitrate Co. v Lagunas Syndicate (1899)**). It is always a question of fact as to whether a person is a promoter and at what stage he becomes or ceases to be one. This is important because, as will be seen below, a promoter has duties in equity towards the company he is setting up.

Functions

A promoter has to prepare the documents for the registration of the company and nominate the directors, auditors, and bankers, and will appoint the company secretary (where the company is to be a public company). He may also buy property on behalf of the intended company; and if it is to be public he may draw up the prospectus.

Duties and Liabilities

In equity, the promoter's relationship towards the company is of a fiduciary nature; so he must not accept bribes or make secret profits, he must keep proper accounts, and make a full disclosure of his interest either to an independent board of directors or to the members *via* the prospectus or other means.

For breach of this duty, the company has the following remedies against him:

(a) **Damages**. It may obtain damages for any loss it has suffered. In **Re Leeds & Hanley Theatre of Varieties Ltd. (1902)** where the promoters failed to disclose that they were the real vendors of property sold to the company, the Court of Appeal held that the company was entitled to damages from them.

(b) **Rescission**. It may rescind the transaction, where the promoter sold to it his own property (i.e. property acquired by him before he became a promoter). In **Erlanger v New Sombrero Phosphate Co. (1878)**, a syndicate, headed by E, bought a lease of an island and then formed a company to take up the lease. They made a substantial profit from the sale, but did not make a full disclosure thereof and of the circumstances of the sale to the company members. The court held that the company could rescind the contract.

(c) **Recovery of profit**. If the company does not rescind the transaction or is unable to rescind it (e.g., because third party rights have been acquired under the contract) the company may recover the profit, where the promoter bought property *after* assuming that office and sold it to the company at a profit without disclosing his interest in the property. In **Gluckstein v Barnes (1900)**, a syndicate was established to promote a company to purchase the Olympia. The syndicate first purchased cheaply existing charges on the Olympia and later purchased the Olympia for £140,000. It then registered the company it was promoting and later sold the Olympia to the company for £180,000. The syndicate disclosed the profit of £40,000 it made on the resale but failed to disclose a further profit of £20,000 it made when charges it had purchased were redeemed. This was discovered four years later when the company went into liquidation. In an action by the liquidator to recover the £20,000, the court held it was a secret profit made by the syndicate as promoter of the company and the syndicate was required to repay the profit to the company.

Pre-Incorporation Contracts

These are contracts made by the promoter on behalf of the intended company before it is registered. The promoter's liability on such contracts is determined by section 51 which states that 'a contract that purports to be made by, or on behalf of a company at a time when the company has not been formed has effect, subject to any agreement to the contrary, as one made with the person purporting to act for the company or as agent for it and he is personally liable on the contract accordingly'. This means that the promoter is personally liable on pre-incorporation contracts.

The promoter's liability under section 51 does not depend on any representation by him that the company was in existence at the relevant time. Thus, he will be liable even though the other party is aware that the company has not yet been registered. In **Phonogram Ltd. v Lane (1981)**, a promoter borrowed money from the claimant under a pre-incorporation contract which he signed "for and on behalf of FM Ltd.". The claimant knew that FM Ltd. was not yet in existence although its formation was contemplated. In fact FM Ltd. was never incorporated. The promoter attempted to avoid liability by contending that there had to be a representation made to the claimant before the section could be invoked. The Court of Appeal rejected this argument.

The third party is equally liable to the promoter if he breaks the pre-incorporation contract. In **Braymist Ltd. v Wise Finance Co Ltd (2002)**, a firm of solicitors entered into a pre-incorporation contract on behalf of a company they were setting up to sell some land to developers. Subsequently, the developers changed their mind about buying the land. The Court of Appeal held that the solicitors could sue the developers for breach of the pre-incorporation contract.

The promoter can avoid personal liability on pre-incorporation contracts in two ways. If the promoter includes a rescission clause in the contract to the effect that he should be allowed to cancel it without liability in the event of the company failing to take up the contract, he will be excused from liability (Denning MR in **Phonogram Ltd. v Lane)**. The promoter can also include a provision in the pre-incorporation contract that his liability should cease when the company, after in-corporation, takes up the contract. The company cannot take up the contract by ratification **(Kelner v Baxter (1866))**. It must make a new contract with the third party after incorporation or else rely on the **Contracts (Rights of Third Parties Act 1999)** (see Chapter 5).

Expenses

A company is under no obligation to repay formation expenses incurred by its promoter and default model articles do not give it authority to meet such expenses. So the company's articles must authorise it expressly. Even then, the repayment of the promoter's expenses is at the discretion of the directors. In **Re English and Colonial Produce Ltd. (1906)**, a solicitor incurred formation expenses at the request of the future directors of the company. The Court of Appeal held that he could not recover these expenses from the company. Where the promoter is the first director of the company, he may deduct such expenses out of the company's funds, subject to disclosure.

Remuneration

A promoter's remuneration is at the discretion of the company. There is no obligation at common law to pay him anything, because the company was not in existence when his services were rendered. Nor does company legislation make any provision for mandatory payments of this nature. Thus if the promoter wishes to be remunerated, the initiative is on him to make the necessary provision. He may enter into a contract with the company for remuneration after its formation; but the contract must be by deed, otherwise it may be set aside on grounds that his services constituted past consideration. Alternatively, he may include a clause in the company's articles providing for remuneration; but he must also become a director to carry the provision into effect.

Where remuneration is payable, it need not take the form of a cash payment. The promoter may be given an option to purchase shares on favourable terms, but not below their par value, within a stipulated time. The usefulness of this inducement becomes apparent when the value of the shares goes up in the interim period. Such an option must be disclosed to the Registrar and noted in the balance sheet. The promoter may also sell property to the company at a profit subject to disclosure. However where the company is a public company and the value of the transaction is equivalent to at least 10 per cent of the company's issued capital, and the promoter is a subscriber to the memorandum, a report must be made by an independent valuer and the members must sanction it by ordinary resolution **(s.598)**. Finally, the promoter may be given fully paid shares for his services. This method of providing remuneration is not available to a public company, since it is now unlawful for such a company to issue its shares for services **(s.585)**.

Chapter 5

Company Contracts

There are five main types of company contracts:

(1) **The Statutory Contract**. This is the contract between the company and its members by virtue of section 33 of the Companies Act. Section 33 provides that the articles have contractual effect between the company and its members, and the members among themselves. The application of this provision was considered fully in Chapter 3. Section 33(2) provides that money owed by a member to the company as a subscriber to the company is to be treated as an ordinary contract debt (6 years limitation period); so that it is enforceable by the company only if consideration was given by the company.

(2) **Pre-incorporation Contracts**. These are contracts made by the promoter on behalf of the intended company. The promoter's liability on such contracts was considered in Chapter 4. The company itself can enforce such contracts against the third party as long as the parties to the pre-incorporation contracts clearly intended to confer a legally enforceable benefit on the company **(Contracts (Rights of Third Parties) Act 1999).** The company is not liable on a pre-incorporation contract, not even if it purports to ratify the contract **(Kelner v Baxter (1866)).** However, it will incur liability if it accepts the contract by novation. 'Novation' means making a new contract on the same terms of the pre-

incorporation contract in which case the old contract is ended and the new contract takes its place. Novation may also be inferred from the conduct of the parties. In **Howard v Patent Ivory Manufacturing Co. (1888),** a promoter entered into a pre-incorporation contract to buy property for the company he was about to form. After incorporation, the company re-negotiated the contract with the vendor of the property whereby the vendor agreed to take part of the purchase money in debentures rather than cash. The court held that the re-negotiation of the consideration was sufficient proof of the formation of a new contract, so that the contract was binding on the company. However in **Re Northumberland Avenue Hotel Co. (1886)**, where the company, subsequent to incorporation, started to erect a building on land which its promoter acquired under a re-incorporation contract, the court held that this was not evidence of a new contract since it was done under a mistaken belief that the company was bound by the pre-incorporation contract.

(3) **Pre-Trading Certificate Contracts**. These are contracts made by a public company after its incorporation but before it receives permission from the Registrar (in the form of a 'trading certificate') to commence business. The company is primarily liable on such contracts; but if it fails to comply with its obligations in connection with the contracts within 21 days from being called upon to do so, the directors will be jointly and severally liable to the third parties for loss resulting from the company's failure to fulfil its obligations **(s.767 (3))**.

(4) *Ultra Vires* **Contracts**. Although a company registered under the 2006 Companies Act has unlimited capacity in the sense that it can enter into any type of activity or transaction

which is lawful **(s.31 (1))**, it may choose to restrict its capacity by including in its articles a clause limiting what the company may do. A company which wishes to register as a charity will have to restrict its objects (i.e., what it can do) under charities legislation; and a community interest company may choose to do so. Where a company has restricted objects, contracts made by the company and which do not come within the scope of its objects are called *ultra vires* contracts. Such contracts are void at common law and cannot be enforced even if all the members purport to ratify them **(Ashbury Rly. Carriage and Iron Co. Ltd. v Riche (1875))**. The *ultra vires* doctrine in relation to a company's capacity has been abolished by section 39 of the Companies Act, except in the case of companies which are charities. Section 39 provides that the validity of any act done by a company cannot be called into question on the grounds of lack of capacity by reason of anything in the company's constitution. In other words, no act of the company can be challenged solely on the ground that it was not within the company's objects (although it could be challenged on other grounds such as that the company's agents had no authority to perform the act in question). Section 39 does not apply where the company enjoys charitable status unless the person dealing with the charity did not know at the time the act was done that the company was a charity, or he gave full consideration for the act and did not know that the act was not permitted by the company's constitution **(s.42 (1))**. 'Good faith' is presumed in favour of the person dealing with the charity **(s.42 (3))**. A charitable company which does not use the word 'charity' or 'charitable' in its name is required to state on all business stationery that it is a charity.

(5) **Unauthorised Contracts**. These are contracts made on behalf of the company by its agents who do not have

authority to make them. The company can sue and be sued on such contracts only if it ratifies them by ordinary resolution. Apart from ratification, the company will not be liable to third parties for unauthorised acts of its agents unless the third parties can rely on:

(a)**The Rule in Royal British Bank v Turquand (1885)**;
(b) **The Doctine of Holding Out;**
(c) **Section 40 of the Companies Act 2006.**

(a) **The Rule in Royal British Bank v Turquand.**
This rule states that an outsider dealing with a company is assumed to have knowledge of the contents of the company's public documents which are kept at Companies Registry (i.e., such knowledge is called 'constructive notice'), but he is entitled to assume that all internal rules of the company have been complied with. Thus if, as in **Royal British Bank v Turquand**, the articles empower the directors to borrow money by sanction of an ordinary resolution passed by its members, then since such resolutions are not normally required to be filed at Companies Registry, and as outsiders do not have any statutory right to examine the minutes book in which proceedings at general meetings are noted, an outsider can assume, upon the directors' representation to this effect, that the resolution has been passed. The rule in **Turquand**'s case is not only a rule of convenience but also a rule of fairness, and it has been held to cover the following types of defects: the defective appointment of a director, or the continuance of a director to act for the company after he ceases to be a director **(Maloney v East Holyford Mining Co. (1857))**; failure to convene a properly constituted board or members meeting to authorise the company to enter into the transaction **(County of Gloucester Bank v Ruday etc.**

Co (1895)); and a disregard of the limitations imposed on the directors' authority by the memorandum or articles **(Royal British Bank v Turquand)**.

The rule in **Turquand** does not apply if the outsider knew that all the internal regulations of the company had not been complied with **(Howard v Patent Ivory Manufacturing Co. (1888))**; if there were suspicious circumstances which ought to put him on inquiry **(Irvine v Union Bank of Australia (1877))**; if the outsider, by virtue of his position in thecompany, is not in the true sense an outsider **(Morris v Kanssen (1946))**; or if the internal irregularity results in the issuing of a document which is forged **(Ruben v Great Fingall Consolidated (1906))**.

(b) The Doctrine of Holding Out

Even though the outsider may not be able to rely on **Turquand** because, for example, there as no irregularity in the internal procedure of the company, he may still be able to bind the company under ostensible authority. This is a form of holding out by the company that the person purporting to act as its agent had the necessary authority; and it may be used to bind the company to an unauthorised act of a single director who does not obtain the consent of the board as a whole. In **Freeman & Lockyer v Buckhurst Park Properties Ltd. (1964)**, Lord Diplock LJ said that four ingredients must be present to bring the doctrine of holding out into play: (i) there must have been a representation that the agent had the necessary authority; (ii) the representation must be made by the company; (iii) the outsider must actually have relied on the representation; and (iv) the contract must have been of a kind which the agent could have entered into on behalf of the company.

For the representation to be made by the company it must be made by the board of directors who have actual authority to manage the company, or it must be contained in the articles. In **Freeman & Lockyer v Buckhurst Park Properties Ltd.**, the articles authorised the appointment of a managing director, but none was appointed. One of the directors, to the knowledge of the board but without its express permission, acted as if he was the managing director. The court held that he could bind the company to his acts, even though the third parties in question had not inspected the articles when dealing with him. Similarly, in **Hely-Hutchinson v Brayhead Ltd (1967)**, the chairman of the company, though not appointed as managing director, acted in that capacity with the acquiescence of the board of directors. The Court of Appeal held that the representation was made by the persons who had actual authority to manage the company; so the company was liable.

Where the representation is contained in the articles, the outsider must have actually seen the articles before entering the contract if he is to make the company liable. In **Rama Corp Ltd. v Proved Tin & General Investments Ltd. (1952)**, the outsider entered into the contract with a director. It was not proved that the board of directors knew of, or acquiesced to, this director acting for the company. The outsider attempted to rely on a provision in the articles which stated that delegation of the management may be made by the board of directors to a single director. The court held that ostensible authority failed because the outsider did not see the articles before entering into the contract; so he could not have been induced by the representation.

(c) Section 40 (1) of the Companies Act.

The position of third parties (outsiders) to bind the company to unauthorised contracts made by the company's agents has

been significantly improved by company legislation. 'Third parties' refers to persons other than directors and members of a company dealing with their own company **(EIC Services Ltd. v Phipps (2003)**.
Section 40 (1) states:

"In favour of a person dealing with a company in good faith, the power of the directors to bind the company, or authorise others to do so, is deemed to be free of any limitations under the company's constitution".

The effect of this subsection is that if a third party in his dealings with the company acted in good faith, the company cannot avoid the transaction on grounds that the directors had disregarded *limitations* under the company's constitution on their powers to bind the company or to authorise other persons to do so. 'Good faith' is presumed in favour of the third party; so it is for the company to establish bad faith. This is a very difficult burden to discharge since section 40 (2)(b)(iii) states that it is not sufficient for the company to show that the third party had actual knowledge that the transaction was beyond the powers of the directors under the company's constitution. Some element of dishonesty by the third party is now required to defeat 'good faith'. Section 40 does not prevent any member of the company who has advanced knowledge that the directors are contemplating an act beyond their powers from instituting injunctive proceedings in the courts to prevent the company from undertaking such transaction. However, no injunction can be granted to prevent the company from completing an act which it has already legally committed to do for the benefit of the third party **(s.40 (4))**. If the third party is dealing with a charitable company, he cannot rely on section 40 (power of the directors to bind the company) unless he has given value *and* does not know that the act is contrary to the company's constitution; or else he is unaware at the time that he is dealing with a charitable company **(s. 42).** If the third party is an "insider" (i.e., a director of the company or its holding company or a person connected with him such as his wife and children or a company in which the director owns twenty per cent of the voting shares) and the transaction exceeds a limitation on the powers of the directors to bind the company, the transaction is voidable at the company's option **(s.41)**. Moreover, the "insider" and any director who authorised the transaction will have to account to the company for any gain he has made directly or indirectly from the transaction and to indemnify the company for any loss or damage resulting from the transaction **(s.41 (3))**, unless the "insider" is not a director and he did not know that the directors were exceeding their powers **(s.41 (5))**. The company's right to cancel the transaction will be lost if its members ratify the transaction by ordinary resolution, or if restitution is no longer possible, or if it will prejudice the rights of innocent third parties for value, or the company is indemnified against any loss or damage arising from the transaction.

In many respects, section 40 would provide the same protection offered by **Turquand** and the **doctrine of holding out**. However under the section, the fact that the third party could have discovered the limitations on the agent's powers by making a search at Companies Registry is no bar to relief because the doctrine of constructive notice as it applies to documents filed at Companies Registry has been abolished except in the case of registration of companies' charges under section 876; a third party is not bound by any limitations in the company's articles including any shareholder resolution or agreement **(s. 40 (3))**; and in his dealings with the company he does not have to enquire whether any limitations are imposed on the board's powers to bind the company or to authorise others to do so **(s. 40 (2) (b) (i))**. Section 40 (2)(b) does not appear to apply where limitations on the agent's powers are imposed by the board of directors (as opposed to the company's constitutional documents) so that the outsider will still have to rely on **Turquand** and **Holding Out**.

Chapter 6

Corporate Finance

There are various ways of funding a company's activities; but in the main, the two most common ways are through the company's own members by an issue of shares or through long term loan creditors, by an issue of debentures. In both cases the law regulates the manner in which such finances can be raised by making a distinction between private and public companies. The relevant law is contained in the Financial Services and Markets Act 2000 and all references to sections in this chapter will relate to that Act unless otherwise stated.

Private Companies

A private company limited by shares (but not an unlimited company or a company limited by guarantee) is prohibited from offering its shares or debentures to the public or from allotting or agreeing to allot any of its securities with a view to their being offered to the public **(s.755) (1) CA)**. There is a presumption that an allotment or an agreement to allot securities is made with a view to their being offered to the public if either an offer of the securities to the public is made within six months after the allotment or agreement to allot, or before the company receives the full payment for the securities **(755 (2) CA)**. 'Public' includes a section of the public; but it excludes cases where the advertisement is of a private nature. An offer aimed at existing or past members and employees and their family, civil partners, or existing debenture holders of the company and trustees, is presumed to be of a private nature unless the contrary is proved **(s.756 CA)**.

An exemption is given where a private company which intends to re-register as a public company offers its securities to the public before the re-registration process is completed, as long as the company acts in good faith, even if re-registration is unsuccessful **(s.755 (3) CA)**. The exemption also applies, if as part of the terms of the offer, the private company undertakes to re-register as a public company within a period not later than six months from the day the offer is made to the public, and it complies with that undertaking.

For breach of section 755 (prohibition of public offers by private companies) the courts must make an order requiring the company to re-register as a public company unless it appears to the courts that the company does not meet the conditions for re-registration as a public company and that it is impractical or undesirable to require the company to take steps to do so, in which case the courts may make a remedial order (e.g., that persons who knew of the infringement should buy the shares at a price to be fixed by the courts) or an order for the compulsory winding up of the company **(s.758 CA)**. Moreover, where the person who contravenes the prohibition is authorised to carry on an investment business by virtue of his membership of a recognised self-regulating organisation (such as the Stock Exchange) or a recognised professional body (such as the Association of Certified Chartered Accountants and the Law Society) or by direct authorisation from the Secretary of State, he will be treated as having breached conduct of business rules with the result that the purchaser of the securities is permitted to rescind the transaction, unless the courts feel that the advertisement was largely irrelevant or that the terms of the transaction were fair. Any allotment of shares or debentures in breach of section 755 does not invalidate the allotment **(s.760 CA)**.

Public Companies
The usual methods used by a public company to offer its shares or debentures to the public are by:

(1) A direct invitation to the public
(2) An offer for sale
(3) Placing
(4) A rights issue

(1) Direct Invitation to Public
This is the most direct form of issue by a company of its shares or debentures to the public, and it may be used by a company which is coming to the market for the first time or by an established quoted company. The company can have the securities listed (i.e., quoted) on a recognised investment exchange in order to make them more marketable or simply offer them as unlisted securities. The law seeks to control such issues by requiring the company to disclose a whole range of information, primarily for the protection on investors.

Part VI of the Financial Services and Markets Act 2000 regulates the admission of securities for listing.

Listed Securities
No securities can be admitted by the Financial Services Authority (FSA) to its official list unless the consent of the corporate issuer (i.e. the company whose securities are to be listed) is obtained **(s.75 (2))** and the listing rules are complied

with **(s.75 (1))**. The listing rules are the conditions laid downby the FSA for the admission of securities for listing and they impose continuing obligations. The rules must be in writing **(s.101(3))** and available to the public with or without a fee **(s.101(4))**. It is a defence to any action for breach of the listing rules to show that a rule alleged to have been broken was not published at the date of the breach.

One of the requirements for listing is that at least 25% of the company's shares must, at the time of admission, have been in public hands (i.e., the shares are held by persons who are not associated with the directors or major shareholders). Another requirement is that the expected market value of the shares for which listing is sought must be at least £700,000. A third requirement is that if the company does not have any securities already listed, it must have published accounts for at least three years prior to its application for listing. Another requirement is that the company should publish a whole range of information about its securities. Such information is contained in listing particulars. The information contained in the listing particulars or the prospectus (a prospectus is necessary where the company is issuing shares for the first time to the public but it is still waiting for permission from the FSA to list them) has to be approved by the FSA and a copy registered with the Registrar of Companies, before they are published. The FSA has up to six months to decide whether to approve the application for listing. It is an offence to publish any information or advertisement in connection with a listing which has not yet been approved subject to the defence of 'innocent issuer' **(s. 98)**. Only persons not involved in an investment (e.g. a newspaper which publishes the advertisement in the belief that it was authorised) can rely on this defence.

The content of the listing particulars is determined largely by the FSA; but the Act also requires two matters to be included in them, namely, (a) the rights attached to the securities to be listed **(s. 86)** and (b) financial information which would enable potential investors to make an informed assessment of the company's assets and liabilities, profit and loss and its prospects **(s. 80)**. The amount of financial information to be disclosed depends on circumstances, such as the nature of the securities, the type of persons likely to buy the securities (e.g., the general public or investment companies) and existing public information **(s.80 (4))**. Only financial information for the listing particulars or which would be reasonable for him to obtain by making inquiries has to be disclosed **(s.80 (3))**.

The FSA can exempt companies from providing financial information if disclosure would be contrary to the public interest (as certified by the Secretary of State) or would be seriously detrimental to the issuer and its omission would not mislead a potential investor as to any essential fact necessary for him to make an informed judgement or, in the case of certain types of debentures, on ground that disclosures would be unnecessary because they are dealt with only by experts in specialised markets **(s. 82)**.

If after the securities are admitted for listing and before commencement of dealings, there is a significant change in circumstances which make the listing particulars no longer accurate or a significant new matter arises which would have had to be included if it had arisen when the particulars were prepared, the issuer has to publish supplementary listing particulars **(ss. 80 and 81)**. Supplementary listing particulars, like listing particulars, also have to be approved by the FSA and a copy registered with the Registrar of Companies before they can be published. Supplementary listing particulars are required only where the issuer knows of the change in circumstances. Persons responsible for the listing particulars are required to inform the issuer if they are aware of such change.

Unlisted Securities

These are securities which are not listed on the official list of the Stock Exchange. They will include shares or debentures which are admitted to dealings on any other approved English or overseas exchange (including the Alternative Investment Market) as well as shares or debentures not dealt on any approved exchange (either because the exchange is not an exchange recognised by the Secretary of State or because there is no formal market for the securities).

The general rule is that no one can offer or advertise for sale unlisted securities (whether for cash or otherwise) which are being offered for the first time to the public in the UK unless a prospectus approved by FSA is delivered to the Registrar of Companies and it is available for inspection by members of the public, free of charge, at an address in the UK **(s.85)**. For breach of this rule an authorised person is treated as having contravened business rules, and an unauthorised person is guilty of a criminal offence, subject to the defence of 'innocent issuer'.

A prospectus need not be issued if the offer is made to fewer than one hundred persons who are not qualified investors; or the issue is a 'small issue' (small issue is where the consideration for the securities is less than 2.5 million euro); or in connection with a *bona fide* underwriting agreement; or is an offer by a private company to existing members, employees or their family, or debenture holders; or an offer in connection with a takeover or merger; or a previous prospectus dealing with shares of the same class as the shares being offered was registered within the previous twelve months.

A supplementary prospectus is required in circumstances similar to those requiring supplementary listing particulars.

Omissions and Misstatements

Section 90 provides a statutory claim for damages to any person who buys the securities (whether directly from the corporate issuer or in the secondary market or from a person who renounces the right to acquire the securities) and suffers a loss as a result of the listing documents omitting some matter required to be included by the listing rules or the Act, or as a result of inaccuracies in the listing documents. A similar claim arises for omissions and misstatements in a non-listing prospectus or supplementary prospectus. No liability can arise under the section if information is withheld lawfully (e.g., on grounds of public interest) even though the non-disclosure makes the information given misleading.

The persons who are liable under section 90 are the persons responsible for the listing particulars (or supplementary listing particulars) and the prospectus (or supplementary prospectus). These persons are the issuer, its directors (including persons who consent to their names being used as directors), and experts who accept responsibility for their own statements **(s. 97)**.

Schedule 10 provides various defences for listing particulars and prospectus liability. A defendant does not incur statutory liability if, after reasonable enquiries, he honestly believed the statement to be accurate (or the omission to be proper); or if he relied on an expert whom he reasonably thought to be competent and the expert consented to the statement being included in the documents. However, in both cases the defendant must also prove that he still held that belief up until the securities were acquired, or else had no time to bring it to the attention of prospective purchasers, or continued in his belief until dealings commenced (in the case of listing particulars) and (in both cases) the securities were acquired after such a lapse of time that he ought in the circumstances to be reasonably excused. There are also defences for inaccurate materials which are extracted from public documents or official persons; and for inaccuracies known to the purchaser at the date of purchase. Finally, for failing to submit supplementary listing particulars or a supplementary prospectus the defendant will not be liable if he reasonably believed there was no need for them.

Quite apart from liability under the Financial Services and Markets Act, various other forms of civil liability exist for a false prospectus (or listing particulars). The corporate issuer is liable for misstatements by its directors and other agents acting within the scope of their authority. The remedies against the company (i.e. corporate issuer) are rescission and damages; and the action will be brought either in the tort of fraud, or under the Misrepresentation Act 1967. Rescission will not be possible if liquidation proceedings have already started against the company **(Houldsworth v City of Glasgow Bank (1880))**; or if the investor has sold his shares; if after discovering the untrue statement, he votes at a shareholders meeting **(Sharpley v South & East Coast Railway Co. (1876))** or pays calls on partly paid shares and accepts payment of dividends **(Scholey v Central Railways Co. of Venezuela (1868))**.

The individuals responsible for the wrong are also liable. The remedy available against them is damages. No action is available against them under the Misrepresentation Act, since the Act admits a remedy only against the other contracting party who, for all intents and purposes, is the company. However, they may be liable in deceit. They may also be liable for professional negligence under **Hedley Byrne Ltd. v**

Heller & Partners Ltd. (1964) where a special relationship exists between the investor and those individuals.

(2) **Offer for Sale**

This method of raising finance is much more common than direct invitations to the public by the company, especially if the company is starting business for the first time or is not well known. The company will sell its entire issue of shares or debentures to an issuing house which, in turn, will offer them by advertisement to the public through the medium of an 'offer for sale' at a higher price. In practice, the issuing house will not be registered as owner of the securities allotted to it but will renounce in favour of members of the public who respond positively to its offer for sale.

An offer for sale requires the registration of a prospectus if the issuing house subscribes for the securities (for cash or otherwise) with a view to offering them to others. In such a case, the issuing house, rather than the company is responsible for the prospectus.

(3) **Placing**

This may take one of two forms. The company's shares or debentures may be purchased by an issuing house which will then 'place' them with its clients, such as insurance companies. This type of placing differs from an 'offer for sale' in that the issuing house does not invite the public at large to take up the securities. With private placing, a prospectus may not have to be registered if the clientele does not exceed 50 persons or if the offer is made to professional investors.The second form of placing arises where the issuing house agrees to 'place' without purchasing. Here it acts as agent (or broker) for the company and invites potential investors to take up the company's securities. Responsibility for the prospectus rests with the company. The consideration given to brokers for their services is called 'brokerage' and it differs from 'underwriting commission' (the consideration given to underwriters to guarantee the success of an issue of securities) in that it is not statutorily regulated.

(4) **Rights Issues**

This method can only be used by an existing company. The company will make an offer to its security holders to take up new securities in the company in proportion to their current holding. In practice, they will offer the new securities at a price slightly below the market price; but they cannot be compelled to accept the offer. The offer may confer on the holders a mere right to subscribe personally (a non-renounceable rights issue) or it may allow them to assign their rights to others in which case it is renounceable. If the shares are listed on a recognised exchange, the right is usually renounceable. However, the circular accompanying the rights issue is a prospectus, so it must be in the prescribed form and be registered.

A rights issue differs from a bonus issue in that with the latter the holders are given free shares and the prospectus requirements do not apply to them. With a bonus issue, also called a scrip issue, the company itself pays for the shares via an internal transaction transferring cash from the Profit and Loss Account, the share Premium Account or the Capital Redemption Reserve Account to the Issued Capital Account. A bonus issue is an indirect way of raising additional capital when the company pays for the shares out of the Profit and Loss Account. A company can only credit its members with bonus shares as fully paid out of profits if authorised by its articles and the members consent by ordinary resolution **(art. 37- private companies; art.78- public companies)**. The shares must then be issued in the same proportion as a dividend payment.

Bonus shares are issued normally for two reasons: to keep the value of the shares in line with the assets value; and to prevent the distribution of reserves which would erode the security of debenture holders.

Restrictions on Allotment of Shares

In contract law an application for shares is an offer, and the allotment letter sent to the applicant is acceptance of his offer. These common law rules have been modified by statutory provisions.

Section 549 of the Companies Act prohibits the directors from exercising any power of the company to allot shares (except to the subscribers of the memorandum in fulfilment of their promise to take up shares, or in pursuance of a employees' share scheme, or if the company is a private company with only one class of shares) unless they are authorised to do so by ordinary resolution passed at a members meeting or power is reserved in the articles **(s.551)**. Authorisation may be given for a particular issue or to issue shares generally and it must specify the maximum amount of shares which may be allotted; and the date when the authority is to expire which must not be more than five years from the date the authority is contained in the articles or the date the resolution to allot shares is passed. The authority may be varied by ordinary resolution. Contravention of the section does not affect the validity of an allotment, but the directors may be liable to a fine.

Section 578 of the Companies Act provides that where the shares of a public company are offered for subscription and are not fully taken up, the company must not allot shares unless the offer states that an allotment will be made even though the issue is under-subscribed. Where an allotment is not made because not enough shares have been applied for under the offer, and forty days have lapsed after the first making of the offer, any money (or consideration) received from applicants must be repaid or returned forthwith to the applicants without interest. If any money (or other consideration) has not been repaid or returned within 48 days after the making of the offer, the directors become jointly and severally liable for repaying it, with interest, unless they can prove that their failure to repay was not due to misconduct or negligence. If instead of returning the application money or consideration the company makes an irregular allotment of shares, the applicant can rescind the allotment within one month of the allotment even if the company is being wound up, and can claim damages from the directors **(s.579 (3))**.

Section 586 of the Companies Act provides that if a public company agrees that the full amount payable for its shares need not be paid up before the shares can be allotted (i.e., the shares will be issued as partly paid shares) no allotment can be made until at least 25 per cent of the nominal value of the shares, together with all premium payable on them, has been paid up. If this section is contravened, the allotment of the shares will not be invalid, but each share allotted will be treated as if an amount equal to one quarter of its nominal value together with the whole premium payable had been received by the company; and the allottee is liable to pay the company that amount less any sum which he has actually paid, plus interest **(s. 586 (3) (a)**. Subsection 3 does not apply to an allotment of bonus shares to members, unless the allottee knew or ought to have known that the shares were allotted in contravention of the section. The restriction imposed by section 586 on public companies where their shares are to be issued as partly paid shares does not apply to shares issued to employees under an employees share scheme **(s.586 (2))**. To qualify as an employees share scheme, a scheme must encourage or facilitate the holding of shares in the company for the benefit of its employees or ex-employees or those of its holding or subsidiary companies.

Return of Allotment

Within one month of allotment ('allotment' means issuing new shares) a company (whether private or public) is required to deliver to the Registrar of Companies particulars of the allotment, including a copy of any contract where the shares are issued for a consideration other than cash, and a new statement of capital **(s.555 CA).** Criminal sanction is imposed for failure to comply with this requirement.

Chapter 7

Shares

The securities which a company can issue fall into two categories:

(a) Shares
(b) Debentures

The legal distinction between the two is that a share may make the holder a member of the company, whereas the holder of a debenture is only a creditor of the company. The money raised by the issue of a share is capital, which the company cannot generally reduce; but that raised on a debenture is a debt which the company may redeem at any time subject to the terms of the debenture. The income from a share is dividend; dividend can only be paid out of distributable profits. The income from a debenture is interest; interest can be paid out of profits or capital. In a winding up the debenture has to be repaid before the return of shareholders' capital. Nevertheless, they are both long-term investments in the company.

Nature of a share
Various attempts have been made to define a share. In **Short v Treasury Commissioners (1948)** Evershed LJ said "It is a chose in action". This definition has been criticised for being too vague, and in any case it merely stresses the contractual rights attached to a share, while ignoring its liabilities. The

definition most widely quoted is that given in **Borland's Trustees v Steel (1911)** by Farwell J:

A share is the interest of a shareholder in the company measured by a sum of money, for the purpose of liability in the first place, and of interest in the second, but also consisting of a series of mutual covenants entered into by all shareholders inter se in accordance with (s.33 of the Companies Act 2006). *The contract contained in the articles of association is one of the original incidents of the share. A share is not a sum of money…but is an interest measured by a sum of money and made up of various rights contained in the contract, including the right to a sum of money of a more or less amount.*

A similar definition is given in **CIR v Crossman (1937)** by Lord Russell of Killowen who said that it is the 'interest of a person in the company, the interest being composed of rights and obligations which are defined by the Companies Act and by (the articles)'.

A share does not, as its name implies, make the holder an owner of the company's assets **(Macaura v Northern Assurance (1925))**, but it gives him certain rights in the company (e.g., right to dividend). Its principal liability is to pay, on call or by pre-determined instalments, any balance outstanding on it.

Types of shares
Basically, there are three types of shares (a) ordinary shares; (b) preference shares; and (c) deferred shares.

(a) **Ordinary shares**. These are the norm. They confer a right to the equity in the company (i.e. a share in the surplus assets in a winding up of the company) and to the extent that members are said to 'own' the company (though not its assets), the ordinary shareholders can be described as the proprietors of the company. Ordinary shares are 'equity shares'. An equity share is a share which does not have any prior limitations place on it as to the amount payable in a distribution of profits while the company is a going concern or of surplus assets in a winding up **(s. 548)**. Both ordinary and certain participating preference shares (see below) will therefore fall within the definition of equity share or equity capital.

It is permissible to issue non-voting ordinary shares but, in such a case, they constitute a class of their own. Unless otherwise indicated, all shares issued by a company are presumed to be ordinary shares and rank equally.

(b) **Preference shares**. As their name implies, they give preference over all other shares as to dividend and /or capital repayment. Where they carry a fixed rate on dividend, it is implied that they are *cumulative*; that is to say, arrears of dividend are accumulated and must be paid before a dividend is paid on other shares, so long as the company is a going concern **(Webb v Earle (1875))**. If the company is being wound up, then in the absence of express provision arrears cannot be paid unless a dividend has been declared **(Re Crichton's Oil Co. (1902))**. Where express provision is made for the payment of arrears in a winding up even though no dividend is declared, such arrears can be paid only out of surplus assets after payment of the company's debts **(Re Sharfedale Brewery Co. Ltd. (1952))**. If the shares are non-cumulative, arrears of dividend are not payable. It was held in **Staples v Eastern Photographic Material Co Ltd. (1896)**, that where it is expressly provided that shares will be preferential to dividend 'out of profits of each year', they will be non-cumulative. The terms of issue may allow preference shares, in addition to their preferential dividend, to have a right to participate in a further dividend dependent, on the company's profits, after the ordinary shareholders have received a specified return of the profits. For example, they may provide that the preference shares shall participate further in any year where a dividend of six per cent has been paid on the ordinary shares **(Re Isle of Thanet Electricity Supply Co. Ltd. (1950))**. Such preference shares are called *participating preference* shares; and as long as they do not restrict the right of the holder of such shares to participate in surplus assets in a winding up of the company, they are a form of *equity* shares.

There is a presumption that where a preferential right is expressly given to shares, the shares will be preferential only to that extent and the right becomes exhaustive. Thus, if shares are given preference to dividend, they are presumed not to be preferential on repayment of capital and will have to rank equally with other (ordinary) shares as regards capital repayment and the sharing of surplus assets in a winding up **(Birch v Cropper (1889))**. Similarly, if the shares are given preference in repayment of capital, they are presumed to be *non-participating*; that is to say they do not carry the right to participate with ordinary shares in surplus assets, since all the rights relating to capital would have become exhausted as a result of the express provision dealing with capital **(Scottish Insurance Corp. v Wilson & Clyde Coal Co. (1949))**.

Most companies treat their preference shareholders as only temporary members whose capital is to be returned if the company has an excess of capital, or if it can raise funds cheaply elsewhere. It is not uncommon to find preference shares being issued as redeemable shares, or liable to be redeemed at the option of the shareholder or the company. To this extent, preference shares are similar to debentures. Neither would then carry the right to share in a capital surplus on liquidation. They both produce a fixed income but no capital appreciation. In addition, preference shares suffer disadvantages which debentures do not have. The earning of any income is dependent on a dividend being declared. Thus, the non-cumulative preference shareholder can lose his year's income for good; but the debenture holder can claim his, if necessary, by enforcing his security. Even if the preference shares are cumulative, the shareholder may have difficulties in securing the arrears if no dividend has been declared before liquidation. Membership rights on preference shares are mostly illusory, since voting rights are, in practice, restricted to matters directly affecting the shares. Thus, preference shareholders are denied the right to participate in the 'democratic' processes of the company.

(c) **Deferred Shares**. These shares are also known as founders or management shares. They often carry multiple votes; but their right to a dividend is deferred until ordinary shareholders are paid a fixed percentage of the profits. Their right to repayment of capital on winding up is also deferred until ordinary shareholders are repaid their capital in full.

Protection of Shareholders rights
Rights or benefits contained in the articles usually fall into three categories. First, there are those which are attached to particular shares (e.g., voting rights, preferential dividend rights and rights to a return of capital in winding up). Secondly, there are those which, although not attached to any particular shares, are nevertheless conferred on the

beneficiary in his capacity as member or shareholder of the company (e.g., as in **Bushell v Faith (1969)** where the articles conferred weighted voting rights on a member if he was to be removed from office as director; or as in **Cumbrian Newspaper Group Ltd. v Cumberland & Westmorland Herald Newspapers Ltd. (1986)** where the articles conferred on a member pre-emptive rights over ordinary shareholders). The third category covers rights or benefits which are conferred on individuals not because they are members but because they are connected with the administration of the company (e.g., as in **Eley v Positive Life Assurance Co. (1876)** where the articles conferred on a member the right to also be the company's solicitor; or as in **Re New British Iron Co. Ex parte Beckwith (1898)** where the articles conferred on the directors a right to receive annual remuneration of £1,000 each).

Only the first two categories are shareholders rights. The last can best be described as "outsiders' rights". The Companies Act provides a method for enforcement of shareholders rights by virtue of the statutory contract under section 33 (see Chapter 3) and gives some protection against the alteration of those rights. The degree of protection given depends on whether the rights threatened with alteration are shareholders' ordinary rights or their special rights (also called *class rights*).

(a) **Ordinary rights**. Where the rights attached to *all* the shares of a company are identical the rights are called shareholders' ordinary rights. These rights are usually attached to ordinary shares. If the rights are in the articles, they can be altered by special resolution under section 21. Dissentients may embark on the general reliefs available for minorities, such as fraud on the minority (see Chapters 14 and 15).

(b) **Class rights**. Where the rights attached to shares are not uniform with all the shares of a company, the shares are then said to belong to different classes **(s.629)** and the rights attached to each class are called 'class rights'. For example, a company may issue shares which have preference over other shares in relation to payment of a dividend or to a return of capital (such shares are called preference shares). The rights attached to such shares are class rights. However, rights attached to shares are not regarded as different from those attached to other shares simply because the shares do not carry the same rights to dividends in the twelve months immediately after their allotment **(s.629 (2))**. The rights attached to ordinary shares are not normally class rights; but they may be, if the ordinary shares are divided into voting and non-voting ordinary shares. Class rights may also be conferred on individuals in their capacity as members or shareholders of the company rather than on shares held by them (e.g., as in the **Cumbrian Newspaper** case).

Class rights may be created by the articles or by the terms of issue of the shares, or by the resolution giving the directors authority to issue shares. If such a document does not have to be filed at Companies Registry (e.g., if the class rights are in an ordinary resolution) the company must send to the Registrar within one month of the allotment of the shares, a statement containing particulars of the rights, unless they are uniform with identical rights of shares already allotted **(s. 637)**.

Class rights can be varied in accordance with the company's articles, or if the articles make no provision for this, then if the holders of at least seventy five percent in nominal value of the issued shares of the class whose rights are affected (excluding any shares held as treasury shares) give their consent in writing informally, or a special resolution is passed at a separate meeting of the members of the affected class to sanction the variation, in addition to any other requirement necessary for the change **(s. 630)**. This means that if the articles contain a less demanding procedure for variation than the statutory regime (e.g., an ordinary resolution passed by the holders of the affected class giving their consent to the variation), then that procedure may be used instead of the statutory procedure. It also means that any other procedure necessary to effect the change must also be complied with. Thus, if the class rights are in the articles, obtaining class consent is not enough, the articles must also be altered by special resolution under section 21 to complete the change. The statutory procedure is stated to be without prejudice to any other restriction in the articles for variation of class rights **(s.630 (3))**. Therefore, if the articles provide a more onerous regime than the statutory procedure for varying class rights, for example, the articles require a higher percentage than the seventy five percent majority in nominal value of the issued shares of the affected class, the company must comply with the onerous regime. Similarly, if the class rights are stated to be entrenched rights, they cannot be varied by using the statutory procedure under section 630. If a provision in the articles for varying class rights is later amended, or such a provision is subsequently included in the articles, this is itself treated as a variation of class rights; so class consent has to be obtained **(s. 630 (5))**.

A variation of class rights is subject to minority protection under section 633. Under this section the holders of at least 15 per cent of the shares of the affected class (being persons who did not consent to or vote in favour of the resolution for the variation) can apply to the courts within 21 days for relief. The courts may cancel the variation if it would unfairly prejudice the members of the affected class, or allow it. Any order made by the courts must be registered by the company within 15 days at Companies Registry.

There is a problem as to what constitutes 'variation'. Some guidance is given by the Companies Act which equates 'variation' with 'abrogation' (e.g., see **s. 630 (6)**). A more helpful guide is found in case law where the courts have drawn a distinction between alterations which vary class rights and alterations which merely affect the enjoyment of those rights. 'Variation' has been interpreted restrictively by the judges to exclude the latter. Thus, as in **White v Bristol Aeroplane Co. Ltd. (1953)**, class rights will not be varied where a company which wants to increase the number of its preference shares issues new preference shares to its ordinary shareholders whereby they gain a majority over the holders of existing preference shares, since the latter will not be losing any right but merely the enjoyment of those rights. Similarly, a subdivision of a class of shares under a power in the articles is not a variation even though it has the effect of altering the voting equilibrium of the classes **(Greenhalgh v Arderne Cinemas (1946))**.

Pre-emption rights
In order to allow existing members to retain control of the company, and to prevent the dilution in value of their shares when new shares are issued to outsiders below their market value, section 561 provides that new equity securities for *cash* (other than those which are to be issued under an employee share scheme or as bonus shares) must first be offered to existing equity shareholders in proportion to the

nominal value of their existing shares (including equity shares held by them under an employee share scheme) before such shares can be offered to outsiders. For the purposes of the section "equity securities" are defined as ordinary shares (and rights to subscribe for or convert securities into ordinary shares); and an ordinary share is any share other than a share which restricts the holder's right to a distribution (of profits while the company is a going concern and/or surplus assets in a winding up) to a fixed amount. The company can communicate the pre-emption offer to shareholders by hard copy or by electronic form; but if a shareholder has no registered address in the EEA or is the holder of a share warrant, the offer must be made by notice in the London, Edinburg or Belfast Gazette as appropriate **(s. 562)**. The offer has to remain open for at least 14 days and it cannot be withdrawn during this period; and where some ordinary shareholders decline to take up their quota, other ordinary shareholders may take up the surplus.

An allotment which contravenes sections 561 or 562 is not invalid; but the aggrieved shareholders may bring an action within two years from the date of delivery of the return of allotment to the Companies Registrar, for damages against the company and the directors in default **(s. 568 (4))**.

There are various ways in which the statutory pre-emption rights may be excluded. They may be **excluded** altogether where the directors, having been given *general* power under section 551 to issue shares, are permitted by the articles or by special resolution to issue equity shares free of these rights. Additionally, the articles or a special resolution may give the directors a discretion to **disapply** (i.e., to use or not to use, or to modify) the statutory pre-emption provisions. The power to exclude or disapply members' pre-emption rights in the above ways is contemporaneous with the power to issue shares, and so it will automatically terminate when the directors' power under section 551 expires or is revoked. Where the directors are given power only for a *particular* allotment, a special resolution from the shareholders is necessary to exclude or modify the pre-emption provisions from that allotment **(s. 571)**. The special resolution in this instance cannot be proposed unless it is recommended by the directors; and together with notice of the meeting at which the special resolution is to be proposed, the directors must circulate a written statement giving their reasons for making the recommendation and the amount the company will receive from the allotment and explain their justification for that amount. Finally, a private company with only one class of shares may include a provision in its articles authoring its directors to issue new shares without having to comply with all (or some of) the statutory pre-emption provisions. **(s. 569)**.

Payment for Shares

Share valuation

There are two ways by which the value of shares may be determined. They may be given an arbitrary fixed value on their issue, known as the *nominal* or *par* value of shares. Alternatively the net worth of the company may be divided into shares, each share representing a fraction of the entire value of the company. These are known as shares at *no par* value.

The advantages of issuing shares at par value are that it ensures that the company initially receives assets at least equivalent to the nominal value of the issued capital (this is particularly important to a public company, which has to raise a minimum capital before it can start trading) and that it determines the extent of the shareholders' liability for the company's debts. If the shares are issued at no par value, this will only make such liability uncertain. The main criticism of shares at par value is that the nominal value does not necessarily reflect the true worth of the company.

English law requires shares in a limited company to be issued at par value **(s. 542)**. The nearest it has come to recognise shares at no par value is when the shares are issued at a premium (i.e., for a sum in excess of their nominal value). The premium is treated as capital.

The par value of the shares can be in any currency; and the company can even have the shares in a mixture of currencies, for example, one class of shares could be denominated in sterling and another class can be denominated in dollars or euros **(s. 542(3))**. However, the initial authorised minimum share capital requirement for public companies must be in sterling (currently set at £50,000) or the prescribed euro equivalent (currently set at E65,000) **(s.763)**. The company can sub-divide or consolidate the nominal value of its shares later, by passing an ordinary resolution, or if the articles require a higher majority **(s. 618)**; but it must notify the Registrar and file a new statement of capital within one month after doing so **(s. 619)**. A new company is not allowed to convert its shares into stock. Old companies which have stock under previous company legislation may reconvert that stock back into fully paid shares of any nominal value by ordinary resolution **(s.620)**; but the registrar must be notified of the alteration of the company's share capital and a new statement of capital must be filed **(s.621)**.

Section 622 allows a company to redenominate the par value of its shares from one currency to another (this is subject to any restriction in the company's articles) by members passing an ordinary resolution **(s. 622)**. The ordinary resolution must specify the spot rate used for converting the nominal value of the shares from one currency to another; and the redenomination must take effect within 28 days after the resolution is passed; otherwise the resolution will lapse. The calculation of the new par value has to be as follows: Step 1 – take the aggregate of the old nominal value of all the affected shares (or shares of that class); Step 2 – translate that amount into the new currency at the rate of exchange specified in the resolution; Step 3 - divide the amount by the number of affected shares (or shares of the class). Where the redenomination will leave the par value in a fractional amount of the new currency, the company may want to obtain the share values in whole units of the new currency. It can do this by capitalising any distributable reserves it has in order to increase the nominal value of the affected shares, or it may reduce its capital by using the procedure under section 626.Section 626 allows a company which redenominates some or all of its shares to reduce part of its share capital by special resolution (there is no need to obtain the courts' permission for this, or for its directors to make a statement of solvency under section 641). The special resolution must be passed within three months of the ordinary resolution effecting the redenomination; but the amount by which the share capital is reduced must not exceed 10% of the nominal value of the company's share capital immediately after the reduction. The company must then transfer the amount by which the share capital is reduced as a result of redenomination into a new non-distributable reserve, called "*the redenomination reserve*" **(s. 628)**. This reserve can only be used to pay for fully paid bonus shares **(s. 628 (2))**. Notice of a reduction of capital under section 626, together with a copy of the relevant resolutions and a statement of capital, must be filed with the Registrar within 15 days. The reduction is not effective until these documents are registered. The company must also file with the Registrar within 15 days a statement by the directors confirming that the reduction in capital does not exceed the 10% ceiling; otherwise there would be a default fine on both the company and its directors

The redenomination of the shares will not affect the rights and obligations of the members under the company's constitution. In particular, it does not affect the members' entitlement to dividends (including entitlement to dividends in a particular currency), voting rights or any liability in respect of amounts unpaid on the shares.

Rules for Payment

1. Price for shares

The basic rule is that shares may be paid for in cash or in kind. 'Kind' includes assets and services; but with public companies, special conditions apply where their shares are issued for a non-cash consideration. Such conditions include:

(a) **Shares for services**. A public company cannot issue its shares for services **(s. 585)**. For breach of this provision, the allottee will have to pay the full price of the shares in cash, together with interest. In addition, any subsequent purchaser who knew of the contravention will also be liable.

(b) **Shares for assets**. A public company which agrees to issue its shares for assets, such as a van, must have those assets independently valued by a person who is qualified to be the company's auditor. The auditor must prepare a report on the valuation for the company within six months before the shares are allotted **(s. 593)**. A copy of the report must also be sent to the proposed allottee.

The auditor need not carry out the valuation himself if it is reasonable to have another person value the assets (e.g., where the auditor is not competent to carry out the valuation personally such as where the non-cash asset is land; or where the auditor is too sick to complete the valuation). The valuation report must include a description of the assets paid for the shares, the method and date of valuation and the extent to which the shares are to be treated as paid up by the assets and in cash. In addition, if the valuation was carried out by some other person than the auditor who prepared the valuation report, the report must state the valuer's name, what knowledge and experience he possesses to make the valuation and why it was reasonable for such person to make the valuation. Finally, the report must conclude that on the basis of the valuation, the amount received by the company is not less that the nominal value of the shares together with the whole of any premium treated as paid up by the assets. A copy of the report has to be filed with the Registrar at the same time as the return of allotment is filed. No valuation is required if a public company allots it shares to the members of another company as part of a takeover arrangement of that company provided the offer to exchange shares is made to *all* the members (or all of a particular class) of the other company**(s.594)**.

For non-compliance, the allottee will have to pay the amount owed on the shares in cash (with interest) if either he did not receive a copy of the valuation report or he knew or ought to know of the contravention.

(c) **Future assets**. Where shares are allotted for non-cash assets which are to be transferred to the public company at a later date, the non-cash assets must actually be transferred not later than five years after the allotment **(s. 587)**. For non-compliance, there is a default fine on the company and its officers; and the allottee will be liable to pay the amount unlawfully credited as paid on his shares, with interest. In addition, the company can enforce the undertaking to transfer the assets unless the courts decide otherwise under section 589.

(d) **Non-cash assets acquired from subscribers**. If within two years after receiving its trading certificate, a public company enters into a transaction, including the allotment of shares, with a subscriber of the memorandum for assets (other than assets used in the ordinary course of its business) and those assets have an aggregate value equivalent to at least 10 per cent of the nominal value of its issued share capital (premium excluded), the assets must be valued in the same way as under section 593 and the members must approve of the transaction by ordinary resolution **(s. 598)**.

For non-compliance, the allottee and any subsequent person with knowledge of the infringement will have to repay the company the consideration with interest.

2. Shares at a discount

The second rule relating to payment for shares is that the shares cannot be issued for a consideration which is less than their nominal value **(s. 580)**. If the shares are issued at a discount the allottee will have to pay to the company the amount of the discount in cash, with interest. In addition, any subsequent purchaser with knowledge of the discount is also liable. Section 580 is not contravened where a company issues its shares to underwriters for underwriting the issue under section 553, or where a private company issues shares in exchange for over-valued assets **(Re Wragg (1897))**.

A public company which intends to make an issue of its shares to the public may ask underwriters to underwrite the issue on terms that any shares not subscribed for will be taken up by the underwriters. The money paid to the underwriters for this service is called 'underwriting commission'; and it can be paid from cash in hand (including cash received from applicants as the price for shares of that particular issue) or by set-off from the shares not taken up by the public and which the underwriters have to subscribe for. If the latter, the surplus shares will be issued to the underwriters at par less the discount. Section 553 permits this provided the company's articles authorise it, and the total commission or discount does not exceed 10 per cent of the issue price of the shares or such smaller limit as may be imposed by the Secretary of State under the Financial Services and Markets Act or by the articles. The 'discount' is then written off in the balance sheet out of capital or profits. If written off from premium, the premium must come from the particular issue of shares for which the commission was paid **(s. 610(2))**.

A private company is allowed in law to issue its shares for a non-cash overvalued consideration unless (i) on the face of the transaction it is clear that the consideration is worth less than the shares **(Re Theatrical Trust Ltd. (1895))**; or (ii) the board of directors made no attempt to assess the money value of the consideration **(Tintin Exploration Syndicate Ltd. v Sandys (1947))**; or (iii) there was evidence of fraud **(Re White Star Line Ltd. (1938))**.

3. Shares at a premium

The third rule is that a company may, without any special powers in its articles, issue its shares for a consideration (cash or assets) which is more than the nominal value of the shares. The excess is called 'premium'. Section 610 states that a sum equivalent to the premium must be transferred into a special account known as the 'Share Premium Account'. This amount also has to be specified in the company's balance sheet under a separate sub-heading.

The share premium account is treated as a capital account and cannot be used to pay a dividend; nor can it be reduced in any other way without leave of the courts except where it is applied in:

(i) paying up new shares of the company to be issued to members as fully paid-up bonus shares; or

(ii) writing off expenses or the commission paid or discount allowed on, an issue of those shares (i.e., shares to underwriters at a discount). This means that the company can use the premium obtained from a *particular* issue of shares only to write off expenses etc incurred in respect of *that* issue;

(iii) providing for any premium payable by the company on the acquisition of its own shares if certain conditions set out in sections 687 (4) and 692 (3) are satisfied.

There may be a situation where a company issues shares in exchange for shares in another company as part of an arrangement providing for the acquisition or merger of the two companies. Then if the shares received by the issuing company represent assets exceeding their nominal value, the issuing company can choose to treat the premium as merger reserves, or if it satisfies section 612 as profits. To treat the surplus as profits, the issuing company must be able to secure 90 per cent of the equity shares of the merged company or, if such shares were divided into classes, then 90 per cent of the shares of each class **(s.613)**. The issuing company is allowed to write down the shares received at their nominal value in the assets section of its balance sheet, thus ignoring the premium element of the shares. The provisions of sections 612 and 613 permit the use of 'merger accounting' under **SSAP 23**.

In determining whether the issuing company has acquired the requisite percentage of equity shares, shares already held by the issuing company in the merged company can be taken into account even though they were not acquired as part of the arrangement.

Similar exemption is given where, in the case of internal group reconstruction, a wholly owned subsidiary allots shares at a premium to a holding company, or to another wholly owned subsidiary of the group, in consideration for the transfer to it of shares in another such subsidiary **(s. 611)**.

4. Shares partly paid up

The fourth rule is that the full amount payable on the shares need not be paid up on allotment. The company may require only part of the price of the shares to be paid on application or allotment. Unlike fully paid shares, partly paid shares must have a distinguishing number; this number is recorded besides each holder's name in the register of members **(s.113 (3)(a))**. Statutory default articles for private companies require private companies to issue fully paid shares only **(art. 21)**. There is no similar provision for public companies; so that unless the articles of a public company restrict it from doing so, the company may issue its shares as partly paid up. However, public companies must receive at least one-quarter of the shares' nominal value and the whole of any premium payable on the shares before they can allot partly paid shares; unless the shares are being allotted to an employees' share scheme **(s.586)**. For non-compliance, the allottee will have to make up the deficiency plus interest at 5 per cent a year. Officers in default will also be committing an offence. The amount paid up on the nominal value of the shares is commonly referred to as '*called-up capital*' and the amount outstanding as '*uncalled capital*'. The amount outstanding may be paid by instalments or by calls (i.e., demand).

In the absence of express provision in the articles, calls cannot be made unless an ordinary resolution is passed at a members' meeting. Statutory default articles for public companies allow directors to make calls by sending out call notices to members requiring them to pay a specified sum of money (a 'call') which is payable in respect of their shares **(art. 53)**. However, call notices cannot require members to pay a call which exceeds the amount outstanding on their shares. Call notices to members cannot require members to pay any call before 14 days have passed since notices were sent out. Any irregularity in the proceedings for making calls will avoid them.

Remedies for Non-Payment of Shares

Moneys which a member is obliged to pay the company under its constitution are debts due to the company. In England and Wales and Northern Ireland, such debts are ordinary contract debts **(s.33 (2))**; so an action under the general law for the principal sum and interest must be brought in the courts within six years otherwise the action will be statute-barred. In addition, other remedies available to a company against a defaulting shareholder are forfeiture, surrender and lien.

(a) **Forfeiture**. This is the process whereby the defaulter loses his shares for not paying some debt on them. The power of forfeiture has to be expressly reserved in the articles, and then only for non-payment of a call or an instalment **(s. 659(c))**. It cannot be used for other debts as this would otherwise amount to an unauthorised reduction of its capital **(Hopkinson v Mortimer, Harley & Co (1919)**, and would be in breach of the general rule against limited companies acquiring their own shares **(s. 658)**.

Draft Articles 57 – 60 for public companies provide the directors with power to forfeit the shares of defaulting shareholders and lay down the procedure by which shares may be forfeited. Notice has to be served on the defaulter to pay the principal sum and interest, and should warn that if the amount is not paid by a date which is not less than 14 days after the date of the notice, the shares are liable to be forfeited. Forfeiture is by resolution of the directors. The directors must exercise this power for the purpose for which it was conferred **(s.171)**, and act in a way they consider, in good faith, would be most likely to promote the success of the company **(s.172)**; otherwise they would be in breach of their general statutory duties to the company.

The procedure for forfeiture is strict, and any irregularity will invalidate it unless third parties in good faith purchase the shares in the meantime **(Art.60 (3))**.

(b) **Surrender**. This is the voluntary return of shares to a company, and it is lawful in two cases. Where a company has power to forfeit shares, it has power to accept a surrender of them in lieu of forfeiture **(art.61)** in order to avoid going through the formalities of forfeiture. Like forfeiture, the power to accept a surrender must be exercised in a way to promote the success of the company; and not simply to relieve a defaulting shareholder from liability **(Bellerby v Rowland & Marwood's Steamship Co. (1902))**. Surrender can also occur where new shares are issued in exchange for existing shares, both having the same nominal value. This type of surrender is permitted only if the old shares are fully paid.

Effect of forfeiture and surrender. The defaulter ceases to be a member of the company and is discharged from later liability on the shares. However, he is still liable to the company for the actual sum defaulted prior to the company repossessing his shares, but that liability can be diminished or extinguished if the forfeited shares are reissued. If the shares are not reissued this may amount to a permanent reduction of capital and is an exception to the general rule that a capital cannot be reduced without the courts' consent.

A public company which forfeits shares or accepts a surrender in lieu of forfeiture has to cancel the shares by means of a directors' resolution unless the shares are reissued within three years **(s.662)**.

(c) **Lien**. This is the right by a company to hold on to a member's shares where some debt due on them has not been paid. The shares may then be sold in the last resort to satisfy the debt; but any surplus money received in excess of the debt has to be returned to the former shareholder.

A company does not have an implied lien on the shares of its members; but where statutory default articles are adopted, articles 51 gives a public company a lien on the shares of each member to secure monies (whether presently payable or not) in respect of his shares. Article 52 requires the company to serve first a lien enforcement notice on the defaulting shareholder and if he fails to pay the sum due on the shares within 14 days after service of the notice, the company may then sell the charged shares and recover the debt. A lien taken by a public company (other than a money-lending public company) is void unless it is on partly paid shares to secure any amount payable in respect of those shares **(s.670)**.

Where a third party advances money to a member and takes an equitable mortgage on his shares as security for the loan, the company will obtain priority over him if its lien arises before he gives notice of his security to it. As a lien for non-payment on shares arises when the shares are issued, and not when the money becomes payable on the shares, it is not possible for the third party to obtain priority in such circumstances. A lien for ordinary commercial debts due from the member to the company (in the case of a private company and a money-lending public company which make special provision in their articles for a lien on members' shares for non-payment of debts incurred in the ordinary course of the company's business) arises only when such debts are incurred; so the third party's equitable interest on the shares will prevail over the company's lien if he notifies the company of his interest before the debt is incurred.

In **Bradford Banking Co. v Briggs (1886)**, the articles of the company gave a 'first and paramount lien and charge' on shares for debts due from its shareholders. A shareholder deposited his share certificate with the bank as security for an overdraft and the bank gave notice of its interest in the shares. Subsequently, the shareholder became indebted to the company for some coal supplied to it. The House of Lords held that the bank had priority over the company.

Procedure for issuing shares. Directors do not have implied powers to issue shares **(s.549)**. Section 551 states that directors can allot shares (or grant rights to subscribe for shares or convert any security into shares) only if they are authorised by the articles to issue shares generally or if the members give them authority by ordinary resolution. Directors do not need authority to issue shares of a private company where the company has only one class of shares, unless the company's articles prohibit them from doing so (see Chapter 6). Where members give authority, the authority may be limited to a particular issue (e.g., to issue shares to fund a certain project) or general authority to issue shares (i.e., prior authority to issue shares in the future). Where prior authorisation is given by the articles or by the members for directors to issue new shares generally, such authorisation can only be given for a maximum period of five years, after which it has to be renewed before additional shares can be issued. Moreover, the authority must state the maximum amount of shares which could be allotted.

Where the shares are to be issued as partly paid shares and the company is a public company, at least one quarter of the nominal value of the shares, together with all premiums payable on the shares, must be paid up before the company is allowed to allot the shares **(s.586)**.

Where the new shares to be issued (allotted) are equity shares for *cash* the directors will have to ensure that the company's equity shareholders waive their statutory pre-emption rights to such shares before the shares can be issued to outsiders

(s.561). The directors also have the duty to act within their powers and for the purpose for which the powers were conferred **(s.171)**; so if they wish to issue shares other than to raise further finance for the company, they will have to obtain the consent of the members.

Where the shares are to be issued at a premium, the premium must be treated differently, using a share premium account.

Share Certificates and Share Warrants

On an allotment of shares (i.e., when the company informs the person who has contracted to buy its shares how many shares he is given), the company must issue the shareholder with either a share certificate or a share warrant. Where it intends to issue a share certificate the company must register the allotment as soon as possible and in any event within two months after the date of the allotment **(s.554)**. The company also has to complete the share certificate and have it ready for delivery to the shareholder not later than two months after the date of the allotment, unless the conditions of issuing the shares state otherwise **(s.769)**. These requirements do not apply where the company issues a share warrant in respect of the shares in question since warrants can only be issued if the articles authorise it **(art.50 – public companies)** and the shares are fully paid up **(s.779)**.

A share certificate is only evidence of title to shares **(s768)**; and its owner becomes a member of the company when his name is entered in the register of members. A share warrant is a warranty by the company that the bearer is a shareholder; and although the bearer of the warrant is never entered in the register, he may still be a member of the company if the articles so provide. Should a share certificate be stolen, no subsequent purchaser in possession of it can obtain a good title to the shares; but since a warrant is a negotiable instrument a purchaser without notice of the theft will obtain a good title. Share warrants are not very common in the United Kingdom because of the obvious disadvantages. The company is unable to get in touch with the shareholder except through newspaper and other advertisements, and unless the shareholder sees the advertisement he loses any right to vote (if the warrant gives the holder a right to vote) and to receive dividends promptly. The owner of a warrant runs more serious risk of loss or theft of his shares than a certificate holder. On the issue of a warrant the company must pay stamp duty of three times the duty that is payable on the transfer of shares in a share certificate. The holder of a share warrant can surrender it to the company for cancellation and the company must then issue him with a share certificate within two months from the date of surrender or within such time as the articles may specify **(s.780)**.

Share Certificates

The modern share certificate is usually printed, and will include the name of the shareholder and the number and description of shares held by him. The company's common seal is affixed and witnessed by signatures; but the articles may dispense with witnesses' signatures. The standard printed wording on a certificate reads:

"This is to certify that (the name of the shareholder) is the holder of (the number and description) shares fully paid of (nominal value) each numbered ... to ... inclusive in the above named company subject to the articles of association thereof".

Reference to the articles is a reminder that this document creates a binding contract between the member and the company and between the members themselves **(s.33)**. Only two other statements in the share certificate have any legal significance: as to who is the holder of the shares, and the amount paid on them.

The statement that the named person is the holder of the shares is a representation by the company that, at the date of issue, that person has a good title to the shares. In **Dixon v Kennaway & Co (1900)**, the secretary purported to transfer to the claimant shares which the secretary did not own, and deceived the directors into issuing a share certificate to the claimant. The company was estopped (prevented) from denying the claimant's title to the shares when the secretary subsequently became bankrupt. The court said that by deluding the claimant into believing that she had a title, the company had prevented her from claiming back the purchase price she paid to the secretary before the bankruptcy made it impossible to recover the whole of it. The claimant was therefore entitled to damages.

The statement in the certificate as to the amount paid up on the shares creates a continuing warranty in favour of an innocent person acquiring them, and will prevent the company from denying the amount stated as paid up. Therefore if the share certificate states that the shares are fully paid, the company cannot later deny the truth of that statement **(Bloomenthal v Foord (1897))**. Even the original allottee may be able, as against the company, to rely on the certificate that the shares are fully paid up. In **Re Building Estates Brickfields Co., Parbury's Case (1896)**, the solicitor responsible for formation of the company caused a share certificate to be issued to the allottee fraudulently, under the pretence that the shares being acquired by him were fully paid. In subsequent liquidation proceedings, the court held that the company was estopped by the statement from making calls on the allottee. An allottee who is aware that the shares are only partly paid up cannot rely on the doctrine of estoppel.

A share certificate will estop the company only if it is the company's certificate. Thus, the company will not be bound by a forged certificate **(Ruben v Gt. Fingall Consolidated (1906))**.

Transfer and Transmission of Shares

Transfer arises by the voluntary conveyance of shares by a shareholder; transmission arises by operation of law (e.g., on the death or bankruptcy of a member his shares automatically pass to his personal representatives or his trustee in bankruptcy).

Transfer of Shares

Unless the articles provide otherwise, every shareholder has a right to transfer his shares to whom he likes. However, the company cannot register the transfer unless a formal document, called an instrument of transfer (usually a Stock Transfer Form), signed by the transferor and duly stamped is delivered to it **(s.770)**; and until this is done and the transferee's name is entered in the register of members, he does not obtain membership of the company. Nevertheless, he acquires an equitable interest in the shares (see post). Shares of publicly quoted companies can be transferred electronically under the CREST system which records the title to shares and makes it easier to transfer the shares. With CREST, the transferee will hold the shares in uncertificated form (known as dematerialised shares); and no share certificate is issued.

With certificated shares (i.e., where the transferor's name is on the shareholder register and he has a paper share certificate), the instrument of transfer may be either in the form prescribed by the company's articles or, if it relates to fully paid shares, as provided by the Stock Transfer Act 1963. The latter provides a simplified form of transfer requiring only the signature of the transferor, which does not have to be witnessed. The instrument should show particulars of the consideration, the nature and number of shares, the names of the parties, and the address of the transferor. It is normally the transferor who has to prepare the instrument of transfer. The instrument of transfer and the share certificate must be forwarded to the company for registration. The same procedure applies on a gift of shares, though no stamp duty may be payable in such cases.

If the shareholder is transferring all of his shares in the share certificate to one transferee, he will hand the share certificate and the instrument of transfer to the transferee. The transferee will pay the stamp duty and then send the documents to the company for registration.

If the shareholder is selling only some of his shares shown in the share certificate to one transferee, he will take the documents himself to the company for registration, since it would be unwise to allow the transferee to have possession of these documents. The company will endorse the instrument of transfer with the words 'certificate lodged', retain the certificate, and return the transfer form to the shareholder. The shareholder then delivers the form to the transferee for stamping and presentation to the company. The endorsement of 'certificate lodged' on the transfer form is known as **'certification of transfer'**. By section 775 this certification is a representation by the company only that the transferor has a *prima facie* title to the shares (or debentures). It is not a warranty as to title. However, if the company fraudulently or carelessly makes a false certification, it will be liable to a purchaser who in good faith acts on the false certification.

The 'certification of transfer' also imposes an obligation on the company to keep the share certificate until the transfer form is returned to it by the transferee. This duty is owed to the certificated transferee alone, and not to the general public. In **Longman v Bath Electric Tramways Ltd. (1905)**, a company certified a transfer and duly registered the transferee as owner of the transferred shares. The company then by mistake returned the old share certificate to the transferor, who used it fraudulently as security for a loan. The court held that the company owed no duty of safe custody to the general public, and so was not liable to the lender for the losses he incurred when the transferor defaulted with the loan.

Restrictions on transfer. Although section 776 requires the company to issue new certificates within two months after the date on which the documents for a transfer of any of its shares (or debentures or debenture stock) is lodged with the company, the directors in certain cases must, and in other cases may, refuse to register the transfer. Where the directors refuse to register a transfer, they must provide reasons for their refusal.

The directors *must* refuse to register the transfer if a proper transfer has not been delivered to the company or if the transfer is an exempt transfer under the Stock Transfer Act **(s.770)**; or if it infringes a pre-emption clause **(Tett v Phoenix Property & Investment Co. (1986))**; or if it contravenes some other clause in the company's articles (e.g., as in **Borland's Trustee v Steel**, where the articles provided that, in the event of a member's bankruptcy he must sell his shares to particular persons at a particular price). In the **Phoenex Property** case, the articles provided that no shares in the company could be transferred if another member was willing to purchase the shares. The executors of a deceased shareholder sold his shares to an outsider without first taking reasonable steps to give the other members a reasonable opportunity to purchase the shares at a fair price. When the outsider applied for registration the directors refused his application and invited bids from existing shareholders, three of whom sent in bids. The Court of Appeal held that the directors had acted properly because they were bound by the pre-emption clause in the articles to refuse to register the transfer to the outsider.

The directors *may* refuse to register a transfer if the articles give them discretion to do so. Where statutory default articles are adopted, article 24 (5) for private companies gives the directors general power to refuse to register a transfer; and article 63 (5) for public companies gives the directors a discretion to refuse to register a transfer of partly paid shares. The directors of public companies do not have discretion to refuse to register a transfer of fully paid shares unless such power is expressly reserved for them in the articles. Where such power exists it may be absolute, or it may be specific (i.e., the directors can refuse to register a transfer only in specific cases, such as if they consider it contrary to the interest of the company to admit the transferee to membership of the company); and it must be exercised in good faith. With specific discretion, the directors may be required to identify the ground of refusal; and with either type of discretion the transferee is entitled to know the reason why the transfer has not been registered **(771 (2))**. Failure to

Shares

provide reasons for refusing to register a transfer will result in a fine on the company and every officer in default **(771 (3))**.

The directors' discretion has to be exercised positively before the company can refuse to register a transfer. Thus, if there is equality of voting at the board meeting when considering the issue of registration of a particular transfer, the transfer must be registered **(Moodie v Shepherd Bookbinders Ltd. (1949))**. If the articles state that a transfer of shares to non-members can take place only with the consent of the directors, and to prevent a particular transfer from being registered a director stays away from the board meeting deliberately to prevent a quorum for the meeting, the courts can require the company to register the transfer **(Re Copal Varnish Co. Ltd. (1917))**.

The directors must exercise their power to refuse to register a transfer within a reasonable time. By requiring the company to provide the transferee (not the transferor) with reasons for refusal to register the transfer within two months of the deposit of the documents for registration, section 771 implies that 'two months' is a reasonable time and that any act outside this period will be invalid for undue delay unless it is not possible for the directors to exercise their powers earlier (e.g., as in **Re Swaledale Cleaners Ltd. (1968)** where it was not possible to constitute a board). For failure to send notice of refusal to register a transfer with the prescribed time, there are criminal sanctions on the company and its officers **(s.771 (3))**. Section 771 only applies to a transfer of shares where a share certificate has been issued in respect of the shares. It does not apply where the company has issued a warrant in respect of the shares under section 779 or in relation to a transmission of shares **(s.771 (5))**. Both the company and its officers will be committing an offence if the company fails to comply with section 771 **(s.771 (3))**.

Effect of an unregistered transfer. There is no implied warranty that a transfer will be registered **(London Founders Association Ltd. v Clarke (1888))**; so unless the transferee bought the shares 'with registration guaranteed' he does not have any contractual remedies against the transferor for failure to obtain registration. In addition, the company is under a statutory duty to regard the person whose name is in the register of members as the only person with an interest in the shares and to disregard other interests attached to the shares unless the courts direct otherwise **(s.125)**. So, the transferor will continue to receive his membership rights (e.g., notice of meetings and dividends from the company).

The unregistered transferee has a mere equitable interest in the shares transferred. This interest requires the transferor to hold all benefits derived from the shares for the transferee, although the transferor is entitled to an indemnity for all calls on the shares subsequent to transfer and to exercise voting rights as he thinks fit to protect his position if the transferee has not fully paid for the shares **(Musselwhite v Musselwhite and Son Ltd. (1962))**. Where the unregistered transferee had not bought the shares but had received them as a gift, he obtains an equitable interest only when the transferor completes all that is required of him to effect the transfer in equity. This normally involves handing over the executed transfer and the share certificate to the company **(Re Rose (1952))**.

The transferee can make the company take notice of his equitable interest by means of a stop notice. A stop notice may be obtained under the Rules of the Supreme Court. The effect of this notice is to prevent the company from registering a transfer (e.g., if the transferor fraudulently re-transfers the shares to a subsequent buyer) or from paying a dividend without first notifying the owner of the equitable interest, who will then have eight days to apply to the courts to stop the company from carrying out the transaction.

Equitable interest in shares. There are various ways in which equitable interests may attach to shares. The shareholder, while remaining on the register of members, may declare himself as trustee of the shares for others. Such action by the shareholder does not infringe a pre-emption clause unless the clause provides for such a situation or if the beneficiary is also given an irrevocable proxy to gain access to company meetings and vote **(Safeguard Industrial Investments Ltd. v National Westminster Bank Ltd. (1982))**. An equitable interest can also arise where the shareholder mortgages his shares by depositing his share certificate with the mortgagee together with '*a blank transfer*' (i.e., a proper instrument of transfer but with the transferee's name left blank, such name to be filled in by the transferee only if the shareholder defaults with the loan). As stated earlier, an equitable interest also arises where the shareholder has sold his shares to an unregistered transferee.

Where several equitable interests attach to shares, priorities will be given to the first in time **(Peat v Clayton (1906))**. In **Ireland v Hart (1902)**, a husband who was trustee of shares for his wife mortgaged them to a third party, who applied for registration. The wife learnt what had happened before the mortgagee became the registered holder of the shares, and applied to the courts for a declaration that her equitable interest prevailed over that of the mortgagee. The courts upheld her claim. It should be observed that her claim would have been defeated had the mortgagee obtained registration before she took the matter to court because a legal interest always prevails over an equitable interest. To prevent third party registration in such a case, it is prudent to serve a stop notice on the company.

Transmission of Shares

With transmission, the shares automatically pass to the personal representatives or to the trustee in bankruptcy; and there is no need to prepare an instrument of transfer. However, such persons do not become members of the company until their names are put on the register, so that they are not entitled to vote until then. Nevertheless, article 25 (for private companies) and article 66 (for public companies) provide that transmittees have the right to dividends and repayment of capital in a winding up; but they are also liable to the company for calls on the shares. Personal representatives such as executors or administrators of the deceased shareholder's estate must first notify the company of the shareholder's death and that they are his personal representatives (this requires evidence of the grant of probate or letters of administration from the Probate Registry) before they can receive dividends on the shares. If the estate is too small to warrant a grant of probate, then a death certificate together with the share certificate and the relevant indemnity is required in order to carry out the transmission. A transmittee can elect either to become registered holder of the shares **(Scott v Frank F. Scott Ltd. (1940)** or to have the shares transferred to another person.

A member is not allowed to arrange for the direct transfer of his shares to a beneficiary, after his death, without a properly executed instrument of transfer. In **Re Greene (1949)**, the articles provided that, on the death of a shareholder, his shares should be registered in the name of the widow. The court held that as a proper instrument of transfer had not been prepared, the widow was not entitled to registration. A trustee in bankruptcy has a right to sell and transfer the bankrupt member's shares or, if they are onerous property, to disclaim them. If they are disclaimed, the company can prove in the bankruptcy for any amount unpaid on the shares.

Forgery and Shares

When forgery affects a company's shares, it may do so in one of two ways. A forged share certificate could have been issued to an innocent allottee by a person without authority purporting to act on behalf of the company; or the company could have been deceived into registering a forged transfer of shares belong to one of its members. In either case the question that arises is what, if any, is the liability of the company to innocent persons affected by the forgery?

A forged share certificate cannot create an estoppel against the company if any of its agents, with no real or apparent authority, should issue a share certificate by forging the directors' signature. In **Ruben v Gt Fingall Consolidated (1906)**, the company secretary issued a share certificate without authority, affixed the common seal, and forged the signatures of the two directors; so that the certificate apparently complied with the company's articles. The House of Lords held that the company was not estopped by the forged share certificate nor was it liable for the secretary's fraud, since the issuing of share certificates was a matter for the directors and not within the scope of the secretary's duties.

At common law a forged transfer is a nullity, and cannot affect the title of the shareholder whose signature is forged. Therefore he can compel the company to put him back on the register **(Barton v North Staffordshire Rly (1888))**. An innocent third party who obtains registration of the forged transfer of shares to himself cannot rely on the new share certificate issued to him by the company since he obtained it by presenting a forged transfer form; but if he transfers the shares to another innocent transferee, the latter may make the company liable on the new share certificate, although the company in turn will be entitled to an indemnity from the person who submitted the forged transfer for registration **(Re Bahia and San Francisco Rly. (1968))**. Alternatively, the company may keep the second purchaser on the register and simply buy other shares to register in the name of the original owner.

In **Sheffield Corp. v Barclay (1905)**, *B* sent to the corporation for registration a transfer of stock which stood in the names of *T* and *H*. The transfer was a forgery because *T* had forged *H*'s signature on the transfer. *B* was ignorant of the forgery. The corporation duly registered the transfer. *B* transferred the stock to third parties to whom share certificates were issued. The corporation was estopped from denying that those registered were in fact stockholders. *H* subsequently discovered the forgery and compelled the corporation to buy him an equivalent amount of stock and pay him the missing dividends with interest. The courts held that *B* had to indemnify the corporation for any damages that it paid out even though he was unaware of the forgery, because he submitted the forged transfer.

Chapter 8

Maintenance of Capital

A company limited by shares has its capital to back its credit. This capital has to be broad-based and of a permanent nature from the viewpoint of the creditors since they cannot claim against shareholders' wealth when the company's assets are not enough to meet its liabilities. The Companies Act seeks to satisfy both needs of the creditors. It defines 'capital' widely to include not only the money invested by the members in the business (i.e., share capital) but also certain other reserves (e.g., share premium, capital redemption reserves, and even the company's unrealised profits). It also lays down rules which ensure that this 'capital' is preserved for the benefit of the creditors. These rules do not prevent the company from using the capital to trade (e.g., to buy assets and stock); but are intended to prevent the company from returning the capital to the members except in a winding up or under relevant statutory procedure. The funds which the company is prevented from distributing to its shareholders but instead to use for the payment of its debts are called *statutory reserves*.

The main capital maintenance rule is found in section 617 of the Companies Act which prohibits a company from altering its share capital except if the purpose is to increase its capital by allotting new shares; or to subdivide or consolidate its shares under section 618; or to redenominate all or any of its shares in accordance with section 662 (see Chapter 7); or to reduce its capital under section 641. Section 617 is not infringed where the company accepts its own shares as an outright gift (provided the shares are fully paid up); or where it acquires the shares under a court order (e.g., section 98 for objection to a resolution to re-register a public company as private, and section 994 for conduct unfairly prejudicial to minorities); or where it forfeits or accepts a surrender of its shares for failure of members to pay sums due on them. In addition, a company is allowed to redeem or purchase its shares under sections 684 and 690 respectively as long as its creditors are not placed in a worse position regarding their security. This is achieved by requiring the capitalisation of distributable profits unless additional share capital is received to match the monies paid out for the redemption or purchase.

Details of the statutory provisions concerning the reduction of capital, together with other capital maintenance provisions, are given below.

1. **Reduction of share capital**

The main procedure for capital reduction is found in section 641. This section permits a company to reduce its share capital by special resolution confirmed by the courts or, in the case of a private company by special resolution supported by a solvency statement. A solvency statement dispenses with the need for a private company to obtain a court order before it can reduce its capital. Section 641 is subject to any provision in the company's articles restricting or prohibiting the company from reducing its share capital. Section 641 (4) specifies three instances where capital might be reduced:

(a) To extinguish or to reduce the liability of members for unpaid capital.
(b) To cancel paid-up capital that is lost or unrepresented by available assets.
(c) To pay off capital in excess of the company's needs.

However, this list is not exhaustive and it was suggested by Lord MacNaghten in **Poole v National Bank of China (1907)** that 'the condition that gives jurisdiction (to confirm a reduction of capital) … arises whenever the company seeking reduction has passed a special resolution to that effect'. The procedure under section 641 also applies to the amounts recorded in the share premium account, the capital redemption reserve and the re-denomination reserve.

In deciding whether to sanction the reduction, the courts have to take into account the interest of the creditors and of the members. A reduction under (a) and (c) will deprive the creditors of funds which could be used to pay off their debts in a winding up. In such cases (and in any other case as the courts may direct), the company must give the courts a list of its creditors and, unless the company has already done so, the courts will advertise for claims to be made by them **(s.646)**. Any creditor who does not consent to the reduction will have to be paid off or given some security before the courts will dispense with his consent. Only creditors who can show that they have an admissible debt or claim and that there is a real likelihood that the proposed reduction in capital would result in the company being unable to discharge their debts or claims as they fall due, can object to the reduction **(s.646 (1)(b))**. A reduction of capital under (b) will be sanctioned by the courts only if the loss is permanent and not merely a temporary fall in the value of some capital assets **(Re Jupiter House Investments (Cambridge) (1985)**.

When considering the interests of the members, the courts must be satisfied that, before the members passed the special resolution, the company had provided sufficient information to the members as to why a reduction of capital was necessary. This is to ensure that members were able to make a real choice as to whether or not to agree to the reduction. The information to members should have been given in a circular accompanying the notice of the members meeting. Moreover, the scheme to reduce the company's capital has to be fair and equitable. If the company wishes to repay excess capital or to reduce the nominal value of its issued shares because of a loss of assets, the reduction should be carried out as in a winding up and the rules of repayment of capital have to be complied with. Thus, if some members are preferential as to repayment of capital they will have to be repaid first, whether or not they agree to it. However, they will bear any loss of capital last. In **Prudential Assurance Co. Ltd. v Chatterley-Whitfield Collieries Ltd. (1949)**, the company had surplus capital, and a special resolution was passed reducing the capital by paying off preference shares which carried a right to the repayment of capital over all other shares. The court sanctioned the reduction even though the preference shareholders wanted to remain in the company which was becoming prosperous.

Any reduction other than in accordance with rights in a winding up will be a variation of class rights, and the courts will not confirm such a reduction unless the variation of class rights procedure is followed. In **Carruth v Imperial Chemical Industries Ltd. (1937)**, the company had issued £1 ordinary shares and 50p deferred shares, both fully paid. The market value of the deferred shares subsequently fell to 25p. The company then proposed to reduce the deferred shares to 25p, so that another resolution passed by the deferred shareholders for converting the deferred shares into ordinary shares, on the basis of 4 deferred shares for one ordinary share, might be more conveniently carried out. The court confirmed the reduction.

Where the courts confirm a reduction they may order the company to publish the reasons for the reduction of capital and the causes that led to the reduction; and they may direct the company to add to its name as its last words "and reduced" during such period as may be specified by the courts **(s.648)**. The confirming order and a new statement of capital (approved by the courts) must be delivered to the Registrar for registration **(s.649)**. The Registrar will then certify the registration of the order and statement of capital. The reduction takes effect on registration. Where a public company obtains a court order reducing its capital below the authorised minimum, the Registrar cannot register the court order making the reduction unless ordered by the courts to do so or unless the company is first re-registered as a private company **(s.650)**. Section 651 allows an expedited procedure for re-registration in such cases.

As an alternative to the court approved procedure for capital reduction, a private company may reduce its capital by passing a special resolution; but each of the directors must then make a statement of solvency, within 15 days, before the date on which the resolution is passed; and the resolution and supporting documents (i.e., a copy of the solvency statement and a statement of capital) must be delivered to the Registrar within 15 days after the resolution is passed **(s.642)**. The solvency statement is a written statement signed by each director stating that in his opinion there is no ground on which the company could be found to be unable to pay, or otherwise discharge its debts; **and** that the company will have sufficient assets to meet its liabilities in full (or as the debts fall due) for the next twelve months. Moreover, if it is intended to wind up the company within that year, the directors must be of the opinion that the company will be able to pay or otherwise discharge its debts within the twelve months of the winding up. It is an offence to make a solvency statement without reasonable grounds **(s.643)**. Where the resolution to reduce capital is to be passed at a general meeting, a copy of the solvency statement must be made available for inspection by the members throughout the meeting; and if the resolution is to be passed as a written resolution, a copy of the solvency statement must be sent to the members at the same time as the proposed resolution. The solvency statement procedure for capital reduction provides a simpler and cheaper means for a private company to reduce its capital; but it can only be used if the company will still have at least one member holding non-redeemable shares left after the proposed reduction. A reduction of capital using the solvency statement route takes effect when it is registered with the Registrar of Companies. A private company which is insolvent, will have to use the court procedure route if it wants to reduce its capital.

Legally, any reserve arising from a reduction of capital may be treated as a realised profit and can be distributed unless the company is prohibited from making such a distribution, for example, by the courts or by the articles. However, accounting guidelines usually treat this surplus as an accounting reserve in order to 'balance the books'.

2. **Redemption of Shares**

Section 684 permits a company, if authorised by its articles (a private company does not need authority in its articles before it can issue redeemable; but the articles may exclude or limit the issue of such shares) to issue shares which are to be redeemed at a fixed date or at the option of either the company or the shareholder. If there is no power in the articles of a public company to issue such shares, power could be included at a later date by the shareholders altering the articles by special resolution. Companies usually issue redeemable shares in order to make the shareholder a temporary member of the company. To ensure that the company will never find itself in a situation where it has no member left, redeemable shares can only be issued (and redeemed) if the company already has in existence issued shares which are non-redeemable. The shares must be fully paid up before they can be redeemed, and the articles must set out the terms and manner for redeeming the shares or else the directors must be allowed either by the articles or by the members by ordinary resolution, to fix the terms and manner for the redemption of the shares (e.g., the time when the shares are to be redeemed).

Shares redeemed are automatically cancelled so that the company must destroy them. The company has to notify the registrar within one month that it has redeemed some or all of its redeemable shares and file an updated statement of capital **(s.689)**.

3. **Purchase of Shares**

Section 690 allows a company to purchase its own shares (including any redeemable shares) as long as the company pays for the shares in full at the time of the purchase. This section is subject to any provision in the company's articles restricting or prohibiting the company from purchasing its shares. Thus, the default rule is that all companies have power to purchase their shares. The shares must be fully paid up before they can be purchased; and the effect of the purchase should not leave the company only with redeemable shares or, in the case of a public company, shares held as treasury shares. In addition, the company must obtain authority from its members to make the purchase. Members' authority is given by resolution. The type of resolution which members must pass will depend on whether the purchase is an off-market purchase or a market purchase.

(a) **Off-market purchase**. This arises where the shares are not listed on the Stock Exchange or otherwise dealt with on a

UK recognised investment exchange. The members must approve by special resolution the terms of the contract before the purchase can be made **(s.694)**; and in the case of a public company, the resolution authorising the purchase must state the date when the authority is to expire (this date cannot be more than five years after the date of passing the resolution). The authority may be revoked, varied or renewed by special resolution. Where the resolution is to be passed at a meeting, a copy of the proposed purchase contract must be made available for inspection by the members at the company's registered office for at least 15 days immediately preceding the meeting and at the meeting, and the identity of the vendor must be disclosed. Any member at the meeting (other than the member whose shares are to be purchased by the company) has a right to demand a poll on the resolution. Where the resolution is proposed as a written resolution a copy of the proposed contract must be sent to the members at the same time that the proposed resolution is sent. Voting rights attached to the shares to be purchased cannot be exercised to secure the passing of the resolution, whether the resolution is to be passed at a general meeting or as a written resolution.

An off-market purchase of its shares by a company may be effected to buy out a dissident member, to retain family control where a member wishes to leave the company, to allow shares under an employee share scheme to be purchased when an employee leaves the company's employment, and to provide a degree of marketability for a private company's shares since the shareholder will have the company itself as a potential buyer.

(b) **Market purchase**. A public company which wishes to purchase its shares on a UK recognised investment exchange must first obtain authority from its members by ordinary resolution. The authority may be general or limited to the purchase of shares of a particular class; and it may be unconditional or subject to conditions. The resolution must state the maximum number of shares that may be purchased, the maximum and minimum prices to be paid, and the date when the authority is to expire (this should not be later than five years from the date the resolution is passed). The ordinary resolution has to be filed at Companies Registry within 15 days as if it were a special resolution **(s.701 (8))**. Stock Exchange rules for listed companies buying back their shares will also have to be observed.

A market purchase of its own shares by a public company may be effected as a means of using surplus cash advantageously, particularly where redeemable shares are listed at below their redemption price; also to re-arrange the company's capital (e.g., by purchasing non-redeemable preference shares to reduce gearing).

A purchase (whether an off-market purchase or a market purchase) is carried out usually by a surrender of shares so that there is no need for a formal transfer. However, section 707 requires the company to file details of the purchase (including information as to whether the shares purchased are of a type which can be held as treasury shares, and if so, whether they are to be cancelled or will be held as treasury shares) with the Registrar of Companies within 28 days of completion; and section 702 requires the company to keep copies of all purchase and option contracts at its registered office or at a place specified by the Secretary of State for inspection by its members (or in the case of a public company for inspection by anyone) for up to 10 years. The tax inspector must also be informed of the purchase. Like redemption, shares purchased are cancelled automatically (unless they are to be held as treasury shares). This would result in the reduction of the company's issued share capital by the nominal value of the shares purchased. Thus, the Registrar must be supplied with an updated capital statement.

A public company which purchases its shares (including redeemable shares) which are listed on the stock exchange or traded on the Alternative Investment Market (or other regulated exchange/market in another EEA state) need not cancel the shares but may hold them as treasury shares and register itself as member of the shares. This allows the directors to raise cash quickly by reselling the shares at some future point without having to get prior authority from the members to issue shares. However, the company cannot exercise membership rights attached to the treasury shares, such as right to vote and to receive a dividend **(s.726 (2))**. Treasury shares can only be purchased out of distributable profits; and if they are later resold by the company the proceeds of sale can be treated as distributable profits (because they were purchased out of profits); but any sum in excess of the price which the company initially paid for purchasing the shares has to be transferred to the share premium account **(s.731 (3))**.

A company which breaches its obligation to redeem or purchase its shares is liable to the shareholder for breach of contract but the shareholder must prove first that the company had distributable profits to fulfil its obligation and failed to use them **(s.735)**. If after the obligation to redeem or purchase has arisen the company goes into liquidation and could have fulfilled its obligation out of available profits, the shareholder may prove as a deferred creditor for any loss suffered (see Chapter 16 on Liquidation).

Financing the Redemption or Purchase

Subject to section 709 which allows a private company to redeem or purchase its own shares out of capital, the money

required for the acquisition of its shares must be provided out
of distributable profits or out of the proceeds of a fresh issue
of shares, or a combination of both **(s.692)**. For companies
which still have an authorised share capital in their articles,
replacement shares may be issued without the need to
increase the authorised capital, where the company had
already issued shares up to its authorised maximum.

If shares are being redeemed or purchased wholly out of
profits, a sum equal to the nominal value of the shares
concerned has to be transferred from profit and loss to a
capital redemption reserve to compensate the creditors for
the reduction in share capital **(s.733 (2))**. This reserve is
treated as part of the company's undistributable reserves
under section 831(4), and it may be applied only in paying up
shares issued to members as fully paid bonus shares **(s.733
(5))**; and, in the case of a private company, to off-set a
loss of capital resulting from the use of section 710. The
application of section 733 (2) can best be understood from
the following example:

BALANCE SHEET OF ALPHA LTD

		£
FIXED ASSETS		
Premises		400,000
Fixtures		40,000
		440,000
CURRENT ASSETS		
Stock	60,000	
Debtors	80,000	
Cash	140,000	
	280,000	
CURRENT LIABILITIES		
Creditors		80,000

		200,000
Net assets		640,000

Financed by
CAPITAL*

Ordinary shares of £1 each	400,000
Redeemable shares of £1 each	20,000
Share premium account	20,000
Revaluation Reserves	60,000
Profit & loss	120,000

Creditors –amounts falling due after more
than one year:

7% debentures	20,000
	640,000

* 'capital' in this context means a liability owed to someone with a proprietary interest (e.g., shareholders) or other long-term interest (e.g., debenture holders) in the business.

Alpha wishes to redeem all of its redeemable shares (20,000 shares) for £40,000 out of profits. The redeemable shares were issued at their par value (£1 each). The adjustments to the balance sheet will be:

(a) Cash will be reduced by £40,000
(b) Redeemable shares will be reduced by £20,000. So no redeemable shares will be left (shares redeemed will be cancelled).
(c) Profit & loss will be reduced by £40,000 (to reflect the use of profits to redeem the shares)
(d) Capital Redemption Reserve of £20,000 will be set up to replace the capital which is cancelled.

Revised Balance sheet of Alpha Ltd.

		£
FIXED ASSETS		
Premises		400,000
Fixtures		40,000
		440,000
CURRENT ASSETS		
Stock	60,000	
Debtors	80,000	
Cash	100,000	
	240,000	
CURRENT LIABILITIES		
Creditors –amounts falling due		
within a year	80,000	
		160.000
		600,000
Financed by		
CAPITAL		
Ordinary shares of £1 each		400,000
Share premium account		20,000
Capital redemption reserves		20,000
Revaluation Reserves		60,000
Profit & loss		80,000
Creditors – amounts falling due after more		
than one year:		
7% debentures		20,000
		600,000

If the shares are acquired wholly or partly out of the proceeds of a fresh issue of shares, and the aggregate amount of those proceeds is less than the nominal value of the shares being acquired, the amount of the difference must also be transferred to a capital redemption reserve **(s.733 (3))**.

Any premium payable by the company to a shareholder on the acquisition of his shares has to be paid out of distributable profits **(s.692 (2) (b))**. If, however, the shares were issued at a premium and are to be acquired out of the proceeds of a fresh issue of shares, the premium may be debited to the share premium account **(s.692 (3))**. The amount that can be debited to the share premium account is the lower of (i) the premium received by the company on the share being acquired and (ii) the current amount of the share premium account (including any sums transferred to that account in respect of premium received on the new shares). The application of section 692 (3) can best be understood from the following example:

BALANCE SHEET EXTRACTS

	£
Ordinary shares of £1 each	2,000
Redeemable shares of £1 each	1,000
Share premium account	500
Permanent capital	3,500
Distributable profits	900
Net assets (including cash)	4,400

The redeemable shares were issued at a premium of £150. The company now wishes to redeem them for £1,200 (i.e., at a premium of £200) and, for the purpose of redemption, issues 600 new ordinary shares of £1 for £650.

CALCULATION

(i) Premium received on original issue   150
(ii) Current amount in share premium
     account (including £50 premium
     received on the new shares)   550

The lowest of (i) and (ii) can be deducted from the share premium account (i.e., £150). The unrelieved balance (£50) has to be deducted from distributable profits.

The amount to be transferred from distributable profits to the capital redemption reserve to replace the issued share capital which is diminished by the redemption is the difference between the nominal value of the shares redeemed and the aggregate amount of the new issue of shares **(s. 733 (3))**. However, this can amount to a reduction of capital as the following illustration shows:

Revised Balance Sheet Extracts

	£
	£
Ordinary shares of £1 each	2,600
Share premium account	400
CRR £(1,000-650)	350
Permanent capital	3,350
Distributable profits £(900-350-50)	500
Net assets £(4,400-1,200+650)	3,850

Any payment made by a company to acquire options to make an off-market purchase or to release its obligation to purchase its own shares (whether in the market or off-market) must also come out of distributable profits **(s.705)**.

Redemption or Purchase out of Capital

A private company which complies with the requirements of section 684 (conditions for the redemption of own shares) or section 690 (conditions for purchase of own shares) and whose distributable profits and proceeds of a fresh issue of shares if any (where a fresh issue of shares was made for this purpose) are not enough to fund the redemption or purchase, can make good the shortfall out of capital **(s.709)**. This power to use its capital in this way is subject to any restriction or prohibition in the company's articles. The lawful use of capital in these circumstances is known as '*permissible capital payment*' (**PCP**).

The main safeguards for members are that the members must approve by special resolution the use of capital for the acquisition (with the same voting restrictions on the shares to be purchased) **(s.716)**, and that no payment can be made for five weeks after the resolution is passed during which time any member who voted against the resolution can apply to the courts to set it aside **(s.721)**.

The main safeguards for creditors are that the directors must make a statement of solvency, within one week before the resolution is passed, specifying the amount of the permissible capital payment for the shares in question and stating that the company will be able to pay its present and contingent debts immediately after the acquisition payment is made, and that the business will continue as a going concern for at least a year. The statement of solvency must be backed by an auditor's report stating that the amount of permissible capital payment has been properly determined and confirming that the directors' opinions as to the financial soundness of the company are reasonable **(s.714)**. The statement of solvency and the auditor's report must be available for inspection both by the members before they pass the special resolution and later, by the members and creditors at the company's registered office during the standstill period of five weeks **(s.720);** and they must be filed at the Registry. Within seven days after the resolution is passed, the company must also publish in the Gazette (and in a national newspaper if its own creditors had not been served personally with notice) details of the proposed capital payment **(s.719)**. The notice to creditors (whether it is personal notice or given by advertisement) must state that a special resolution to permit the company to acquire its own shares out of capital has been passed, that a statement of solvency backed by an auditor's report is available for their inspection at the company's registered office, and that any creditor can apply to the courts with five weeks from the date of the resolution to have the resolution set aside. Where an objection is made to the courts by any dissentient member or creditor, the courts may confirm, amend or cancel the resolution, require the company to purchase the shares of the objector, and insist on additional protection for the creditor **(s.721 (4))**.

The payment out of capital has to be made between five and seven weeks after the resolution date. If the company is wound up within one year after the capital payment, the persons whose shares were acquired out of capital and the directors who signed the statement of solvency (unless those directors had reasonable grounds for their belief) will be liable to repay the amount paid out of capital **(s.76 IA)**.

The accounting requirements relating to shares redemption or purchase out of capital depend on whether the permissible capital payment (and the proceeds of any fresh issue of shares, if one was made) is less than, or greater than, the nominal value of the shares redeemed or purchased. If it is less than the nominal value of the shares redeemed or purchased, the amount of the difference must be transferred to the capital redemption reserve. However, if it is greater, the excess can be deducted from any capital redemption reserve, share premium account, fully paid share capital, or revaluation reserves account (representing net unrealised profits of the company). The effect of using unrealised profits for this purpose is to reduce the amount available for distribution when the profits become realised, as they will have been utilised already. The effect of this will be to reduce the net assets as the following illustration shows:

BALANCE SHEET OF BETHA LTD.

		£
FIXED ASSETS		
Premises		300,000
Fixtures		40,000
		340,000
CURRENT ASSETS		
Stock	60,000	
Debtors	40,000	
Cash	80,000	
	180,000	
CURRENT LIABILITIES		
Creditors	80,000	
		100,000
Net assets		440,000

Financed by
CAPITAL
Ordinary shares of £1 each	360,000
Redeemable shares of £1 each	50,000
Share premium account	10,000
Profit & loss	20,000
	440,000

The company issues 15,000 £1 ordinary shares at par to provide part of the funding for redeeming all the redeemable shares. The cost of redeeming the shares is £40,000.
The permissible capital payment is:

	£	£
Cost of redemption		40,000
Less: distributable profits	20,000	
Proceeds of fresh issue	15,000	
		35,000
Permissible capital payment		5,000

The adjustments to the balance sheet will be:
(a) Reduce cash by £25,000 (i.e., £40,000 - £15,000)
(b) Reduce redeemable shares by £50,000
(c) Increase ordinary shares by £15,000
(d) Reduce profit and loss by £20,000
(e) Create capital redemption reserves of £30,000*

	£	£
*Nominal value of shares redeemed		50,000
Less: permissible capital payment	5,000	
15,000 proceeds of fresh issue	15,000	
		20,000
		30,000

Revised Balance Sheet of Alpha Ltd.

	£	£
FIXED ASSETS		
Premises	300,000	
Fixtures	40,000	
		340,000
CURRENT ASSETS		
Stock	60,000	
Debtors	40,000	
Cash	55,000	
	155,000	
CURRENT LIABILITIES		
Creditors	80,000	
		75,000
Net Assets		415,000
Financed by		
CAPITAL		
Ordinary shares of £1 each		375,000
Share premium account		10,000
Capital redemption reserves		30,000
Distributable profits		0
		415,000

If the cost of redeeming the shares was £75,000 then the permissible capital payment would have been £40,000 (75,000- 20,000-15,000); and as the aggregate of the PCP and the proceeds from the fresh issue of shares £(40,00+15,000) would be greater than the nominal value of the shares being redeemed £(50,000), the excess (£5,000) could be written off to the share premium account. Thus the revised balance sheet extract would be:

	£
Ordinary shares of £1 each	375,000
Share Premium £ (10,000 – 5,000)	5,000
Permanent capital	380,000
Distributable profit	0
Net assets	380,000

4. Financial Assistance for Purchase of Own Shares

Section 678 makes it unlawful, subject to a few exceptions, for a public company (or its subsidiary) to give financial assistance for the purpose of the acquisition of its shares; and section 679 prohibits a public company (or any other subsidiary) from giving financial assistance to acquire shares in its private holding company. These sections are not infringed if the assistance is an incidental part of some larger purpose and is given by the directors in good faith for the benefit of the company (e.g., where the company gives money to X principally to purchase goods supplied by him and X uses the money to buy its shares). The prohibition on financial assistance only applies to UK public companies and their UK subsidiaries. Thus, no offence is committed under section 678 where an overseas incorporated subsidiary gives financial assistance for the purchase of shares in its UK incorporated public holding company, even if the assistance reduces the value of the subsidiary's shares held by the UK holding company, and thus the holding company's net assets **(AMG Global Nominee (Private) Ltd. v SMM Holdings Ltd. (2008)**. Also, a private company may give financial assistance freely for the purchase of its own shares.

'Financial assistance' is elaborately defined and includes any gift, loan, guarantee or indemnity, security, release or other assistance which materially reduces the net assets of the company. 'Net assets' here means the aggregate amount of the company's assets less the aggregate amount of its liabilities. Moreover, it makes no difference whether the assistance is direct or indirect, or whether it is given before or after the acquisition of the shares. However, post-acquisition assistance (i.e., where financial assistance is given after the acquisition of the shares) is only unlawful if the assistance is given at a time when the company is a public company. This means that if a person takes a loan from a bank to purchase shares in a public company and later the company re-registers as a private company and then gives the borrower financial assistance by acting as a surety for the loan, no offence is committed by the company under the section. On the other hand, if the company was a private company when the shares were acquired, but at the time the assistance is given it has re-registered as a public company, the prohibition in section 678 will apply.

The following transactions are not caught within the ambit of the basic prohibition **(s.681)**: those relating to the payment of a dividend out of profits (e.g., where a third party lends X money to purchase shares in the company and the company subsequently declares a dividend on those shares, which X uses to repay the loan); distributions made in the course of a winding up; allotment of bonus shares; reduction of capital approved by the courts; redemption or purchase of shares under sections 684 and 690; and certain transactions incidental to reconstruction, amalgamation and liquidation under relevant company legislation.

The following three transactions made by a public company although caught within the basic prohibition, are exempted by section 682 provided the financial assistance does not reduce the company's net assets (e.g., where the assistance is a loan); or if it does (e.g., where the assistance is a gift), to the extent that the assistance is provided out of distributable profits: (i) a loan by a money-lending company in the ordinary course of business to a customer who uses it to purchase the lender's own shares. A loan given expressly to purchase the lender's own shares is not a loan in the ordinary course of business **(Steen v Law (1964))**; (ii) the provision of money by a company for the purchase of its shares under an employee share scheme. It is not necessary to appoint trustees before a company can benefit from this exception; and (iii) a loan by a company to any of its employees (other than directors) to enable them to own shares in the company or its holding company.

For the purposes of section 682, 'net assets' means the amount by which the aggregate of the company's assets exceeds the aggregate of its liabilities. The amount of both assets and liabilities is the amount stated in the company's accounting records immediately before the financial assistance is given. 'Liabilities' include a reasonable sum retained by the company to meet prospective liabilities (i.e., liabilities which the company will have to meet in the future although the amount or the date on which they arise is uncertain).

Sanction for non-compliance. If unlawful assistance is given by a public company criminal sanction is imposed on the company and every director who is knowingly a party to the breach. The transaction is void for illegality (unless, as in **Carney v Herbert (1985)**, the courts can sever the illegal elements from the rest of the transaction), and any security or guarantee given in connection with the transaction will be invalid **(Selangor Rubber Estates v Cradock (1967))**.

The company will obtain a beneficial interest in the shares where the person to whom the assistance was given did not acquire the shares by subscribing for them but purchased them, when they were fully paid up, from a third party with the intention of holding them on trust for the company **(s.660)**.

5. **Effect of Shares Acquired by a Company**
(i) **Lawful acquisition**. Although as a general rule a limited company is prohibited from acquiring its own shares, whether by purchase, subscription or otherwise **(s.658)**, the prohibition does not apply (and so no offence is committed under the section by the company and its directors) where the company acquires or has a beneficial interest in the shares in the following ways:

(a) It redeems or purchases its shares under relevant legislation or a court order.
(b) It forfeits the shares or accepts a surrender of them in lieu, in pursuance of its articles, for failure to pay any sum payable in respect of the shares.
(c) It accepts as an outright gift its fully paid shares.
(d) It obtains a beneficial interest in fully paid shares held by its nominee who acquired them from a third party for the company, and without any financial assistance being provided from the company for the acquisition (e.g., as in **Re Castiglione's Will Trust (1958)** where a member in his will left his fully paid shares to a nominee of the company on trust for it).

In case (a) the shares are cancelled automatically (unless they are to be held as treasury shares). In cases (b), (c) and (d) if the company holds the shares on a balance sheet date, the shares must be shown as investments in the assets section of the balance sheet and, if the company is a public company, an amount equal to the value of the shares must be transferred out of profits available for dividend to a reserve fund ('*the reserve for own shares*'). This fund is a statutory reserve which cannot be used to pay a dividend **(s.669)**. A public company should reissue shares it acquires in cases (b), (c) and (d) within three years **(s.662 (3))**. If it fails to reissue them within the time limit it must cancel the shares by directors' resolution. On cancellation of the shares, the share capital must be reduced by the nominal value of the shares cancelled **(s.662 (2) (a))**.

Where the effect of a cancellation of such shares is to bring the nominal value of the company's allotted share capital to below the authorised minimum (i.e., £50,000), the company is obliged to apply for re-registration as a private company **(s.662 (2) (b))**. There is a default fine for failing to cancel shares and to re-register.

A company which fails to re-reregister is still treated as a public company except that it cannot have its shares dealt in on a recognised exchange or advertise its shares for sale. Thus it will still have to file full accounts, its shares cannot be issued for services and its ability to make distributions out of distributable profits is still restricted. A public company cannot exercise any voting rights on shares required to be cancelled.

(ii) **Unlawful acquisition**.   This can arise where (a) the company acquires as an outright gift its shares which are only partly paid up; or (b) it obtains a beneficial interest in partly paid shares held by a nominee who acquired them from a third party for the company, and without any financial assistance being provided from the company for the acquisition.

In case (a) the acquisition is void and the company and its officers are liable to a fine (with possible imprisonment of those officers). In case (b) the shares are to be treated as held by the nominee on his own account (i.e., the company is regarded as having no beneficial interest in them).

6. Distribution of Profits and Assets

Section 830 prohibits a limited company with a share capital from making a distribution to its members unless the distribution comes out of profits available for distribution. Distribution means giving the company's assets, whether in the form of cash (e.g., dividends) or otherwise to members. Thus, gifts of company assets (other than cash) to members, such as where the company transfers an asset to a member for a consideration which is below the asset's book value, will come within the ambit of the section, and so the company must have an equivalent amount of distributable profits to cover the distribution **(s.845)**. If the company has no distributable profits to cover the shortfall, this would be an unlawful distribution contrary to section 830. If the consideration for the asset exceeds the asset's book value, the amount of the distribution is zero. Where the company had revalued the asset before transferring it and the revalued asset includes an unrealised profit in the company's accounts, the unrealised profit may be treated as realised for the purpose of making the distribution lawful **(s.846)**. Section 830 excludes the following acts done by a company: issuing bonus shares; redeeming, purchasing or giving financial assistance for the purchase of shares under company legislation; reducing capital under established procedures; and distributing assets to members in a winding up.

In determining whether the company has 'profits available for distribution', the company has to satisfy the *realised profits test*. This test applies to the company's profit and loss account. It provides that the 'profits available for distribution' will be the company's accumulated realised profits (revenue and capital) in so far as they have not been previously utilised by a distribution or capitalisation, less its accumulated realised losses (revenue and capital) in so far as they have not been previously written off in a reduction or reorganisation of capital. Realised profits are the amount by which the revenue from sales of company assets in a financial year exceeds the expenses of sale. If the expenses of sale exceed the revenue from sale then there is a realised loss for that financial year. Unrealised profits cannot be used to declare a dividend, or to pay up debentures or amounts unpaid on issued shares **(s.849)**; but they may be used for paying up bonus shares **(s.835(3))**. Unrealised profits arise where the assets appreciate in value and the new value is recorded in the accounts. They will be shown in the accounts as *revaluation reserves*. If there is an overall decrease in the book value of the company's assets, this unrealised loss will be shown in the accounts as a debit balance in the revaluation reserves.

Where a company makes provision in its accounts, other than revaluation provisions, (e.g., provision for bad debts, or for depreciation of a fixed but wasting asset) that provision is to be treated as a realised loss **(s. 841(2))**. A 'provision' is an amount set aside to meet a known liability, the amount of which cannot be determined precisely. In the case of provision for depreciation of assets, that provision may be calculated at original cost (i.e., historical cost) so that if the asset is revalued any increased provision relating to the increase in value of the asset can be treated as profit. For example, if in **2004** a company purchased an asset with a life expectancy of 50 years for £100,000 and set aside in the accounts a sum of £2,000 a year for depreciation, and in **2014** the asset is revalued at £200,000 and the sum included in the accounts for depreciation is increased to £4,500 (£180,000 divided by 40 years = £4,500), the difference between £80,000 (the sum which would have been retained originally for depreciation of the asset) and £180,000 (the sum now retained as a result of an increase in value of the asset), namely £100,000, is treated as a realised profit made over that period of 40 years. Thus, £2,500 per year may be added back to reserves in order to determine the company's accumulated realised profits. If there is no record of the original cost of an asset, the directors may use the earliest record of value available to them.

Where, on a revaluation of all fixed assets (or all except goodwill) there is a diminution in value of a fixed asset, any increase in the provision for that asset need not be treated as a realised loss if there is an overall increase in value of all the fixed assets **(s.841(5))**. The revaluation of all the fixed assets need not be formal but only need to be considered by the directors **(s.841(4))**. However a note in the accounts must state that the directors have considered the value of all fixed assets, without actually revaluing them; that they are satisfied that the aggregate value of the fixed assets is not less than their value as stated in the accounts; and that the asset that has diminished in value is recorded in the accounts after providing for that decline in value.

Public companies. As well as satisfying the realised profits test, a public company must also satisfy the *net assets test*. This test applies to the company's balance sheet; and it prohibits a public company from making a distribution if its net assets (assets minus liabilities) are less (or would be less after the distribution) than the aggregate of its called up capital and its undistributable reserves. Undistributable reserves are the share premium account, capital redemption reserves, the excess of accumulated unrealised profits over accumulated unrealised losses, and any other reserve which the company is prevented from distributing by law (e.g., redenomination reserves) or by its constitution **(s.831).** The effect of the *net assets test* as laid down in section 831 is that a public company must also make good its net unrealised losses before it can declare a dividend to shareholders. The application of section 830 (*the realised profits test*) and section 831 (*the net assets test*) can best be understood from the following example:

BALANCE SHEET EXTRACTS

		Company A £		Company B £
Ordinary Shares of £1 each		100,000		100,000
Share Premium		5,000		5,000
CRR		5,000		5,000
Revaluation reserves/ (deficit)		75,000		(15,000)
Permanent capital		185,000		95,000
Profit & loss reserves				
b/f	(20,000)		40,000	
Profit for year	60,000		80,000	
less:				
Realised loss	(20,000)		(60,000)	
		20,000		60,000
Net assets		205,000		155,000

Distributable profits
(a) If private company	£20,000	£60,000

(b) If public company:

£(205,000 – 185,000)   £20,000   £45,000

In the case of Company B plc, the net assets test prevents the company from distributing £60,000 as dividends, since the net assets, £95,000 (155,000 - 60,000) would be reduced to below the aggregate of the called up capital and statutory reserves, £110,000 (100,000 + 5,000 + 5,000). Company B can only distribute £45,000, since its net unrealised loss will first have to be offset from its net realised profits.

Investment companies. If the constitution of an investment company prohibits the company from distributing capital profits, the company can made a distribution out of its accumulated realised revenue profits less its accumulated revenue losses (whether realised or unrealised); but only if the effect of the distribution would not reduce the assets to less than one and a half times the aggregate of its liabilities **(s.832)**.

An investment company is a public company, whose shares are quoted on a recognised exchange, and whose business consists of investing its funds mainly in securities mainly with the aim of spreading investment risk.

Insurance companies. In determining its distributable profits all amounts shown in its profit and loss account must be treated as though they are realised (even though this is not really so). An insurance company is a company registered under the Insurance Act 1982 and which carries on long term business.

Consequences of an unlawful distribution. By section 847, any member who receives an unlawful distribution and who knows or ought to know that it has come out of undistributable funds is liable to repay the amount he has received. If that amount cannot be recovered from the member, then every director who is knowingly a party to the payment is jointly and severally liable to pay the account with interest.

In practice, recovery of the unlawful distribution will be sought from the directors rather than the member since the latter is unlikely to be aware of the lawfulness or otherwise of the distribution, especially if the company is a public company. Thus, in **Bairstow v Queen's Moot Houses plc (2000)**, the directors who made an unlawful payment of a dividend were required by the courts to repay the dividend since they were aware that the annual accounts were not prepared in accordance with the Companies Act.

Dividends

The question of declaration and payment of dividend is usually dealt with by the articles. Where statutory articles are adopted, Article 70 of model articles for public companies, and article 30 model articles for private companies give the directors the sole power to recommend to the members whether a dividend should be declared and if so, how much that dividend should be; and, except for an interim dividend, the dividend has to be approved by the members by ordinary resolution. The members cannot approve a dividend unless it is recommended by the directors; nor can they approve a dividend exceeding the amount recommended by the directors. A dividend so declared and approved becomes an enforceable debt from the date the resolution is passed.

Directors have power to declare an interim dividend without having to obtain the consent of the members; but this must be justified, usually by reference to the company's last set of annual accounts which must be prepared to give a true and fair view of the company's financial affairs. If a distribution on the basis of the last accounts would make the dividend unlawful (e.g., because they show a net loss), the directors may justify the interim dividend on the basis of the company's interim accounts. Interim accounts are usually prepared where the company has started to make profits again and does not want to wait until the next set of full accounts before it declares a dividend. Interim accounts must be prepared in just the same way as full accounts; but they need not be audited. However, in the case of public companies, interim accounts must be filed at Companies Registry before any distribution can be made. Directors may cancel an interim dividend before payment **(Lagunas Nitrate Co. v Schroeder (1901)**.

Although members cannot insist on directors recommending a dividend, in some cases refusal to recommend a dividend may be used as a ground for a compulsory winding up order under the 'just and equitable' ground of the Insolvency Act 1986 s.122 (1)(g) **(Loch v John Blackwood Ltd. (1924))**. Additionally, it may constitute 'unfair prejudicial conduct' resulting in relief to minorities under section 994 of the Companies Act.

7. Serious Loss of Capital

Where the net assets of a public company have been reduced by losses to half or less of the amount of its called up capital, the directors are required to convene an extraordinary general meeting within 28 days to consider the company's financial position and whether it should re-register as a private company **(s. 656)**. The meeting must be held not later than 56 days from the day the directors were aware that the company had suffered a serious capital loss. Directors who knowingly fail to comply with section 656 will have committed an offence and liable to a fine.

Chapter 9

Debentures

The usual method of raising long-term loans is for a company to issue debentures, or debenture stock, to persons prepared to lend it money. A **debenture** is a document evidencing a debt, and it may be secured by a charge over some property of the company. A legal charge of land by a company is a debenture **(Knightsbridge Estates Trust Ltd. v Byrne (1940))**. A debenture is indivisible, and it usually provides for repayment at specified dates. Debenture stock constitutes one composite debt, and is created by trust deed. It can be transferred in fractional amounts, and is often made repayable in the event of a winding up of the company or by its default. Unlike debenture holders, debenture stockholders are not creditors of the company but only beneficiaries under a trust.

For isolated transactions, such as to obtain a loan or overdraft from a bank, the company simply will issue single debentures. But with larger public issues, the debentures are issued in series, all ranking equally with each other. Public issue of debentures and debenture stock are governed by the same rules as those governing shares; thus, for example, a formal prospectus has to be registered at Companies Registry. Debentures are issued in accordance with the articles, usually by directors' resolution. Stock can be issued only if they are fully paid. Section 741 requires a company to register an allotment of debentures as soon as practicable, but in any event not later than two months after their allotment; and section 769 requires it to complete and issue certificates to debenture holders (or debenture stockholders) within two months of an allotment or of a transfer being lodged, unless the issue otherwise provides. Such holders also have a right to obtain a copy of any debenture trust deed, on payment of a fee **(s.744)**. A company is not obliged to keep a register of debenture holders; but if one is kept, it must be kept in the same country as the company's registered office **(s.743)**, and it must be opened to inspection by any person except when duly closed. The total period for which the register is closed in any year cannot exceed 30 days **(s.744 (5))**. Members of the public requesting to inspect or to be provided with a copy of the register must provide the company with their name and address and the purpose for which the information will be used. The company has 5 days to comply with the request unless it applies to the courts to set aside the request on grounds that the information is sought for an improper purpose **(s.745)**. A company which keeps a register of debentures must notify Companies Registry of the place where such register is kept available for inspection and of any change of that place **(s.743 (2))**; so that it will be of public knowledge.

Trust Deed

Debenture stock and debentures issued in series are issued usually by a trust deed whereby the assets charged as security are transferred by the company to trustees, normally a trust corporation like an insurance company, for the benefit of the lenders.

The normal trust deed would include provisions dealing with the following matters: appointment and powers of the trustees; description and terms of the debenture or debenture stock; the type of security and circumstances in which it will be enforced; the obligations of the company.

A trust deed has several advantages. First, it enables the security to be by way of specific mortgage or charge on the company's land, rather than just by way of floating charge. By giving the security to trustees, the prohibition by the Law of Property Act 1925 that a legal interest in land cannot be vested in more than four persons is thus circumvented. Secondly, where the security is a specific charge on shares in a subsidiary company, the presence of trustees ensures that persons independent of the holding company will exercise any right to vote. Thirdly, trustees with necessary powers are able to intervene promptly in the event of default by the company. Fourthly, since debenture holders often lack the skill, interest and financial resources to safeguard their interest properly, the expertise of trustees is a considerable advantage to them.

Registered and Bearer Debentures
Debentures can be in registered form, transferable by a duly stamped instrument of transfer like shares, or payable to bearer, in which case they are negotiable instruments and coupons are attached to them representing right to interest.

If registered, they will have to be issued under the company's common seal, and their contents will deal with two matters, namely, the repayment of capital on a specified day, and interest in the meantime; and endorsed conditions such as a promise to keep a register of debenture holders, and a statement that only the registered holder will have title to the debentures and that they will be paid without regard to equities. The last condition is necessary since, unlike shares, a company will be bound by trusts on debentures whether it knows of them or not.

Redeemable Debentures
Debentures may be issued as redeemable or irredeemable. If redeemable, they will be redeemed according to the terms of issue. Basically, there are three methods of redeeming

debentures. It could be done by 'annual drawing' of a fixed number by lot; or by the company buying the debentures in the market; or by the company redeeming them out of a sinking fund or out of the proceeds of a fresh issue of debentures.

Where secured debentures are issued to banks, section 753 provides that the debentures are not redeemable merely because the company's account ceases to be in debt. Redeemable debentures may be re-issued, but their date of redemption on re-issue cannot be later than the date of the original debentures.

If irredeemable, the loan is repayable only on default by the company or in the event of a winding up; and they will not be invalid simply because the date of repayment is postponed for too long a time **(s.193)**. In **Knightsbridge Estates Trust Ltd. v Byrne** where a company raised a loan secured on 75 houses and other property and where it was agreed that the loan was to be repaid in instalments spread over 40 years, the company was not allowed to repay the loan earlier by contending that the provision preventing it from doing so was void because it conflicted with the general rule in equity that a mortgagor has a right to pay off his loan and discharge his mortgage earlier than the repayment date. The court said that the company's mortgage was in effect a debenture and so was saved by what is now section 193.

Convertible Debentures

Debentures may be issued on terms that they can be converted into shares at fixed dates, or at the option of the debenture holder. This is a particularly useful device for enticing persons to lend money to the company, since it enables such persons to acquire shares at prices below their market value and to switch their securities when the option to convert exists. Nevertheless, debentures issued at a discount cannot be made immediately convertible into paid up shares of the full par value since this would constitute indirectly issuing shares at a discount **(Mosely v Koffyfontein Mines Ltd. (1904))**.

Charging Secured Debentures

In the exercise of its borrowing powers a company may create a mortgage or a charge on all or any of its undertakings or property, including its uncalled capital, as security for the loan. A mortgage differs from a charge in that with a mortgage the title (legal or equitable ownership) of the company's property is transferred to the creditor, whereas with a charge title of the property remains with the company. A legal mortgage requires the formal transfer of title of the company's property to the lender, with the right of the company to get back ownership of the property once the loan is repaid. If the company defaults with the loan the lender (creditor) can sell the property mortgaged without the concurrence of the company. However, the company has a right to redeem (discharge) the mortgage even where the contract date for repayment of the loan has passed (this right is called the equity of redemption of mortgages) unless the courts have ended (foreclosed) the right. With a charge, title of the property charged remains with the company; but the lender has certain rights over the property such as the right to prevent the company from selling or using the property charged without his consent (as in the case of a fixed charge). Unlike a mortgage, the lender himself has no implied right to sell the property charged. A charge given by the company can be a fixed or floating charge or a combination of both.

A fixed charge is a charge given on specific assets such as the company's freehold and leasehold property, fixed plant and machinery, and goodwill. '*Goodwill*' is the difference between the assets value of the company and the overall value of the company to a purchaser. A purchaser may be willing to pay more than the value of the real assets of the company because of factors such as customers' loyalty and location of the business. A fixed charge may be legal or equitable and, if legal, a first legal charge will prevent the company from dealing with or disposing of the security without the concurrence of the debenture holder.

A floating charge is a charge of unspecified assets owned by the company from time to time such as the company's undertaking and after-acquired stock. It embraces all or most of the company's resources, and has the effect of making the resources available for securing the debt of one of the company's creditor at the expense all the other unprotected creditors. The floating charge 'floats' over the resources and becomes a fixed charge when it crystallises (i.e., when it attaches to the assets which make up the security); so that the company will no longer be able to use the secured assets in the ordinary course of its business without the consent of the creditor. Crystallisation takes place either when the company ceases business or the chargee intervenes. Crystallisation can also occurs where the terms of the charge provide for 'automatic crystallisation' on the happening of specified events (e.g., as in **Re Brightlife Ltd. (1986)** where it was provided that the chargee could, at anytime, by serving notice on the company convert the floating charge into a fixed charge).

The characteristics of a floating charge were stated in **Re Yorkshire Woolcombers Association (1903)** to be a charge on both present and future assets which are, in the ordinary course of business, changing from time to time; and until the owner takes steps to enforce the security, the company can carry on business and deal with the assets charged. The crucial element of a floating charge is that the company is free to use the assets charged in the ordinary course of its business. A floating charge is always equitable in nature. A charge on future book debts is invariable a floating charge **(Re Spectrum Plus Ltd. (2005).**

Value of Floating Charges

A debenture secured by a floating charge is often said not to be a very good security because the law has placed various curbs on its effect. A percentage of the assets secured by the floating charge has to be set aside for the payment of the company's unsecured debts (see Chapter 16). In addition, a floating charge suffers from the following drawbacks:

(a) **Priorities**. A fixed charge on property already subject to a floating charge will have priority over that floating charge unless the fixed charge was made expressly subject to the floating charge, or the floating charge contained a provision that no later charge will have priority and the creditor with the later fixed charge had notice of that provision. Inclusion of the restrictive provision with the particulars of the charge in the file at Companies Registry does not give constructive notice of the existence of such a provision **(Wilson v Kelland (1910))**; but it is useful to do so, since most creditors do in fact search the file at the Registry before taking a charge. Thus, anyone searching the file is treated by the courts as having notice of the restriction even though he actually overlooks it.

(b) **Preferential debts**. Debts, such as employee's wages (four months' wages up to a maximum of £800 per employee and accrued holiday pay) are preferential in a winding up and must be paid before debts secured by a floating charge **(s.175**

IA). The same priority is given to preferential debts where an administrative receiver (see later) is appointed by the courts, but the company is not in the course of a winding up **(s.40 IA)**.

(c) **Execution and distress**. If property of the company is seized and sold by the sheriff in execution of a judgement obtaind by an unsecured creditor, or distress (i.e., seizure and sale of the company's property) is levied by a landlord for rent owed by the company, both execution and distress take priority before crystallisation of the floating charge. The same is true with liens on the company's property, and the right of set-offs by unsecured creditors. In **Rother Iron Works v Canterbury Precision Engineers Ltd. (1973)**, the claimants owed £124 to the defendants who later ordered goods valued £159 from them. After the goods were delivered but before payment a bank appointed a receiver under a floating charge over the claimants' property. The Court of Appeal held that the defendants were liable to pay only £35 to the bank, being entitled to set-off the debt of £159 which was incurred before crystallisation

(d) **Reservation of title clauses**. Where a supplier of goods to the company has reserved title to those goods until he is paid the purchase price, he is able to recover his goods in the hands of a receiver appointed under a floating charge and may be able to trace the proceeds of sale if the goods were resold. In **Aluminium Industrie BV v Romalpa Ltd. (1976)**, AIV sold aluminium foil to Romalpa and reserved the ownership of the foil until the buyer met the purchase price. The conditions of sale included, *inter alia*, a term requiring the foil to be stored separately. On the insolvency of

Romalpa, the Court of Appeal held that that particular term
imputed a fiduciary relationship between the contracting
parties, with the result that the foil still held by Romalpa and
the proceeds of the foil sold could be recovered by AIV under
a tracing order.

To acquire rights against the proceeds of sale, the contract
must state expressly that if the buyer resells the goods he
resells them as agent of the seller. A reservation of title
clause which states that if the seller's goods are mixed with
other goods by the buyer to make a new component the seller
will have the legal ownership of the new component, will
not extend the seller's title to the new component but may
give him a valid charge on the new component if the charge
is registered under the Companies Act **(Borden (UK) Ltd.
v Scottish Timber Products (1979))**. However, the seller
may be able to retain ownership of his own goods if they are
readily detachable from the new component **(Hendy Lennox
Ltd. v Graham Puttick Ltd (1984)).** A reservation of title
clause is only effective if it reserves legal (rather than
equitable) title in the goods **(Re Bond Worth Ltd. (1979))**.

(e) **Pre-existing debts.** Under section 245 of the Insolvency
Act the liquidator can set aside a floating charge given by a
company to secure an existing unsecured debt if the company
was not solvent when the charge was created and it went into
liquidation within 12 months thereafter. If the person to
whom the charge was given was connected with the company
the period is extended to two years preceding the
commencement of winding up and it makes no difference
whether or not the company was solvent at the relevant time.

The provisions of section 245 apply equally where the
company is in administration (see later). In addition, the
administrator can set aside any floating charge created by the
company between the presentation of the petition for an

administration order and the making of the order unless consideration was given for the charge.

Despite its vulnerability, a floating charge may nevertheless be a useful security to its holder. Certain types of creditors secured by a floating charge can apply to the courts for the appointment of a receiver to manage the company. Moreover, only a creditor secured by a floating charge, in addition to the company itself, can make an out of court appointment of an administrator for bankruptcy protection purposes. This is done by putting the company into administration. Administration allows all debts enforceable against the company to be freezed for a period of time, while allowing the company to carry on its day to day operations. Also, a floating charge on stock and book debts, present and future, is in no way affected by disposal of existing stock and payment of book debts, since after-acquired stock and book debts will fall within the charge until crystallisation. This may result in the appreciation of the security. Likewise, preferential debts are preferred only to the extent that they arise before the floating charge crystallises. Once crystallisation takes place, the charge ranks before subsequent preferential debts, though not before those existing at the date of crystallisation **(re Griffin Hotel Co Ltd. (1941))**.

Registration of Charges
Charges (including mortgages) created by a company on its property are required to be registered in the company's own register of charges **(s.876)** and, if they fall within the ambit of section 860, with the Registrar of Companies. With the latter, the charge must be registered within 21 days from the day after its creation **(870 (1) (a))**; otherwise it will be void

against the company's administrator, liquidator and all of its
creditors, though the advance itself is not affected and the
loan becomes immediately repayable **(s.874)**. It is the duty of
the company to send the necessary particulars of the charge
to the Registry for registration; but in practice the lender
himself will do so to ensure registration within the prescribed
time.

Only charges created by a company on its property in the
course of raising money have to be registered under the
section **(Stoneleigh Finance Ltd. v Phillips (1965))**. By
section 860 (7) all floating charges have to be registered;
most fixed charges also have to be registered except fixed
charges on stock and shares, on life policies, on produce and
bills deposited to secure an advance (unless the charge was
created for the purposes of securing an issue of debentures).

For registration purposes, the charge has to be accompanied
with a brief summary showing the date of creation of the
charge (if the company acquired property already subject to
an existing charge, the date that the company acquired the
property), the amount secured by the charge, the property to
which the charge applies, and the name and address of the
person entitled to it. Additional particulars may be included,
but this does not make them known by constructive notice to
anyone unaware of them. In **Wilson v Kelland**, a company
issued by trust deed debentures for £100,000 secured by a
floating charge on present and future property, which
prohibited the creation of any charge ranking in priority to or
pari passu with it. Particulars of the trust deed and debentures
were registered in accordance with the Companies Act. The
company later created a fixed charge on its property. Eve J.
held that the creditor with the fixed charge had constructive
notice of the floating charge but not of the special provision
contained in the charge restricting the company from dealing

with its property in the usual manner, since the latter was not information which it was obligatory to register .

Certificate of Registration. When the Registrar registers a charge, he will issue a certificate of registration. This certificate is conclusive evidence that the requirements of the Act as to registration have been complied with **(s. 869(6)(b))**. Therefore evidence will not be admitted to dispute the fact of registration once the certificate of registration is produced. In **Re C. L. Nye Ltd. (1970)**, a company asked its solicitor to register an undated bank charge in accordance with the Companies Act. The charge was not registered in the prescribed time, and in order to obtain registration the solicitor inserted a false date of creation of the charge so that it could fall within the prescribed time. A Registrar's certificate was given. The Court of Appeal held that although the charge was not registered within 21 days and the date was incorrect on the certificate, the certificate was conclusive evidence that the requirements of registration had been complied with and it was therefore valid. The maxim that no one should take advantage of his own wrong had no application, since no creditor had given credit to the company between the dates when the charge should have been registered and the date when it was registered.

The Registrar's certificate is also conclusive evidence that the Registrar has entered the prescribed particulars on the register; but it is no authority that the contents of those particulars submitted for registration are accurate. Thus, to discover the exact terms of the charge, prospective creditors have to look at the document creating the loan. In **Re Mechanisation (Eaglescliffe) Ltd. (1966)**, the particulars registered described inaccurately the amount secured by the charge as £18,000, when it was in fact £23,000. The courts held that the charge covered the actual loan, and the

Registrar's certificate was conclusive evidence that the charge had been duly registered. Inaccuracy of the registered particulars could not alter the legal position.

Apart from subsequent secured creditors, no other person is deemed to have notice of the registered particulars unless notice is imputed by some other statute, such as by section 198 of the Law of Property Act 1925 which provides that registration of a floating charge on a company's land under section 860 of the Companies Act will serve as notice of the charge to all persons who may be interested in the land since it is equivalent to registration under the Land Charges Act 1972.

Late and Further Particulars. The courts have power to give leave for a charge to be registered outside the prescribed time **(s.873)**; but they will do so only if the omission is accidental, or due to inadvertence or some other sufficient cause, or is not of a nature to prejudice the creditors or shareholders, or on the ground that it is just and equitable to grant relief.

Relief is often granted where failure to register was due to some conveyancing muddle in a solicitor's office, or bad legal advice or where the parties simply forgot to register. In **Re Kris Cruisers Ltd. (1949)**, the courts extended the time for registration where the secretary thought that the company's solicitors had registered the charges, and the solicitors thought the secretary had done so.

An application for late registration is not normally granted if the company is in liquidation or is insolvent and on the verge of liquidation or if the chargee, having discovered that his charge is not registered, delays his application for late registration in order to see which course would be to his best advantage. In **Re Ashpurton Estates Ltd. (1982)**, the chargee discovered that by some oversight his charge had not been registered within the prescribed time. Instead of applying for immediate relief, he decided to delay since he did not wish to alarm other creditors and so precipitate a collapse of the company. Eventually he applied to the courts for an extension of time but only did so because notice had been served to convene an extraordinary general meeting to put the company into winding up. The Court of Appeal refused his application on account of his undue delay and as winding up was imminent.

The effect of registration outside the prescribed time is to make the charge valid from the date of its creation subject to the right of the courts to impose such conditions as seems just and convenient. It is standard practice for the courts to attach a 'proviso' to a late registration order protecting rights of intervening secured creditors. The wording of the 'proviso' usually only protects rights acquired against the company's property during the extension period (i.e., between the end of the 21 days within which the statute requires registration and the date of actual registration). A subsequent chargee is protected notwithstanding that he had knowledge of the unregistered charge before his charge was acquired **(Re Monolitic Building Co. (1915))**. If the subsequent charge was created and registered within the statutory time limit allowed for registration of the first charge (i.e., within 21 days), the subsequent charge does not obtain priority by reason of the 'proviso'. In **Watson v Duff Morgan and Vermont (Holdings) Ltd. (1974)**, two charges were registered consecutively on the same day, the second being registered within 21 days and the first sometime later under a court order containing the usual 'proviso'. It was held that the 'proviso' did not protect the priority rights of the second charge over the first charge when the first charge became void for non-registration within 21 days.

Where the company acquires property which is already subject to an existing charge, the company must register the charge within 21 days after the day in which the acquisition of the property is completed; but unlike section 874, non-registration of the charge by the company does not render the charge void, but only results in a fine on the company and its officers in default **(s.862)**.

Remedies of Debenture Holders

The remedies of a debenture holder where the company defaults with the loan will depend on whether the debenture holder is secured or not.

(a)**Unsecured debenture holder**. He may sue for the sum due together with interest on it. If the judgement is unsatisfied he can levy execution against the company. As an alternative to the above remedy, he can petition for a winding up of the company on grounds of insolvency **(s. 122(1)(f) IA)** or apply for an administration order under Part II of the Insolvency Act.

(b) **Secured debenture holder**. He has additional remedies. Subject to section 72 of the Insolvency Act, he (or the trustees where there was a trust deed) may take steps to enforce the security and exercise any powers conferred by the debenture or the trust deed (e.g., the power of sale and the appointment of a receiver) without reference to the courts. If the debenture (or trust deed) did not contain such powers, he (or the trustees) may apply to the courts for the appointment of a receiver or a receiver and manager or an order for sale or foreclosure.

Receivers

A receiver is a person appointed to take possession of property which is subject to a charge and to deal with it primarily for the benefit of the holder of the charge. A receiver differs from a trustee of debenture holders, a liquidator and an administrator in that he is appointed only when the company defaults with secured debts. He must also be an individual, not a corporation. Moreover, once he is able to pay off those debts, he must vacate office and the company can continue business as before. A trustee is appointed by the company when the debenture trust deed is executed and he can be a corporation. A liquidator is appointed to wind up the company and terminate its existence. An administrator is appointed in the interest of creditors and members to save a company which is in financial difficulties from liquidation.

The courts have power to appoint a receiver on application of any secured creditor if the principal sum or interest is in arrears, or the company is being wound up, or the security is in jeopardy. Security is said to be in jeopardy if the company is threatening to dispose of its entire undertaking **(Re Tilt Cove Copper Co. (1913))**; or if another creditor is about to levy execution against property which forms part of the security **(Re London Pressed Hinge Co. Ltd. (1905))** or to petition for a compulsory winding up of the company **(Re Victoria Steamboats Co. (1897))**. However, security is not in jeopardy simply because the assets charged are found to be less in value than the amount of the debt secured by the charge **(Re New York Taxicab Co. (1913))**. Where the security is the company's business the courts will provide the receiver with power to manage the business or appoint a manager to assist him.

Court appointed receivers to enforce a charge are rare since most debentures or trust deeds contain express power to make an appointment. Moreover, all mortgages by deed contain an implied power under section 101 of the Law of Property Act to appoint a receiver of income. Where the security is the company's business, a manager will be appointed by the creditor to run the business either by virtue of a power in the debenture or by application to the courts. A receiver or manager of the whole (or substantially the whole) of the company's property appointed by or on behalf of creditors secured by a floating charge is called an 'administrative receiver' **(s.29(2) IA)**. An administrative receiver has statutory powers to manage the business. Only a person qualified to be an insolvency practitioner may be appointed administrative receiver. To be an insolvency practitioner a person must be qualified under the rules of a recognised public body to act as such and must have proper insurance bonding. An ordinary receiver need not be an insolvency practitioner. Subject to some limited exceptions, section 72A of the Insolvency Act 1986 has now taken away the power of creditors to appoint an administrative receiver under a floating charge created on or after September 15, 2003. Thus, for all intents and purposes, administrative receivership ceases to be a major insolvency procedure and new floating charge holders now have to enforce their security by appointing an administrator (see post). It is unclear whether section 72A also affects the appointment of an administrative receiver by the courts on application by creditors secured by a floating charge.

The appointment of a receiver will be invalid if the debenture under which he is appointed can be set aside on grounds that the charge is a transaction at undervalue **(s.28 IA)**; or a voidable preference **(s.239 IA)**; or it is a floating charge granted gratuitously by an insolvent company within one before insolvency proceedings commence **(s.245 IA)**; or it is void for non-registration at companies Registry **(s.395 CA)**. A receiver who takes possession of company assets under an invalid appointment is a trespasser **(Ford and Carter Ltd. v Midland Bank (1979))**; but the courts may order the appointor to indemnify him against liability resulting solely out of the defective appointment **(s.34 IA)**.

A receiver who decides to accept an appointment must do so not later than the end of the next business day after receiving the document of appointment **(s.33 IA)**. The appointor must then notify Companies Registry of the appointment within seven days who then has to enter this fact in the Register of Charges **(s.409 CA)**, and all company documents must state that a receiver has been appointed **(s.39 IA)**.

The appointment of a receiver/manager by the courts will result in the dismissal of the company's employees **(Reid v The Explosives Co. Ltd. (1887))**. The directors' powers over the security are suspended; but they still remain in office and so are liable to file annual returns and other documents at Companies Registry.

The receiver will be personally liable for contracts which he makes on behalf of the company. However, existing contracts made by the company before his appointment remain binding on the company but not on the receiver unless he adopts them after re-negotiation **(Parsons v Sovereign Bank of Canada (1913))**.

A receiver cannot dishonour existing trading contracts even though they may be unprofitable to the company since this would damage the company's goodwill **(Re Newdigate Colliery Ltd. (1912))**. However if their performance can only be effected by borrowing more money ranking in priority to the debenture holder whom he represents and are unprofitable, the receiver can refuse to honour them. In **Re Thames Ironworks Co. Ltd. (1912)**, a receiver of a shipbuilding company was given permission to dishonour a shipbuilding contract, since the ships which were half built could be completed only by borrowing more money, and the performance of the contract was unprofitable to both the company and the debenture holder. The obligation to honour current trading contracts only arises if the company will have sufficient assets to carry on business once the secured debts are discharged.

Where the receiver refuses to honour a trading contract, the company can still be sued for damages **(Telsen Electric Co. Ltd. v Eastick & Son (1936))**; but the claim will rank as an unsecured debt and can only be met if the insolvent company will have sufficient assets left after the secured debts are discharged **(Airlines Airspares Ltd. v Handley Page Ltd. (1970))**. Nevertheless such an action is still useful for set-off purposes where the company has a cross-claim, and also if the contract is of a type where specific performance can be ordered against the receiver, as in the case of a contract for the sale of land **(Freevale Ltd. v Metrostore Holdings Ltd. (1984))**.

Where liquidation follows receivership the receiver's powers to hold and dispose of the property forming part of the security or to use the company's name for this purpose is not affected. A company which is in receivership can be put into liquidation by unsecured creditors if there will be surplus assets after receivership.

A receiver must vacate office on the appointment of an administrator. A receiver has a right to be indemnified out of the company's assets in which he was appointed for expenses and liability incurred in the proper performance of his tasks. Remuneration, expenses and indemnity take priority over the security of the debenture holder.

Administrators

Part II of the Insolvency Act contains a procedure which allows the courts to freeze the debts of a company in financial difficulties and to appoint an insolvency practitioner as administrator to manage the company to achieve its survival, and thus avoid bankruptcy. This procedure is known as 'administration' and it protects companies from their own creditors, allowing them to re-arrange their finances while still trading. Only the company in general meeting, its directors or creditors (secured or unsecured) can apply to the courts for an administration order **(s. 9 IA)**. The procedure is not available to individual shareholders or to **BIS**.

The courts' power to make an administration order is exercisable if the company is unable to pay its debts and the order is likely to achieve the company's survival as a going concern, or will provide a better way of realising its assets than would be likely if the company was put into liquidation (bankruptcy), or will be a better way of realising the company's assets in order to make a distribution to one or more secured or preferential creditors **(Sch. B 1 of the IA)**.

The filing of an administration petition has the effect of freezing all actions against the company until the petition is considered. The company cannot then be put into liquidation, and none of its creditors can take steps to enforce any security against the company or repossess any goods under a hire purchase or similar agreement **(s.10 IA)**. If the petition is granted all company documents and its website must state that the company is in administration and the administrator must, under penalty, give notice of his appointment to the Registrar of Companies and the company's creditors of whom he has notice within 14 and 28 days respectively.

Part 10 of the Enterprise Act now allows the holder of a floating charge, the company itself or its directors to appoint an out of court administrator without having to petition the courts to appoint one. The holder of a floating charge can appoint an out of court administrator on filing 2 days notice with the courts, and the company or its directors on filing 5 days notice. The conditions for an out of court appointment are that the company is likely to become unable to pay its debts and that the administrator believes that the purpose of administration can reasonably be achieved. However, a floating charge holder need not establish that the company is or is likely to be unable to pay its debts before he can make an appointment; but his floating charge must be enforceable at the time notice of appointment is filed with the courts. An administrator is in a similar position to that of an administrative receiver. Thus, the directors' powers to manage the company are suspended in so far as their exercise would interfere with his powers; but employees' contracts are not affected on his appointment. The administrator can dispose of any property subject to a floating charge and, with the courts' consent, property subject to other charges; although the creditors in question still retain their priority on the proceeds (s.15 IA). In addition, an administrator has power to replace the directors with new ones (s.15 IA) and, like a liquidator, can set aside floating charges which were created by the company to secure existing debts (s.245 IA), transactions at undervalue and preferences (ss.238, 229 IA), and extortionate credit transactions (s.244 IA). An administrator is an agent of the company; but he must perform his functions in the interests of all the creditors.

The administrator's main task is to prepare proposals for achieving the purpose of the administration. Such proposals must be sent to members of the company and the Registrar of Companies within eight weeks of the company going into administration, and to a creditors' meeting within 10 weeks. If the creditors' meeting should accept the proposals, the administrator will continue to manage the company in accordance with the proposals. If the creditors' meeting rejects the proposals the administrator can file notice with the Registrar to convert the administration into a creditors' voluntary winding up or to the courts to dissolve the company (where the company's survival cannot be achieved).

Administration cannot last for more than a year, subject to a six months extension by the creditors or to such longer time as the courts may direct.

Section 27 of the Insolvency Act provides minority relief where the administrator is acting in a manner unfairly prejudicial to the creditors or the shareholders. Anyone of them may apply to the courts for an order regulating the administrator's future conduct or for his discharge. The administrator is entitled to be paid his remuneration and expenses in priority to creditors secured by a floating charge.

Voluntary Arrangements

As an alternative to administration and liquidation, section 1 of the Insolvency Act allows the directors of an insolvent company to make proposals through a nominee, who must be a qualified insolvency practitioner, for the company and its creditors to reach a voluntary arrangement whereby the creditors take a smaller sum, paid over a reasonable period of time, in satisfaction of their debts. The nominee must, within 28 days of receiving the proposals from the directors, apply to the courts for permission to summon a members and creditors meeting to consider the proposals if he feels they are worth pursuing **(s.2 IA)**.

If members and creditors at their separate meetings agree, with or without modification, to identical terms of the proposals their decisions must be reported back to the courts and unless an objection is lodged within 28 days after the courts receive the report, the arrangement takes effect as if made by the company at the creditors meeting and binds every person who had notice of, and was entitled to vote at, the meetings **(s.5 IA)**. Dissentient members and creditors, and even the nominee himself, can object to the proposals within the prescribed time on grounds of prejudice or material irregularity at or in relation to either of the meetings **(s.6)**. The courts may dispense with their objections, and even amend or suspend the proposals. A binding arrangement is implemented by the nominee who becomes its supervisor. He takes orders from the courts and has power to apply for an administration or liquidation order if the arrangement is broken or cannot be achieved.

A company voluntary arrangement (CVA) can be either a composition in satisfaction of the company's debts (i.e., where all the creditors promise to take a proportion of what is owned to them) or a scheme of arrangement of its affairs (i.e., where the company's property is transferred to another to be managed for the benefit of the creditors). However, it is subject to the rights of secured creditors to enforce their security and to preferential creditors **(s.4 IA)**.

Where the company is already under administration or in liquidation, the administrator or liquidator can also propose a voluntary arrangement; and if he intends to supervise the composition or scheme himself he does not have to apply to the courts for permission to summon the relevant meetings. Nevertheless, the decisions of the meetings must still be reported to the courts and the administrator or liquidator has a similar right under section 6 to object to the terms as agreed by the meetings. If the administrator or liquidator intends another insolvency practitioner to be supervisor, the procedure is the same as with proposals from directors, namely, the nominee will have to apply to the courts for permission to summon meetings to consider the proposal.

The Insolvency Act 2000 introduces another form of voluntary arrangement which is similar to the arrangement mentioned above except that it provides the company with a moratorium whereby no creditor can enforce any legal right he has against the company while the moratorium exists. On receipt of the proposal by the nominee the directors can secure a 28 days stay of action by the creditors if the nominee files certain documents with the courts and advertises the fact of the moratorium by notice in the press and with the Registrar of Companies. The moratorium ends (unless it is extended for a further two months by the creditors) when the meetings of creditors and members take place to consider the proposal. The main drawback of this type of arrangement is that it results in adverse publicity to the company.

Chapter 10

Membership and Meetings

Acquisition of Membership

Section 112 provides that a person may become a member of a company by agreeing to become a member such as by an application and allotment or by a transfer from an existing member or by a transmission on the death or bankruptcy of a member. This person's name must be entered in the register of members. A subscriber to the memorandum becomes a member when the company is registered, rather than when his name is entered in the register. If a member holds shares in a company and his name is entered in the register of members, he is called a 'shareholder'.

A minor may be a member of a company unless the articles provide otherwise; but his contract of membership is voidable during his minority or within a reasonable time after attaining his majority. If he repudiates his shares, he cannot recover monies paid on the shares unless there was a total failure of consideration **(Steinberg v Scala (Leeds) Ltd. (1923))**. A personal representative or trustee in bankruptcy of a member may become a member of the company unless there is any contrary provision in the articles; but their names must be put in the register.

A company may, if authorised by its memorandum, become a member of another company, and may attend meetings and vote by appointing a personal representative or a proxy. Section 323 allows a corporate shareholder to authorise by resolution of its directors any natural person to act as its representative at a company's meeting and he can exercise on behalf of the company the same powers which the company could exercise if it was an individual shareholder. Most companies will therefore appoint a representative rather than a proxy to represent them at another company's general meeting because proxies are not free to act as they please (see 'proxies').

Register of Members
Every company is required to keep a register of members **(s.113)**. This register must include the following matters: the names and addresses of members (joint owners of shares are treated as a single member and although their names must be included in the register only one address needs to be shown), number of shares or stock, the amount paid as consideration, and the date when each person was entered in the register. The register need not be kept as a bound book but may be kept as micro-film or computer record as long as adequate precaution is taken against its falsification. If the company has more than 50 members and the register of members is not itself in such a form as to arrange in name order, the company must also keep an index of the members' names and it must be made available at the same time as the register **(s.115)**.
The register and not the share certificate is the document of title to shares; and it must be made available for inspection during business hours. Members may inspect the register of members without charge, and any other person on payment of a fee **(s.116)**. Also for a fee, any person (including a member) can obtain a copy of the register or part of it from the company. Where a request is made to inspect the register or to make copies of it the company must comply with the request within five days; unless it applies to the courts to set aside the request on grounds that the request is not for a proper purpose **(s.117)**. Persons requesting to inspect the

register or to make copies of it must provide their names and addresses, whether the information obtained will be disclosed to others, and the purpose for which they require the information **(s.116 (3) and (4))**.

The register can be kept at the company's registered office or at a place permitted by the Secretary of State under regulations made under section 1136 **(s.114)**. The courts have power to rectify the register if it contains an omission or inaccuracy **(s.125)**. In the case of a public company, if as a result of its investigation under section 793, it finds that the names of persons who had interests in its shares carrying unrestricted voting rights had not been disclosed to the company, or the names of present holders of such shares are unknown, the company must also keep a '**Register of interests in shares disclosed**' **(s.808)**. Moreover the company must be notified in writing of any change in interest within five days. Interests of the individual's spouse and minor child and interests held by a company in which the individual holds at least one-third of the shares or controls its directors are treated as part of his interest.

Shareholder communications

Shareholders take decisions by passing resolutions at meetings, by written resolution, or by informal unanimous consent. A public company must always hold a general meeting to pass a resolution, except that if all the members are in support of the resolution then, at common law, the resolution is deemed to be passed on account of the unanimous consent of the members **(Cane v Jones)**. A private company can pass a resolution at a general meeting or outside the framework of a general meeting, by use of the written resolution, or by unanimous consent. The main disadvantage of having to pass a resolution at a general meeting is that the resolution is only passed if the company follows the correct procedures at the meeting **(s.301)**.

A company can communicate with its shareholders in hard copy form such as by sending the document by post to the shareholders' address, or electronically. Electronic form communication can be used by a company only if the shareholders agree in general meeting to such communication or there is a provision in the company's articles for it. In addition, shareholders must be contacted individually to agree to receive electronic form documents or information. A shareholder can insist in receiving information in hard copy form; but he must indicate this to the company. If a shareholder does not respond within 28 days of being contacted, the company can assume that he has no objections to receiving information in electronic form. Electronic form communication is subject to any provision of the Companies Act which requires information to be supplied in particular ways.

Meetings

'Meeting' implies the coming together of two or more persons. Thus as a general rule a single member cannot constitute a meeting (per Plowman J. in **Re London Flats Ltd. (1969)**). In that case a private company had two members left, and they convened a meeting to appoint a liquidator. The other member left the meeting; the first member continued the meeting on his own, and subsequently appointed himself the liquidator. The court held that the meeting ceased to be a meeting when the minority member left; so the appointment was invalid.

The general rule is subject to three exceptions. The courts may direct that one member present, whether personally or by proxy, can constitute a meeting **(s. 306)**; the **Rule in East**

v Bennett (1911) provides that where only one member of a class of members is left, that member may constitute a class meeting; and in a single member company, that member may hold and constitute a meeting.

The Companies Act recognises two types of general meetings: the annual general meeting (AGM) and other general meetings.

(a) **Annual General Meeting**

This meeting has to be held by a public company within 6 months after the end of the company's last financial year **(s.366)**; and it may be in addition to any other meeting held in that year. A private company does not have to hold one (unless its shares which carry voting rights are traded on a regulated market in an EEA state with the company's consent); but if it does hold one (because its articles require one to be held), the meeting will be treated as an ordinary general meeting.

The normal (ordinary) business transacted at the annual general meeting includes the declaration of a dividend (if any); consideration of the company's annual financial statements; the election of the directors in place of those retiring by rotation; and the re-appointment and fixing of remuneration of the auditor. Also, members representing at least five percent of the total voting rights of the members entitled to vote on a resolution they intend to propose at the meeting (or at least 100 members holding shares on which there has been paid up on an average sum per member of not less than £100) can compel the company to include the proposed resolution in the agenda and to give notice of the resolution to all members **(s.338)**; and to circulate to other members their views on that resolution or on other matters to be dealt with at any general meeting as long as the statement is not defamatory, frivolous or vexatious and does not exceed

1000 words **(s.314)**. In order to compel the company to comply with section 338 and 314, the members must lodge a notice of their proposed resolution at the company's registered office at least six weeks before the annual general meeting (or if later, before the company gives its members notice of the AGM); or lodge the requisition to circulate their views on any matter to be dealt with at the meeting, not less than one week before the meeting. The members making the requisition must meet the expenses incurred by the company in circulating notice of the resolution and members' statements on the matter (unless the company resolves otherwise); but if the requests sufficient to require the company to circulate notice of the resolution and/or statements are received before the end of the financial year preceding the meeting, the company itself will have to meet the expenses of circulation **(s.340 and s.316)**. Members of a private company which is a trade company have to satisfy similar conditions to get a resolution put in the agenda of the company's Annual General Meeting; but they need only give the company 14 days notice before the meeting, instead of the six weeks notice, and the company must meet the cost of circulating the resolution.

If a public company defaults in holding an annual general meeting every officer in default is subject to a fine. Moreover, the company may be directed to do so by **BIS** acting on the application of a member; but **BIS** has no statutory power to convene the meeting. In addition, repeated failure to hold such meetings could be the subject of a section 994 petition by aggrieved shareholders for unfair prejudicial conduct **(Re A Company, ex parte Shooter (1990))**.

(b) **Other General Meetings**

These are general meetings of the members other than the annual general meeting. The directors may convene a general meeting when they think fit **(s.302)**, but must do so within 28 days where the net assets of a public company fall to half or less of the company's paid up capital **(s.656)**; and also at the direction of the auditor where the auditor resigns and there are circumstances which he considers should be brought to the notice of the members of the company **(s.518)**.

Minority shareholders can also compel the directors to call a general meeting. Section 303 gives a statutory right to minorities holding at least 5% per cent of the company's paid-up capital carrying the right to vote to require the directors to call a general meeting. The request for such a meeting must state the general nature of the business to be dealt with at the meeting and may include the text of any resolution that may properly be moved and is intended to be moved at the meeting. A resolution may properly be moved at a meeting unless, it would, if passed be ineffective (because of inconsistency with any enactment, the company's constitution, or otherwise), or it is defamatory of any person, or it is frivolous or vexatious. On receipt of the requisition, the directors must give notice to members within 21 days convening the meeting (the meeting does not have to be held within that time limit). The notice convening the meeting must include the text of any resolution proposed by the requisitionists and which is to be moved at the meeting; and where relevant, members' statements under section 314 must be circulated. The meeting must be held within 28 days of the date the notice of the meeting is sent out **(s.304)**. Thus the directors must hold the meeting not later than 49 days after receiving the request for the meeting. If the directors do not send out notice to members for the meeting within the 21-day period, the requisitionists (providing they represent more than half of the total voting strength of the company) may themselves convene the meeting within three months of the requisition date at the company's expense **(s.305** and **s.306)**.

The courts too have power under section 306 to order a general meeting to be called where it is impracticable to call one, to hold and conduct the meeting in such manner as they see fit, and to give any ancillary direction as they think expedient (e.g., that a single member in person, or by proxy, shall constitute the meeting). The courts may exercise this power either on their own motion, or on the application of any director or any member of the company. This power has been used to resolve problems which arise if for some reason a private company has no director; or where shareholders refuse to attend a meeting, and so rendering the meeting invalid for lack of a quorum. Shareholders of private companies often refuse to attend meeting in order to prevent the majority shareholder from resolving an issue in a particular way. In **Re El Sombrero Ltd. (1958)**, the company had three members of whom two were directors holding ten percent of the shares. The articles provided for a quorum of two members. The majority shareholder wanted to call a meeting under what is now section 168 to remove the directors, but they frustrated his efforts by refusing to attend such a meeting. He therefore made an application to the courts to call the meeting and to dispense with the need for a quorum. The application was granted. Also, in **Re Whitchurch Insurance Consultants Ltd. (1993)**, a husband and wife were the directors and only shareholders of a small company, each holding 666 and 334 of the issued shares respectively. The parties subsequently quarreled and the wife simply absented herself from meetings, rendering them inquorate and preventing her husband from removing her as a director, as he was entitled to do under section 168. Again the courts ordered a meeting to be held without her. By ordering the meeting in this way, the courts prevent absent shareholders from gaining an effective veto over company business.

Notice of Meetings

To enable members to exercise their powers at general meetings, the directors must send notice in writing or by electronic communications to each member who is entitled to attend and vote of the details of the meeting. Section 310 (1) states that notice must also be sent to the directors, and any person entitled to a share as a result of the death or bankruptcy of a member (although the articles may restrict the right to vote to persons whose names are entered in the register of members). Although not a member, the auditor of the company has a statutory right to receive notice of any general meeting during his term of office, or of the general meeting at which his term of office would have expired had he not being removed from office as auditor before that meeting **(s.502)**. Article 28 (for public companies) provides that if the company has less than two directors and the remaining director does not call a general meeting to appoint additional directors, any two or more members may call the meeting by serving notice of the meeting to other members. Any person who does not attend a meeting, after being given a reasonable opportunity to do so, will be bound by the decisions taken by those members who attend the meeting.

'Notice' is written intimation to persons entitled to notice summoning them to attend a particular meeting at a named place, date and time. It must specify the general nature of any special business to be dealt with at the meeting; and where the meeting is convened to pass a special resolution or an ordinary resolution requiring special notice, the notice must specify either the text of the resolution or the entire substance of the resolution **(Re Moorgate Mercantile Holdings Ltd. (1980))**. If the company is a traded company, the notice must also include the matters listed in section 311 A(1) such as a statement of the procedures which members must comply with in order to be able to attend and vote at the meeting, rights of members to ask questions at the meeting, details of forms to be used for appointment of proxies, and the address of the website on which the information required by the section is published.

Notice must be sent to the last known UK address of every person entitled to attend the meeting **(s.310)**. Failure to serve notice on a person entitled thereto will invalidate the proceedings at the meeting even if the person to whom notice was not sent was not entitled to vote at the meeting. A member is entitled to notice even if he had previously indicated that he would not be able to attend the meeting. In **Young v Ladies Imperial Club (1920)**, a member of the club was expelled by a resolution passed by the appropriate club committee. Another committee member was not given notice of the meeting because she had previously informed the chairman that she would not be able to attend. In an action concerned with the validity of the expulsion, the court held that failure to send notice of the meeting to the other committee member invalidated the meeting and the expulsion void.

To mitigate the harshness of the rule that failure to give notice, even to one member, will invalidate the meeting, section 313 (1) provides that any accidental failure to give notice of a meeting to a member entitled to it is to be disregarded for the purpose of determining whether notice of the meeting or resolution (as the case may be) is duly given. Except in relation to notice given under section 304 (notice of meetings required by members), section 305 (notice of meetings called by members) and section 339 (notice of resolutions proposed by members at a public company's annual general meeting), section 313 (1) is subject to any provision of the company's articles. Section 313 (1) only protects the validity of the meeting where failure to give notice is 'accidental'. In **Re West Canadian Collieries**

(1962), the omission to give notice of a meeting to a few members occurred because the address plates of those members were inadvertently kept out of the machine which printed the envelopes. The court held that it was an accidental omission within the article of the company and so did not invalidate the meeting. However in **Musselwhite v G.H. Musselwhite & Son Ltd. (1962)**, where the directors deliberately failed to send notice of a general meeting to some members because the directors erroneously believed that they were no longer members (the members had sold their shares to a purchaser but the purchaser's name had not yet been entered in the register of members), the court held this was not an accidental omission to give notice, but a mistake of law. So the meeting was invalid.

Length of Notice
Section 307A lays down certain periods of notice, depending on whether or not the company is a traded company and on the type of meeting to be summoned. A 'traded company' is a public or private company whose voting shares are admitted to trading on a regulated market in an EEA state and the admission to trading is by or with the consent of the company. The section provides that notwithstanding any contrary provision in the articles, a general meeting of a traded company requires advance notice of at least 21 days (or longer if the articles provide for longer notice) to be given to the members before the meeting can be validly held. However, the traded company can give at least 14 days notice for a general meeting (other than an AGM) if its members are allowed to vote by electronic means accessible to all the members, and an earlier general meeting (either the preceding annual general meeting or a general meeting held since the last annual general meeting) have agreed, by a special resolution, to allow shorter notice for future general

meetings, up to the next annual general meeting. For a non-traded company, the company must give its members advance notice of at least 21 day (or longer if the articles provide for longer notice) for an annual general meeting and for other general meetings at least 14 days notice. The length of notice must be 'clear days' notice. This means the required period excludes the day when notice is sent out and the day that the meeting is to be held. The Combined Code requires listed companies to give 20 working days notice for annual general meetings.

Shorter notice for an annual general meeting of a public company (other than a traded company) can be given only if all the members entitled to attend and vote agree to such notice **(s.337)**. For other general meetings of non-traded companies, shorter notice can be given if a majority in number of members holding 95 per cent of the voting shares agrees to shorter notice. The threshold is reduced to 90% for a private company, unless its articles specify 95%.

Special Notice

Exceptionally, special notice is required for a resolution to be passed at a general meeting for certain purposes. These purposes are: to remove a director before his term of office expires **(s.168)**, and to remove the auditor from office, or to appoint an auditor other than the retiring auditor **(s.510)**.

Special notice means notice by members of their intention to move the resolution; and the notice must be given to the company at least 28 days before the meeting at which the resolution is to be moved **(s.312 (1))**. The company must then give notice of the resolution to members at the same time that it sends out notice of the meeting (or if it is not possible for good reason to do so, the company must give at least 14 days' notice by advertisement in a newspaper with appropriate circulation or by any other method allowed by the articles). If, after the company receives the special notice, the directors should call the meeting before the 28 days notice period has expired, the special notice is still deemed to have been given properly. If the proposed resolution is to be considered at a public company's annual general meeting, the directors cannot be compelled to circulate notice of the resolution to members (and thus it will not be included in the agenda for the meeting) unless the member complies with section 338 (see ante). In **Pedley v Inland Waterways Assoc. Ltd. (1977)**, the claimant wanted to propose a resolution to remove the directors at the annual general meeting. He gave the company secretary 28 days notice of the resolution he intended to propose, but the claimant did not hold at least five per cent of the voting shares. The courts held that the claimant would have to comply with what is now section 338 before he could compel the company to include his resolution for circulation.

Procedure at Meetings

Even though proper notice of the meeting and of resolutions to be passed at the meeting is given, matters transacted at the meeting will be valid as long as the meeting is properly conducted **(s.301)**. This means that there must be a quorum for the meeting; a chairman must be appointed to preside over the meeting; decisions must be reached fairly, if necessary by resolution after adequate discussion; and voting must be conducted properly. Each of these requisites for a valid meeting will now be considered.

Quorum

The quorum is the minimum number of persons entitled to attend a meeting and to vote, and who are actually present in person or by proxy at the time when the meeting proceeds to business. Unless the articles provide otherwise, in the case of a company limited by shares or guarantee and having only one member, a quorum for all company meetings is one 'qualifying persons' present in person at the meeting **(s.318 (1))**. In any other case, subject to the provision in the company's articles, the quorum is two qualifying persons present at the meeting **(318 (2))**. 'Qualifying persons' means a member, a corporate representative and a proxy; but not two or more corporate representatives or proxies of the same person.

Where statutory articles are adopted, Article 33 (plc) provides that if within half an hour after the meeting is due to start a quorum is not present, the meeting is adjourned to the same day, time, and place as may be specified by the chairman of the meeting or as may be fixed by the directors. If the continuation of the adjourned meeting is to take place more than 14 days after it is adjourned, the company must give members at least 7 clear days notice of it. If during the meeting a quorum ceases to be present the meeting stands adjourned in the same way as if there had been no quorum at the beginning of the meeting. However, business transacted before the meeting becomes inquorate remains valid **(Re London Flats Ltd.)**.

Chairman

The articles determine who shall be chairman. Article 40 (private companies) provides that if the directors have appointed a chairman, the chairman shall chair the general meeting if present and willing to do so; and article 31 (public companies) state that the chairman of the board of directors shall act as chairman of the general meeting. In the absence of the chairman, the directors present at the meeting may appoint one from among the directors or the members. If there are no directors present, then, subject to any provision of the company's articles as to who may or may not be chairman, the members can elect a chairman from among themselves **(s.319 (1))**. The members in general meeting may even appoint a proxy at the meeting to be the chairman of the meeting **(s.328)**.

The duties of the chairman are to preserve order, to call on members to speak and to decide on points of order such as the acceptability of amendments. The chairman does not have implied power to adjourn a meeting at his own will and pleasure (Chitty J. in **National Dwellings Soc. v Sykes (1894)**); but he can do so for a short time if there is disorder at the meeting **(John v Rees (1970))**. If he adjourns the meeting improperly, it can continue under another chairman. The chairman of the general meeting has no casting vote in the event of equality of votes on an ordinary resolution at the meeting unless the articles give him one and the provision for a casting vote was in the articles before 1 October 2007. The chairman of a general meeting of a traded company no longer has a casting vote even if such provision was included in the articles before 1 October 2007.

Proxies

A 'proxy' is an agent appointed by a member of a company to represent him at a meeting at which the member is entitled to be present and to vote. The term is also used sometimes to describe the instrument which gives the agent authority to act for a member.

Section 324 (1) gives every member of a company with a share capital, having a right to vote at a meeting, a right to appoint another person as his proxy to attend and vote instead of him. A member with more than one share can appoint more than one proxy to exercise his rights attached to different shares held by him. Moreover, any provision in a company's articles which provides that a member voting by proxy will have fewer votes than if he votes in person at the meeting will be void **(s.329)**. The proxy must be appointed by notice in writing (proxy notice) in accordance with the articles **(art. 46:** private companies; **art. 38:** public companies**)**; but the articles cannot require the instrument appointing the proxy to be deposited with the company more than 48 hours before the meeting **(s.327)**. In counting the 48 hours, weekends, Christmas Day, Good Friday and any bank holiday are excluded. Where a company invites proxies by issuing proxy forms, it has to issue them to all members, and not just to those members who are expected to support the directors.

A proxy has a right to speak and vote at a general meeting. Where a proxy is general (i.e., given a discretion as to how to vote) he can vote as he thinks fit; but if he is a special proxy (i.e., instructed to vote in a particular way) he cannot abstain.

A corporate member (e.g., a company) may, by resolution of its directors or other governing body, appoint a person(s) to act as its representative(s) at any meeting of another company in which it is a member **(s.323)**. It will usually appoint a representative rather than a proxy, since the former has power to make on-the- spot decisions.

A member who has appointed a proxy can still attend the meeting and vote in person, thus revoking the appointment **(Cousins v International Brick Co. (1931))**; but if the member does not vote on a resolution at the meeting, the proxy may do so **(Ansett v Butler Air Transport (1958))**.

Resolutions

Members reach decisions by resolutions; and they have a right to demand that a resolution should be considered at a meeting and that notice of the resolution and their views on it are circulated to other members before the meeting **(ss. 313,**

338), or (in the case of a private company) to propose a written resolution **(s. 292)**. In most cases decisions are made by **ordinary resolution** which is a simple majority of the votes cast at the meeting. Sometimes (such as for alteration of the company's articles) the law requires members to pass a **special resolution** which is seventy five per cent majority of the votes cast at the meeting. Amendments to resolutions are allowed if proper notice is given. On-the–spot amendments at meetings can be considered only if they do not cause a substantial change in the resolution. Whether or not a change is 'substantial' will depend on whether a reasonable shareholder who had decided after receiving notice of the resolution not to attend the meeting would have attended the meeting had he received notice of the amended resolution. If the chairman of the meeting does not put a valid amendment to the vote the resolution will be void **(Henderson v Bank of Australia (1890))**.

Voting

Unless a company's own articles provide otherwise, voting in the first instance is by a show of hands; and each member will have one vote only, irrespective of how many voting shares he holds in the company. Minority shareholders always prefer this form of voting as they will have equal voting power on decision making with their company's majority shareholders. In a vote on a show of hands, the declaration of the chairman that the resolution is carried is conclusive evidence of that fact without proof of the number of votes recorded for and against the resolution; although it can be challenged by a demand for a card vote or if it is manifestly wrong. In **Re Carratal (News) Mines (1902)**, a special resolution was put to the vote on a show of hands. The chairman counted the hands raised for and against and said "six for and 23 against but there are 200 votes by proxy and I declare the resolution carried". This declaration was challenged in the courts. The courts said that although the chairman's declaration of the result of a vote when it is by a show of hands is conclusive, the declaration could still be challenged if it was fraudulent or manifestly wrong. As proxies could not vote on a show of hands, the declaration was invalid. Once the result of a vote on a show of hands is declared, any member can demand a poll. Members can also demand a poll before the meeting is started.

When voting is by poll (i.e., a card vote), the number of voting shares held by a member will determine his number of votes. Poll voting is done at the meeting itself; but the articles may also provide for votes on a resolution to include votes cast in advance of the meeting. The articles usually will set out the provisions for a poll; but any provision which excludes the right to demand a poll at a general meeting other than on the election of a chairman or the adjournment of the meeting will be void **(s.321(1))**. Similarly, any provision that a poll may be allowed only if the requisitionists exceed five members, or hold more than one-tenth of the paid up capital will be void **(s.321(2))**. In addition to the right given under section 321 to demand a poll any member can demand a poll to pass a special resolution for an off-market purchase by the company of its own shares **(s.695 (4)(b))**, and for a purchase or redemption of its shares by a private company out of capital **(s.717(4)(b))**.

In exercising his voting rights a member may vote as he pleases even if it is to the detriment of the company **(North-West Transportation Co. Ltd. v Beatty (1887)**. However, if he and his supporters hold the majority of shares his ability to vote as he pleases is restricted by the common law rule that voting rights must be exercised in good faith and not for an improper purchase, such as with the alteration of the articles. In **Dafen Tinplate Co. v Llanelly Steel Co. (1920)**, the majority included an expropriation clause in the articles to enable them to expel a a member because he had stopped purchasing steel from the company. The court held that it was fraud on the minority. Also, if the majority shareholders control the company and use their votes to misappropriate the company's assets, this will also be fraud on the minority **(Cook v Deeks)**; though in such a case, if the majority shareholders are also the company's directors they will be in breach of their general statutory duties to the company under section 171 (to act within their powers) and section 172 (to promote the success of the company). Where the wrongdoers are not also the company's directors, minority shareholders will have to bring an action under section 994 (proceedings for protection of members against unfair prejudice). Finally, section 239 prevents interested directors and persons connected with them from exercising their votes as shareholders on ratification decisions (but not on authorisation decisions). 'Ratification decisions' arises where a wrongful act such as directors' breach of duty has already occurred and the shareholders decide by resolution (or unanimous consent) to excuse the wrongdoer for that wrongful act (see Chapter 11). 'Authorisation decisions' arises where the shareholders decide in advance to permit an act which would otherwise have been a wrongful act.

Minutes

These are the written record of the proceedings of a meeting. They constitute evidence of the proceedings, but are not conclusive evidence unless the articles so provide. They must be signed by the chairman at the same or the next succeeding meeting.

All companies are required to keep minutes of all general and directors meetings and to enter them in specific books **(s.248)**. The minute book of the general meetings must be kept at the company's registered office and be open to inspection by members without a charge **(s.358)**. The company must provide copies to members on request, but there is a charge for this service. Minutes must be kept for a minimum of 10 years **(s.355)**.

Where minutes are not kept, there is a fine on the company and its officers in default. Where an inspection of the minutes is refused on request, the courts may order that the request be satisfied.

Website publication of financial matters

Section 527 gives members of a quoted company who hold at least 5 per cent of the total voting shares (or 100 members with £100 of shares each) the right to require the company to publish on its website a statement setting out questions to be raised by members about the accounts, or about the departure of the auditor, at the next general meeting where the accounts are to be considered. The company or any other person such as a director or the auditor can apply to the court to avoid having to comply with this request, where members are abusing this right **(s.527 (5))**. Results of polls taken at general meetings of quoted companies must also be disclosed on its website **(s.341)**.

Written Resolutions

In order to make it easier for a private company to operate, the Companies Act 2006 allows members to take decisions outside the framework of a general meeting or a class meeting by signifying their agreement to written resolutions. The company will send copies of a written resolution proposed by the directors to each eligible member at the same time for him to approve the resolution or, if it can be done without delay, circulate the same copy of the resolution to each eligible member. If members holding the required percentage of votes (50% + 1 for an ordinary resolution and 75% for a special resolution) agree with the resolution, the resolution is deemed to be passed. Where the resolution is proposed as a written special resolution, the resolution must state that it is proposed as a special resolution and members must have at least fourteen days notice of it. The company can send copies of the written resolution to members by e-mail or by other electronic means such as websites; but there must be an accompanying statement informing members how to signify their agreement to the resolution and the date by which the resolution must be passed if it is not to expire. Where the written resolution (or a statement relating to the resolution) is sent by means of a website, the resolution or statement is not validly sent unless the resolution is available on the website throughout the period beginning with the circulation date and ending on the date on which the resolution lapses **(s.299)**. Members need not sign a proposed written resolution to signify their agreement to it. They can signify agreement by e-mail or other electronic means if the company allows electronic form communication or if it is deemed to allow it because it has given an electronic address in a document containing or accompanying the proposed resolution. If electronic form communication is not allowed, members may signify agreement to a proposed written resolution in hard copy by identifying the resolution and indicating agreement **(s.296)**. The eligibility of members to vote on a written resolution is fixed on the circulation date of the resolution which is the date on which copies are sent to members (if copies are sent on different days, the first of those days). Members will have the same number of votes on a proposed written resolution as they would have had had they voted by a card vote at a general meeting **(s.285 (3))**.

The members have 28 days (or such time as the articles may specify) from the date the resolution is first circulated to members to communicate their agreement to the resolution **(s.297)**. Once a member has signified his agreement to the resolution, he cannot change his mind and withdraw his agreement.

Members also have a statutory right under section 292 to propose written resolutions and to compel the company to circulate the resolutions (together with any accompanying statements of not more than 1000 words about the subject matter of the resolutions) within 21 days to all eligible members; but the requisitionists must hold at least 5% of the total voting rights (or such lower percentage as the articles may specify) and they must lodge any deposit requested by the company to meet the costs of circulation. The company need not circulate any accompanying statement with a written resolution proposed by members if the courts, on application of the company, relieve the company of its obligation to circulate such statement because the requisitionists are abusing their right to require circulation of statements such as where a statement is defamatory of any person or it is frivolous or vexatious **(s.295)**.

The written resolution procedure cannot be used to pass an ordinary resolution to remove a director or an auditor before his term of office expires. In such a case, the company must hold a general meeting to pass the resolution. Such meeting can be requested by the holders of 10% of the voting shares (or 5% if the company did not hold, within the last twelve months, a similar meeting before which the requisitionists had a right to circulate the resolution) under section 303.

Section 355 requires a company to keep records comprising copies of resolutions passed outside the framework of general meetings (which would include all written resolutions) for a minimum of 10 years.

Chapter 11

Directors

A company being an artificial person cannot manage itself. It needs natural persons to exercise its managerial powers. These persons are called directors. Every company must therefore appoint at least one *natural* person to be its director **(s.155).** This requirement is met if the office of director is held by a natural person as a corporation sole or otherwise by virtue of an office. Thus, a company cannot be a sole director of another company. A natural person must be at least 16 years of age before he can take up his appointment as director of a company **(s. 157)**. Subject to this requirement being satisfied, a company or a firm which is a legal person (i.e., a **LLP**) can be a director of another company. A private company must have a minimum of one director; and a public company must have at least two directors **(s.154)**. There is no statutory maximum; so that a company may have as many directors as it wishes. Where a company does not comply with sections 154 and 155, the Secretary of State can direct the company to do so; and if the company fails to comply, it will be guilty of an offence **(s.156)**. The test of whether a person is a director within the meaning of the Companies Act is functional – section 250 stresses 'any person occupying the position of director', rather than the title he goes under (e.g., as a "governor"). Thus, the term 'director' includes not only a person who is formally appointed as director (i.e., a *de jure* director); but also a person who assumes the functions of a director even though he has not been formally appointed as one (i.e., a *de facto* director). The liability of a *de facto* director is not affected by the fact that he could not have been validly appointed as a director because of his age **(s.157 (5))**. A director is a company officer and can be, but is not necessarily, an employee of the company. A director of a public company can also act as company secretary; and he will still be counted as part of the statutory minimum number of directors required for public companies.

Types of Directors

There are generally five types of directors. An *executive director* is one who is appointed as a director and holds an executive position in the company (e.g., as director of finance, marketing director, or managing director), on a full-time basis and usually with a service contract. Article 5 of default model articles for both private and public companies makes it possible for the board of directors to appoint individual directors to executive positions in the company; and article 19 (private companies) and article 23 (public companies) permit the board to fix the remuneration of such directors for their service. However, despite what the articles may say, directors are not allowed to have service contracts for more than two years without shareholders' approval **(s.188)**. An executive director is an agent of the board and so he is answerable to the board of directors; but he owes his duties to the company. A *non-executive director* is one who is appointed as director but who does not devote his full working time to the company's business; so that he does not form part of the executive management team. However, he serves on the same board as those employed full-time, and he has both an advisory and a supervisory role. A non-executive director is an agent of the company. An *alternate director* is one who is appointed as a director by another director to represent him at board meetings when he is unavailable to attend such meetings. Article 25 gives a director of a public company power to appoint an alternate director; but if the person to be appointed as alternate director is not an existing director of the company, board approval is required before that person can be appointed alternate director. An alternate director is not an agent of the director who appointed him and is responsible for his own acts and defaults **(art. 26)**. An alternate director ceases to be a director if his appointor ceases to be a director (except where the appointor retires by rotation and is immediately reappointed by the general meeting}; and also when the alternate's appointor revokes the appointment by written notice to the company **(art.27)**. A *nominee director* is one who is appointed by an individual shareholder or a lender or some other person with an external interest in the company to represent his interests in the company. Such a director is an agent of the person appointing him but he owes his duties to the company, and not to the appointor. In **Hawkes v Cuddy (2009),** the Court of Appeal held that although a nominee director is entitled to take into account the interests of the person who appointed him, the company's interests will always prevail over the appointor's interest. A *shadow director* is a person who is not appointed as director, but on whose instructions the formally appointed directors are accustomed to act **(s.251)**. Professional advisers such as lawyers and accountants, and holding companies giving instructions to directors of their subsidiaries, are not normally shadow directors. A shadow director has no right to attend directors' meetings. A person who is deemed to be a shadow director is affected by the following provisions which apply to formally appointed directors:

(a) **General statutory duties of directors**. The general statutory duties of directors under sections 171 – 177 (e.g., to promote the success of the company for the benefit of the members, care and skill, disclosure of interest, direct or indirect, in contracts with the company) apply to shadow directors but only to the extent that the common law rule or equitable principles which the statutory rules replace, applied to them **(s.170 (5))**. Thus, where the common law rule or equitable principles did not apply to shadow directors, the general statutory duties equally will not apply to them. The courts are left to develop this area of the law on shadow directors.

(b) **Directors' long-term service contracts**. Any service contract with the company (or subsidiary of the company) likely to exceed two years and which cannot be terminated by notice must be approved by the members of the company or in the case of a director of a holding company, members of the holding company, before it can bind the company **(s. 188)**. 'Service contract' is defined by section 227 to include a contract of service, a contract for service and a letter of appointment as director.

Where members' approval is not obtained, the company can terminate the service contract by giving reasonable notice.

(c) **Inspection of directors' service contracts**. Service contracts of director and shadow directors, whether the contracts are long term or not, must be kept by the company for at least one year after they have expired and must be available for inspection by the members without a charge at the office where the register of members is kept **(s. 228)**.

(d) **Substantial property transactions**. A company needs approval from its members before it can buy or sell to a director (or shadow director) or a director of its holding company (or persons connected with the director such as his spouse or 'live-in partner', his children or his parents, or a company in which the director and persons connected with him own at least 20% of the share capital or voting rights) a non-cash asset where the value of the asset exceeds £100,000 or else is equivalent to at least ten per cent of the company's net assets (as long as the latter figure exceeds £5,000) **(s.190)**. Members' approval is given by ordinary resolution; but the articles may require approval to be given by a higher majority. The directors may vote as members at the meeting on the resolution giving approval for them to enter into the transaction with the company. No approval is required for substantial transactions between a holding company and its subsidiaries where the holding company is the director of the subsidiaries; or for transactions between directors and their non-UK registered companies; or for transactions which are made by a company in administration or in insolvent liquidation. Where members' approval is required but not obtained the transaction becomes voidable at the option of the company unless restitution is not possible, or rights have been acquired by innocent third parties for value, or the transaction is affirmed by the company in general meeting within a reasonable time.

(e) **Loans to directors**. A company needs approval from its members *before* it can make a loan to its directors (including shadow director) or directors of its holding company **(s.197)** or persons connected with the directors **(s.200)**. Members' approval is also required before the company can give any person a guarantee or provide security in connection with loans to its directors and their connected persons. Where the directors are directors of the company's holding company, the transaction must also be approved by the members of the holding company. If the company is a public company or a company associated with a public company, the requirement for members' approval on loans and collaterals extends to quasi-loans (i.e., where the loan is given *via* third parties such as where the company pays a travel agency for a holiday for its directors on condition that the directors repay the loan to the company), and to credit transactions (e.g., the company supplies land. goods, or services to its directors in return for periodical payments) between the company and its directors or their connected persons **(ss.198 - 201)**. Thus, members' approval is necessary *before* quasi-loans and credit transactions can be made to or in favour of directors of public companies; and for loans, quasi –loans and credit transactions to be made to persons connected with directors of such companies.

The following loans etc. do not need members approval: a loan made by a money-lending company to its directors on ordinary commercial terms; a small loan or quasi-loan not exceeding £10,000 per director (or a small credit transaction not exceeding £15,000); a loan or a quasi-loan to meet expenditure on company business as long as it does not exceed £50,000 per director; a credit transaction made in the ordinary course of the company's business; and a loan to enable a director to defend the costs of legal proceedings or in connection with any regulatory action or an investigation of the company by BIS. Home-loans by a money-lending company to its directors or to connected persons who are employees of the company are permitted only if the loans are on normal commercial terms and the home-loan scheme is open to all employees.

Where members' approval is required for loans, guarantees, quasi-loans and credit transactions, the company must prepare a memorandum of the terms of the transaction and provide it to its members before the members give their approval (whether approval is sought by written resolution or by resolution at a general meeting). The company must also disclose in notes to its accounts loans and credit facilities to its directors. For failure to obtain members' approval for loans and credit facilities to directors and their connected persons, the transaction is voidable at the option of the company unless restitution is no longer possible **(s.213)** or the members of the company have affirmed the transaction by resolution within a reasonable time **(s.214)**.

Appointment of Directors

First directors. A company's first directors are the persons named in the statement of proposed officers signed by all the subscribers to the memorandum and filed at the Registry on registration of the company **(s.12)**. Their appointment takes effect from the date of the company's incorporation, which is the date specified in the certificate of incorporation **(s.16 (6))**.

Subsequent directors. The appointment of the directors when the company is operational is regulated by the default model articles which provide, in effect, that:

(i) The board of directors has power to appoint a new director whether to fill a casual vacancy or as an additional board member **(Art.17 – private companies; Art.20 – public companies)**. Even if the board consists of only one director, it may appoint another person as director in order to make up the minimum number of directors required for public companies. Where the board appoints a person as director of a public company, that person must present himself for re-election at the next annual general meeting **(Art.21 (2) (a))**. This is not the same with private companies which do not have to hold annual general meetings.

(ii) The members have power to appoint directors by ordinary resolution **(Art.17 – private companies; Art.20 – public companies)**. Public company directors elected in general meeting must be voted on individually unless the meeting has beforehand unanimously agreed to waive this rule **(s. 160)**. Where, as a result of death, a private company has no shareholders and no directors left, then the personal representatives of the last shareholder to have died have the right, by written notice, to appoint a person to be a director **(Art. 17(2))**. For the purposes of Article 17 (2), if the only shareholders die in circumstances rendering it uncertain who was the last to die, the younger shareholder is deemed to have survived the older shareholder **(Art.17 (3))**.

By section 161, the acts of a director whose appointment is procedurally defective (e.g., because the person who was appointed as director was disqualified from holding office, or he was not entitled to vote on the matter in question, or he was appointed director of a public company and the appointment of the company's directors was not voted on individually), so that strictly speaking he is not a director at all, are not invalidated. Innocent third parties may therefore treat those acts as if they were those of a properly appointed director.

Removal of Directors

This is governed by the articles or by legislation. Statutory provisions for removal of directors have been stepped up by legislation, broadening the scope of the Companies Act, notably the Company Directors Disqualification Act 1986.

In the following circumstances a director may be removed from office:

(a) **By the articles**. Statutory default articles **(Art. 18 – private companies; Art. 22 – public companies)**, list the following as grounds for a person ceasing to be a director:

  (i) that person ceases to be a director by virtue of any provision of the Companies Act 2006 or is prohibited from being a director by law;

 (ii) a bankruptcy order is made against that person;

(iii) a composition is made with that person and his creditors in satisfaction of that person's debts;

(iv) a registered medical practitioner who is treating that person gives a written opinion to the company stating that that person has become physically or mentally incapable of acting as a director and may remain so for more than four months;

(v) by reason of that person's mental health, a court makes an order which wholly or partly prevents that person from personally exercising any powers or rights which that person would otherwise have;

(vi) notification is received by the company from the director that that director is resigning or retiring from office, and such resignation or retirement has taken effect in accordance with its terms.

(b) **By the courts**. The courts have wide powers under the Company Directors Disqualification Act 1986 to disqualify directors from taking part in the management of a company or being concerned in the promotion, liquidation or receivership of a company. In some cases disqualification can last for up to 15 years. The Act gives the courts a *discretion* to disqualify a director in the following cases: where a director has been convicted on indictment of a company offence (e.g., fraud); where there have been persistent breaches of company legislation, most notably in not delivering accounts and making annual returns; where there has been fraudulent trading or any other fraud or breach of duty in relation to the company which is revealed in a winding up; where a director has been convicted summarily on at least three occasions within a period of five years for failing to make returns to Companies Registry; where the Secretary of State, following a **BIS** report, refers the matter to the courts in the belief that a disqualification order would be in the public interest.

Under section 6, the courts *must* make a disqualification order, if, during insolvency proceedings, the Secretary of

State (or if the company is in compulsory liquidation, the official receiver on behalf of the Secretary of State) applies for one against a person involved in the management of an insolvent company (e.g., a director, shadow director or administrative receiver) and the courts are satisfied that the conduct of that person makes him unfit to be concerned in the management of a company. 'Insolvency proceedings' means the company is in insolvent liquidation, or an administration order is made in relation to the company, or an administrative receiver is appointed. 'Unfit' is not defined by the Act; but it clearly includes incompetence and dishonesty. In **Re City Investment Centres Ltd. (1992),** two directors attempted to resist an application by the official receiver for a disqualification order under section 6 against them by saying that they had left the running of the company to a third director. The court still disqualified them because their attitude displayed "a woeful ignorance of the duties attached to the office of a director of a company." The minimum period of disqualification under section 6 is two years and the maximum is 15 years. For a section 6 order to be made, three conditions must be satisfied, namely, (a) the company must have been insolvent when the individual concerned was a director; (b) the Secretary of State must have instituted court proceedings for a disqualification order (every liquidator, administrator or administrative receiver must report to the Disqualification Unit of the Insolvency Service, an arm of **BIS**, of persons who are likely to be caught within the ambit of the 1986 Act; and the Unit will then decide whether to apply for a disqualification order); and (c) the courts must be satisfied that the individual concerned was unfit to be a director.

The Insolvency Act 2000 now gives the Secretary of State power to accept an undertaking from a director that he would no longer be concerned in the management of any company for a period of time (to be determined by the Secretary of

State) without the need for the Secretary of State having to apply to the courts for a disqualification order. However, the director concerned must admit that he was unfit to manage the company.

It is a criminal offence for a person who is disqualified from acting as a director by a disqualification order (or because he is an undischarged bankrupt), to act as such without the courts' permission. Moreover, he will be personally liable for the company's debts incurred while he was involved.

(c) **By rotation**. At the first annual general meeting of a *public* company all the first directors must retire (thus none of the first directors can continue as directors without the agreement of the meeting); and from the third annual general meeting any director who was not appointed at any of the two previous general meetings must retire. The retiring directors may offer themselves for re-appointment **(Art.21)**.

(d) **By the members**. Members have a statutory right under section 168 to remove a director from office by ordinary resolution (see post).

The Position of Directors

Directors are not servants of the company; but they are often described as organs, agents or quasi-trustees of the company. In exercising the company's managerial powers the directors are its organ, and become the company's motive force and its controlling mind. In **H.L. Bolton & Co. v T.J. Graham & Sons (1957)**, Denning J. said: "A company may in many ways be likened to a human body. It also has hands which hold the tools and act in accordance with directions from the centre. Some of the people in the company are mere servants and agents who are nothing more than hands to do the work, and cannot be said to represent the mind or will. Others are directors or managers, who represent the directing mind and will of the company and control what it does. The state of mind of these managers is the state of mind of the company and is treated by the law as such. So you will find that in cases where the law requires personal fault as a condition of liability in tort, the fault of the manager will be the personal fault of the company. So also in criminal law, in cases where the law requires a guilty mind as a condition of a criminal offence; the guilty mind of the directors or the managers will render the company itself guilty".

As agents of the company, the directors must act within the powers conferred on them by the articles; and so long as they do so, they will not generally be liable on contracts made on the company's behalf. Occasionally, the directors will be regarded as agents of the members, in which case the members rather than the company will be liable for the directors' acts. In **Briess v Woolley (1954)**, the members of a company who authorised the manager director to negotiate the sale of their shares to another company were held liable for his fraud.

In some respects, directors are like trustees in that they owe the company similar duties as those owed by trustees to their beneficiaries. Nevertheless, they are not strictly trustees, since the legal ownership of the company's property is vested in the company itself, rather than in its directors.

Nature of Directors' Duties

Directors' duties to the company have now been written down in statutory form. Directors have specific statutory duties as organs of the company. They also have general statutory duties as agents and quasi-trustees indicating how they are expected to behave. The general statutory duties are based on certain common law rules and equitable principles and they have to be interpreted and applied in a way that reflects the rules and principles which they have replaced **(s.170 (4))**. Moreover, section 178 provides that the remedies for breach of the directors' general statutory duties are the same as those available for breach of the common law and equitable principles (i.e., damages, restitution of company's property, account of profits made by directors, and rescission of the transaction where directors fail to disclose their interest in the transaction). The general duties are owed to the company itself, and not to individual members or to third parties. Thus, if the directors are in breach of these duties, only the company can sue them. This can be done by the board of directors instituting legal proceeding; by the general body of shareholders after a special resolution is passed to commence legal proceedings in the company's name; or by the liquidator or administrator under formal insolvency proceedings. An individual member can only sue on behalf of the company if he obtains permission from the courts by instituting derivative proceedings (see Chapter 15).

(a) **Specific statutory duties**. These statutory duties include the duty to keep records of resolutions and meetings for at least ten years from the date of the resolution, meeting or decision **(s.355)**, the duty to produce and file annual accounts of the company's financial position and reports on their management of the company with the registrar within the period for filing **(s.441)**, the duty to deliver annual returns within 28 days after the return date **(s.854)**, and the maintenance of certain statutory registers such as a register of directors **(s.162)**. In most cases, sanctions are imposed on the directors for the company's failure to comply with such statutory requirements.

(b)**The general duty to act within their powers (s.171)**. This duty deals with two aspects of directors powers. First, it requires directors to act in accordance with the company's constitution **(s.17(a))**. For the purposes of directors' duties, the term 'constitution' includes not only the company's articles but also decisions taken in accordance with the articles and decisions of members (or a class of them) if they are to be regarded as decisions of the company such as informal unanimous decisions of the members **(s.257)**. Thus, the directors will be in breach of this duty if they act *ultra vires* or if they fail to observe decisions taken under it. Secondly, this duty requires directors to exercise their powers for the purposes for which they were conferred **(s.171(b))**. Thus, directors will be in breach of this duty if they use their powers improperly to secure an advantage for themselves or for a third party or for a certain section of the shareholders at the expense of the company. In **Re W & M Roith (1967)**, a director who was in poor health wished to make provision for his widow without leaving her his shares. On advice, he entered into a service agreement with the company whereby on his death she was entitled to his pension for life. The court set aside the agreement, after his death, because the sole object was to make provision for his widow; no thought had been given to the question whether the agreement was in the company's interest. On these facts, the director would also have been liable for breach of section 172 (duty to promote the success of the company).

If directors have power to issue shares they must exercise this power principally to raise capital and not for some ulterior motive, such as to alter the power structure of the company. An issue of shares will be invalid if the directors are motivated by other interests (e.g., to fight a takeover bid). In **Hogg v Cramphorn (1966)**, the directors issued new shares on trust for the company's employees to prevent a takeover which was supported by the majority of members. The new issue was declared invalid by the courts. However, in **Bamford v Bamford (1969)**, on similar facts, the issue was upheld because it was ratified by the members, the holders of the new shares not voting thereat. In **Howard Smith Ltd. v Ampol Petroleum Ltd. (1974)**, directors issued new shares to facilitate a takeover bid which they honestly believed was in the company's interest, but which was opposed by the majority of members. The new issue was declared void. Lord Wilberforce said "It must be unconstitutional for directors to use their fiduciary powers over the shares in the company purely for the purpose of destroying an existing majority or creating a new majority which did not exist".

(c) **The general duty to promote the success of the company (s.172).** This duty requires directors to act in a way which they consider, in good faith, will best enable them to promote the success of the company for the benefit of all the members. For a commercial company, Lord Goldsmith QC, the then Attorney-General said 'success' would normally mean long-term increase in value of the company. However, for a non-commercial company such as a charity and a community interest company, 'success' may mean achieving the purposes for which the company was formed. In complying with this duty the directors must pay attention to a wide range of matters when making decisions such as they must have regard to the interests of the company's employees, also the likely consequences of any decision on the long term, the need to foster the company's business relationships with suppliers, customers and others, the impact of the operation of the company on the community and the environment, the importance of the company maintaining high ethical standards, and the need to act fairly between the company's members **(s.172 (1))**. Provided the directors take these matters into account, and do so honestly, their decision as to how best they can promote the success of the company will not be interfered with by the courts.

The duty to promote the success of the company for the members is modified if the company is insolvent or on the verge of insolvency **(s.172 (3))**. In such a case, the directors must act in the best interests of the company's creditors

(West Mercia Safetywear Ltd. v Dodd (1988). Thus, in the case of an insolvent company, not only will the directors be in breach of their duty to the company if they fail to take account of the creditors' interests, but they may also have to contribute towards the company's debts under the statutory provisions relating to fraudulent trading **(s.213 IA)** and wrongful trading **(s.214 IA)**.

Directors will not be in breach of their duty to promote the success of the company if they exercise their statutory power under section 247 to make provision for the company's existing or past employees or those of its subsidiaries in connection with the cessation or transfer of the whole or any part of the company's business. Thus, voluntary payments to employees over and above their state redundancy entitlement cannot be challenged by dissentient shareholders on grounds that the directors are not performing their duty to promote the success of the company **(s.247 (2))**. The exercise of the section 247 power needs the approval of the members by ordinary resolution (the board can authorise the payments to employees only if the articles allow it) and the payments must be made out of profits available for distribution and before the commencement of winding up of the company (provisions for employees after winding up commences are allowed by section 187 of the Insolvency Act which has its own conditions to comply with).

(d) **The general duty to exercise independent judgement (s.173)**. This duty requires directors to have an independent mind and to ignore all considerations not relevant to the task in hand. However, this duty does not mean that the directors cannot seek and rely on the advice of others; it only means that when deciding how they treat such advice, the final judgement has to be the directors' own judgement. This duty is a restatement of one aspect of directors' fiduciary duties, namely, that the directors should not do anything which would 'fetter their discretion'. If directors enter into an agreement with a third party to the effect that they will exercise their future discretion in a certain way, they will be in breach of this duty unless at the time they make the agreement, they do so in good faith and in the company's interest **(Fulham Football Club v Cabra Estates plc (1994)**. This duty is not broken if the directors act in a way authorised by the company's constitution such as where the articles allowed them to delegate the management of the company to others (provided they have adequate internal control in place) **(s.173 (2)(b))**.

(e) **The general duty to exercise care and skill (s. 174)**. This duty requires directors to exhibit reasonable care, skill and diligence when they are carrying out their managerial tasks. This duty replaces the common law duty laid down by Romer J in **Re City Equitable Fire Insurance Co. (1925)** that only a director's own personal skills should determine the standard of care and skill which may be expected of that director. Section 174 (2) now provides that a director's conduct, as to whether he has used reasonable care, skill and diligence in the management of the company is to be judged by the higher of two standards, namely, (x) the standard which would be expected of a reasonably diligent person carrying out the same functions as the director in relation to that company (an *objective* test), and (xx) the experience that that director has (a *subjective* test). Thus, the standard will depend on the type of company with which the director is connected and the personal experiences and skills which the director possesses. The director's own experiences and skills will fix the standard expected of that director only if they improve on the objective standards of the reasonable director. If directors are in breach of this duty they will be liable to the company for any loss which it suffers as a result of their negligence. In **Dorchester Finance Co. Ltd. v Stebbing**

(1989), the company's three directors were all accountants; but only one was an executive director. The other two were non-executive directors and signed blank cheques which the executive director used to make loans to his friends. When the loans became unrecoverable, the courts held that the non-executive directors were equally liable with the executive director for the loss to the company because they did not show the necessary care and skill expected from accountants when they signed blank cheques.

A director is not required to give his full-time attention to the company's affairs unless he has a contract to do so. Nevertheless, such a director is expected to keep himself informed of the company's financial position; otherwise he runs the risk of being disqualified under the Company Directors Disqualification Act as 'unfit' to run a company (see **Re City Investment Centres Ltd. (1992)**), and also probably will be in breach of his duty under the objective/subjective test to act with reasonable care and skill.

Where the management of the company is delegated to others, a director will not be liable for their negligence if the delegation was made in good faith and it was consistent with the company's articles. Nevertheless, as overall responsibility for the management of the company remains with the directors, the director and his fellow directors must supervise the discharge of the delegated functions; otherwise they may be considered unfit to be directors if things go wrong, and could be disqualified from holding office (**Re Barings plc (No.5) (1999)**).

(f) **The general duty to avoid conflicts of Interest (s.175)**. This duty requires directors to avoid any situation where their personal interests or duties to others will (or are likely to) conflict with their duties to the company, unless approved by the company. This duty applies to those cases where the company is not a party to the transaction or proposed transaction as in the case of third party dealings by directors which may result in a conflict of interest. Conflicts of interest may arise where the directors compete with their company; where they make personal use of the company's property, corporate information or opportunity without the company's knowledge and consent; where directors hold directorships in other companies (this could result in a conflict between the company's interests and the interests of the other companies) and where directors are appointed by individual shareholders (i.e., the directors are *nominee* directors).

Where directors exploit corporate resources and opportunity, which have come to them in their capacity as directors, for their own use, they are accountable to the company for any profit made; and it is immaterial that the company would not have taken advantage of the resources or opportunity **(Regal (Hastings) Ltd. v Gulliver (1967))**. In **Bhullar v Bhullar (2003)**, the director of a family company, whose objects included the acquisition of property for investment, saw an opportunity during his lunch break to purchase private premises for himself, with a view to starting a similar business as the company after the company ceased to trade. The Court of Appeal held he was in breach of the 'no conflict rule' notwithstanding that the company had decided not to buy any more property for investment and to stop trading. The directors' duty under section 175 continues even after they cease to be directors as regards the exploitation of corporate opportunity of which they became aware when they were directors of their company **(s.170(2) (a))**. In **Industrial Development Consultants Ltd. v Cooley (1972)**, the managing director of a company resigned and took up a contract which his own company was unable to acquire. The court held that he was accountable to the company for the benefit as he had broken the no conflict rule.

Section 175 (3) excludes any conflict of interest which may arise where a transaction or arrangement is made (or to be made) *with the company* and the director has a personal interest (direct or indirect) in the matter. In such a case, the transaction or proposed transaction or arrangement does not have to be approved by the members or by the board. Instead, only the director's interest in the matter has to be *disclosed* to the board (interest in transactions or arrangements in which the company was a party must be declared under section 182, and interests in *proposed* transactions and proposed arrangements under section 177).

Section 175 is not infringed if the situation cannot *reasonably* be regarded as likely to give rise to a conflict of interest; or if the matter which amounts to a conflict of interest has been authorised by the other directors in accordance with the requirements set out in the Companies Act. Fellow directors of the same company can only authorise the matter if they are independent directors (in the sense that they have no direct or indirect interest in the matter). In the case of a private company, as long as nothing in the company's constitution invalidates such authorisation, the authorisation may be given by the other directors. If the company is a public company, the company's articles must contain express provision enabling the other directors to authorise the matter since default model articles for public companies do not make provision for this (if no provision for authorisation by the board is contained in the articles, authorisation can only be given by the members in general meeting). Where authorisation by the board is permitted, the authorisation is only effective if, at the board meeting at which the matter is being considered, the director concerned does not vote (or if he does vote, the matter would still have been agreed to if his vote had not been counted) and his presence is not counted as part of the quorum for the board meeting. Board authorisation is not permitted with regards benefits which a director receives from a third party; only the members can authorise the director to keep the benefit (see post).

(g) **The general duty not to accept benefits from third parties (s.176)**. This duty prohibits directors from using their position as directors to accept personal benefits (including bribes) from third parties and which are likely to result in a conflict of interest unless the members of the company authorise the directors to accept such benefits. Whether or not benefits conferred on directors by third parties can reasonably be regarded as likely to give rise to a conflict of interest is a question of fact. Thus, directors who accept gifts or are taken for dinners and provided with other entertainment by third parties who hope to do business with the company, where this practice is considered in the business world as ordinary business hospitality, may very well be in breach of this duty. However, it would depend on the regularity and financial value of the benefits.

Section 176 only applies to benefits conferred by third parties on directors because they are directors or because of something the directors do or do not do. The section does not apply to benefits directors receive from their own company, or from any associated company, or from persons acting on behalf of such companies. A person who ceases to be a director continues to be subject to this duty as regards things done or omitted by him before he ceased to be a director **(s.170 (2)(b))**.

Where the acceptance of benefits from third parties may give rise to a conflict of interests, the directors concerned will be in breach of this duty as well as the general duty to avoid conflicts of interest under section 175, and depending on the facts, failing to exercise independent judgement under section 173.

(h) **The general duty to declare interest in proposed transactions or arrangements with the company (s.177)**. This duty applies to the situation where the company *proposes* to enter into a transaction or arrangement with a director or with a third party with whom the director has an interest (because the third party is the director's spouse or a member of his family, or a company in which the director is a shareholder). The director is under a duty to disclose the nature and extent of that interest to the other directors before the company enters into the transaction or arrangement (disclosure to the members and obtaining their consent is not necessary unless the articles require it). The director must *disclose* his interest at the earliest board meeting or by notice in writing or by general notice; and a shadow director must disclose his interest by written notice or general notice to the board. In **Guinness plc v Saunders (1990)**, the court held that 'disclosure to the board' means disclosure to the full board, and not just disclosure to a committee of the board. However, if the company only has one director, no disclosure is necessary; unless the company was required to have more than one director in which case a declaration of interest in existing transaction must be made in writing under section 182 (see post).

Information need not be disclosed if it is already know to the other directors, or if it cannot reasonably be regarded as likely to give rise to a conflict of interest, or if it concerns the terms of the director's service contract which are to be considered by a meeting of the directors or by a committee of the directors appointed for the purpose under the company's constitution such as a remuneration committee **(s.177 (6))**. Substantial property transactions (i.e., where the assets involved value at least £100,000 or their value is equivalent to at least ten per cent of its net assets) between the company and its directors (or persons connected with the directors) still need members' approval. Also, if the company is a charity, disclosure of interest is not enough; the directors must obtain board or shareholder authorisation before they can keep the interest, unless the charitable company's articles allow for mere disclosure of self-dealing transactions **(s.181)**.

(i) **The general duty to disclose an interest in existing transactions or arrangements (s.182).** If the transaction or arrangement in which the director has an interest (direct or indirect) has already been entered into by the company, the director is under a duty to disclose the nature and extent of his interest in that transaction or arrangement as soon as is reasonably practicable to do so. This situation may arise where a company in which **X** is a member had entered into a transaction with "**Company A**" and before the transaction could be fully performed, **X** becomes a director of the "**Company A**". **X** must disclose to "**Company A**" his (indirect) interest in the transaction after he becomes its director. The disclosure could be at a board meeting, or by notice in writing to all the directors (in accordance with the provisions of section 184), or by general notice (in accordance in accordance with the provisions of section 185). General notice is notice given to the other directors that the director in question has an interest (as member, officer, employee or otherwise) in another body corporate or firm or is connected with the person with whom the company has entered into the transaction or arrangement (e.g., a member of the director's family as defined by section 253 such as spouse, civil partner, children or step-children, the director's live-in partner's children under 18 years of age, and the director's parents).

If the company has only one director, the sole director need not comply with section 182 (disclosure of interests in existing transactions with the company); but if the company was required to have more than one director (e.g., because it is a public company or because its articles require the company to have more than one director) the sole director must record in writing the nature and extent of his interest in the transaction made by the company **(s.186)**. The duty under section 182 to disclose any interest in existing transactions or arrangements that have been entered into by the company also applies to shadow directors **(s.187)**. Shadow directors must disclose the nature of their interest by general notice. If after making a disclosure, the director's interest in the transaction or arrangement changes, the director must make another disclosure updating the earlier one.

The director need not disclose his interest under section 182 if he had already done so under section 177 at the time the transaction was proposed, or if the nature of his interest is such that it could not have given rise to a conflict of interest, or if the other directors were already aware or ought reasonably to have known of his interest, or if his interest concerns the terms of his service contract which was considered or to be considered by the board or relevant remuneration committee. Failure to disclose interests in transactions under section 182 is a criminal offence **(s.183)**.

Transactions requiring members approval

Even though directors have complied with their general statutory duties, certain transactions involving directors also require the approval of the members before they can be binding on the company. The transactions which require members approval are set out in Chapter 4 of the Companies Act, and they are: directors' long term service contracts, **(s.168)**; substantial property transactions **(s.190)**; loans to directors **(s.197)**; quasi loans to directors **(s.198))**; and compensation to directors or persons connected with the directors for loss of office **(s.217))**. The general duties and the Chapter 4 requirements are exclusive of each other; so that directors have to comply with both sets of requirements. Thus, if the board makes a valid loan to one of its directors under section 197 (i.e., the company obtains members' approval for the loan or the loan comes within the exceptions where members' approval is not necessary) the loan must be made for the company's benefit; otherwise the directors will be in breach of their duty to promote the success of the company. However, section 180 provides that where the Chapter applies and approval by the members is given under the Chapter (or an exception applies under the Chapter dispensing with the need for members approval), the directors do not have to comply with the general duty to avoid conflicts of interest under section 175 or the duty not to accept benefits from third parties under section 176.

Apart from the Chapter 4 requirements, section 366 requires directors to obtain prior authorisation from the members before they can make political donations to political parties or incur political expenditure. If authorised by the members,, the authority lasts for four years, unless the articles prescribe a shorter time. Donations not exceeding £5,000 in any twelve month period do not require prior authorisation.

Reliefs Available for Directors

Directors may be relieved from liability for breach of any of their duties in several ways, namely:

(i) **By ratification of the breach by shareholders.** Some breaches by directors such as negligence, default, breach of duty and breach of trust can be excused by the members passing an ordinary resolution; but the directors in default and connected persons such as their family cannot use their votes as shareholders to secure a pardon when the members are considering the matter **(s.239)**. If the resolution is proposed as a written resolution neither the director (if he is a member of the company) nor any member connected with him can take part in the written resolution procedure; and if the resolution is proposed at a meeting, he and his connected persons can take part in the meeting and count towards the quorum for the meeting but they cannot vote on the resolution **(s.239 (3) and (4))**. This does not affect the unanimous consent rule, so that if all the members of the company including the defaulting directors and connected persons vote to ratify the breach, the vote is still effective.

Some breaches, such as giving unlawful financial assistance by public companies and conduct amounting to fraud on the creditors, cannot be excused even by unanimous consent.

(ii) **Relief from liability by the courts**. Under section 1157, the courts may grant directors a full or partial indemnity for breach of duty if the courts are satisfied that the directors have acted honestly and reasonably and that, having regard to all the circumstances, they ought fairly to be excused. Except for criminal liability against the company's officers for specific duties imposed by the Companies Act, the courts can grant an indemnity under section 1157 only if the action is brought against the directors by the company or on its behalf or its liquidator for their personal breaches of duty. Thus, the section is not applicable if the action is brought by a third party in his own right against the officers in default **(Customs and Excise Commissioners v Hedon Alpha Ltd. (1981))**.

In **DTI v Bollins Café Ltd. (1975)**, a criminal prosecution was brought on behalf of the Secretary of State against the company and its officers for failing to file annual returns over a number of years. The courts granted a partial indemnity to the directors for breach of their statutory duty because they had paid accountants to deal with this matter and had no reason to believe that their instructions were not being carried out. In **Re Duomatic (1969)**, the liquidator brought a civil action to recover a number of payments made by the directors (who were the only voting members of the company) to themselves. These payments included compensation for loss of office by the directors but not disclosed to non-voting members, and remuneration paid in advance before the members meeting, according to previous practices. The courts held that an indemnity could not be given for failure to disclose the compensation for loss of office to all the members (as required by the Companies Act), since the directors did not act reasonably in this matter; but the remuneration paid in advance of approval by members, though irregular, could be excused under section 1157.

(iii) **Provision in the articles.** Although any provision in the articles which excludes directors' liability for negligence, default, breach of duty or breach of trust in relation to the company is void **(s.232)**, the company may lawfully include a provision in its articles allowing it to indemnify its directors in respect of legal proceedings brought by third parties against the directors for liability incurred by the directors to the third parties (but not for liability incurred to the company unless the directors successfully defend the action against them or else obtain an indemnity from the courts under section 1157). Also section 232 does not prevent the company from purchasing and maintaining insurance for its directors against their liabilities **(s.233)**. Moreover, it is possible for the company to define in its articles what would not be regarded as giving rise to a conflict of interest if it had previously been lawful before the Companies Act 2006 was passed **(s.232 (4))**.

Board Meetings

Directors of a company exercise their powers collectively either by majority decision taken at formal board meetings convened and conducted in accordance with the company's articles or outside the framework of a formal meeting by means of a unanimous agreement. If statutory default articles are adopted, article 7 for public companies requires that directors' decisions which are taken unanimously outside the framework of a formal meeting must be taken by written resolution; and article 18 (1) states that the resolution is adopted when all the directors who have received notice of it have signed one or more copies of it, provided that those directors would have formed a quorum at a formal directors meeting. Model articles for private companies make it possible for private companies to take unanimous decisions outside the framework of a formal board meeting without a written resolution. Article 8 for private companies limited by shares provides for directors to take unanimous decisions 'by any means' such as by e-mails, tele-messages and fax, and not just by a written resolution.

Board meetings may be held without all the directors having to be at the same place **(Art.10 (2) – private companies, Art.9 (2) - public companies)**. Board meetings must be called at a reasonable time and place and directors must be given sufficient notice of the meetings unless no director objects by giving notice to the company within 7 days after the date on which the meeting is held that he is waiving his right to notice **(Art.9 (4) – private companies; Art.8 (6) – public companies)**. So in **Barron v Potter (1914)**, where the only two directors of the company one of whom was the chairman with a casting vote, met accidentally at a railway station, and the chairman insisted on a directors meeting despite protests by the other, the courts held the meeting to be invalid. The courts will not intervene where an irregularity at a board meeting can be cured by the members. In **Bentley-Stevens v Jones (1974)**, an irregularly convened board meeting summoned a general meeting to remove a director from office. The court held that as the general meeting could cure the irregularity, the general meeting was valid.

The quorum for a board meeting of both private and public companies is two; but the directors may set a higher quorum if they wish **(Art. 11- private companies; Art. - 10 public companies)**. This rule does not apply where a private company has only one director **(Art. 7)**. Where there are not enough directors for a quorum, the directors may appoint new sufficient directors to make a quorum or they may call a members meeting to appoint additional directors **(Art.11 (3) - private companies; Art. 11(2) - public companies)**. Where the board meeting fails to agree (the chairman of a company automatically has a casting vote; but it cannot be exercised if the company's own articles specify that the chair should not be counted for quorum and voting purposes) or the board meeting cannot be held (e.g., it always lacks a quorum), the general meeting has a residual power to use the company's powers and by-pass the board (Lord Hailsham in **Alexander Ward & Co Ltd. v Samyang Navigation Ltd. (1975))**.

Minutes must be taken at board meetings; and the minutes must be kept for at least ten years from the date of the meeting **(s.248)**. Every officer in default of the obligation to record and keep minutes will be liable (but not the company) to a fine. Once the minutes are signed by the chairman of the meeting or by the chairman of the next board meeting, they become strong evidence of the proceedings at the meeting, unless the contrary is proved **(s.249)**.

Chairman of the Board of Directors.

Article 12 of both private and public companies gives the directors power to appoint the chairman of the board and to terminate his appointment at any time. Article 12 (3) allows the board to appoint other directors as deputy to chair the board meeting of a public company in the absence of the chairman. Where the articles give the board power to appoint the chairman, the members of the company cannot make an appointment **(Clark v Workman (1920))**.

The chairman of the board has a casting vote unless the company's own articles provide otherwise. **(Art.13 – private companies; Art.14 - public companies)**.

Remuneration and Expenses for Directors

Directors are not entitled to be paid for acting as directors unless such payment is approved by the members or it is provided for in the company's articles. Statutory default articles **(Art.19 (2)– private companies; Art. 23 - public companies;)** allow the directors to fix their remuneration for services as directors to the company; and Article 20 (private companies) and Article 24 (public companies) require the company to meet reasonable expenses (e.g., travelling and hotel expenses) properly incurred by directors in connection with the business of the company. Where the articles set out the amount of remuneration the directors may enforce it by implied contract **(Re New British Iron Co., Ex Parte Beckwith (1898))**.

Directors' pay (fees) in the above cases is not a preferential debt when the company is in liquidation; so that the directors will have to prove as ordinary creditors. Even if the directors have separate contracts for remuneration, pay already due will not be a preferential debt if the contracts relate solely to the office of director (which requires attendance of board meetings and willingness to be associated openly with the company). Such contracts are called 'purely directorship contracts' to distinguish them from 'contracts of service' which enable directors to work as employees of the company (e.g., as executive director or office manager). In **Sec. of State for BIS v Neufeld (2009)**, the Court of Appeal said that a director may be an employee of his company even though he is the company's only director and owns or controls all of its shares, as long as his contract of service is genuine and not a sham. Pay due under contracts of service is a preferential debt.

Directors' pay has to be disclosed in a note to the annual accounts and in the directors' report; and where the company is a quoted company in a directors' remuneration report. The amount of information relating to directors' pay to be disclosed varies, depending on the type of company. A quoted company must identify each paid director and the pay package he receives; and it must prepare and file a separate directors' remuneration report in addition to a directors' report. A small sized private company need not disclose its directors' pay in the accounts it files with the Registrar. Non-contractual payment of compensation (this includes benefits otherwise than in cash) to directors for loss of office (e.g., when they cease to be directors on retirement or on removal from any office or employment in connection with the management of the company or any of its subsidiaries) is lawful only if it is approved by the members in general meeting, after proper disclosure has been made **(s.217)**. Small payments not exceeding £200 for loss of office do not require members' approval. In **Taupo Totara Timber Co. Ltd. v Rowe (1978)**, a director who had a service contract for five years was forced to resign before his term expired as a result of his company being taken over. The courts held that there was a valid contractual obligation to make the payment; and so it did not require the approval of the members in general meeting.

Members Control over the Board

The directors' powers to manage the company are found in the articles; and where statutory articles are adopted, Article 3 of default model articles for both private and public companies gives the directors authority to exercise all the powers of the company. Members may exercise control over the board in the following ways:

(a) **Alteration of articles**. The members may limit the directors' powers in the articles by special resolution **(Art. 4 –private and public companies)**. The effectiveness of this method of control is greatly reduced by the *Rule in Royal British Bank v Turquand* and by section 40(1) of   the

Companies Act which enable third parties to bind the company to unauthorised transactions made by its directors.

(b) **Re-appointment of directors**. The members may refuse to re-appoint the directors when they come up for re-election. In this way, the members may exercise indirect control over the directors' day to day activities.

(c) **Circulation of members' views**. Members holding at least five per cent of the voting capital or at least 100 members (whether entitled to vote or not) can insist on a resolution being put at the annual general meeting if they give six weeks notice to the company before the meeting; and they can require the directors to circulate their views on any matter coming up at any general meeting if they give at least one week's notice to the company and are prepared to meet the costs incurred by the board for doing so **(s.338)**. In this way, members can influence policy decisions at the meeting.

(d) **Removal of directors**. In the last resort, members may remove the directors from office by ordinary resolution **(s.168)**; but the directors concerned have a right to defend themselves both by written representations (which have to be circulated to members) and by addressing the meeting at which the resolution is to be proposed **(s.169)**. Section 168 overrides any clause in the articles aimed at entrenching the position of directors; but a number of factions restrict its use. First, if the directors hold shares in the company, they may enter into an agreement with all (or a majority) of the shareholders as to how each party to the agreement will vote at general meetings such as that the parties to the agreement will always vote for the directors every time their re-election as directors is in issue and to vote against any resolution to remove them from office **(Russell v Northern Bank Development Corpn. Ltd. (1992))**, or how a quorum for a general meeting shall be determined **(Harman and Another v BML Group Ltd)**. Such a shareholder agreement will be upheld by the courts (see Chapter 3). Secondly, the articles may give the directors weighted votes (i.e., more than one vote for each share they possess) and this may make it difficult for the other shareholders to get enough votes to pass an ordinary resolution to remove the targeted directors from office. In **Bushell v Faith (1969)**, a company had three members, all of whom were directors holding 100 shares each. The articles provided that in the event of a resolution being proposed at a general meeting of the company for the removal from office of any director, each of that director's shares will carry the right to three votes per share. A motion to remove one of the directors was proposed; two directors voted in favour, and the director in question against. The votes in favour were thus 200, and those against 300. The courts held that it was permissible to have weighted voting rights, and directors could be removed only if the resolution was carried. In this instance, the ordinary resolution was defeated. Thirdly, where a section 168 resolution is intended to be put before an annual general meeting, the directors may refuse to include it in the agenda for the meeting unless the proposer of the resolution also complies with section **338 (**see **Pedley v Inland Waterways Association Ltd. (1977))**.

The consequences of the removal of a director under section 168 may also be serious. In the case of small private companies, a director's removal may constitute a breach of an understanding that the director should always have a right to participate in the management; its breach amounting to a ground for a compulsory winding up order under the 'just and equitable' rule of section 122(1)(g) of the Insolvency Act 1986 (see **Ebrahimi v Westbourne Galleries Ltd. (1972))** or for other relief under section 994 of the Companies Act for conduct unfairly prejudicial to the interest of minorities (see Chapter 15). Also, a director's removal without cause will constitute a breach of his service contract as an employee and will enable him to claim damages from the company. Therefore, if the director has a long term service contract for which prior approval was given by the members, this may make it very expensive for the company to get rid of him. However, the courts cannot grant an injunction to prevent the use of section 168 where it leads to a breach of contract.

Publicity Concerning Directors

Section 162 requires a company to keep a register of its directors. The register will contain particulars of each person who is its director. However, in order to protect directors, it need not give the directors' residential address, but only a service address for communications to them (the service address is usually the company's registered address). Where the director is a company or a LLP its registered or principal office must also be registered

The register of directors must be open to public inspection; but the company may charge a prescribed fee for public inspection. The company's own members have a right to inspect the register without a charge. The company must also keep a register of directors' residential address **(s.165)**; but this register is not open to public inspection. The Registrar of Companies has to be notified of any changes in the register of directors and the register of directors' residential address within 14 days.

Chapter 12

Company Secretary

Appointment

Section 271 requires every public company to have a secretary. A private company may only have one if it chooses to do so **(s.270)**. Where a private company decides to have a company secretary, the secretary will have the same authority and responsibilities as company secretaries and will have to be registered at Companies Registry. A sole director can act as company secretary; but where an act is required by some statutory provision to be done by a director and the secretary of the company, the provision is not satisfied by it being done by the same person acting both as director and as, or in place of, the secretary **(s.280)**.

The directors have power to appoint the secretary **(s.274)**; but the first secretary of the company is invariably appointed by the promoter. Section 12 provides for a statement of the name and particulars of the first secretary, with his signed consent to act, to be delivered to the Registrar on the registration of the company. A private company which intends to take advantage of the exemption given under section 270 (1) in not having a secretary does not have to provide any details of a secretary on registration of the company. If the person actually appointed as the first secretary is not the same as the person in the application for registration of the company, then the appointment is void, and for all intent and purposes, the person so named will be deemed to be the first secretary **(s.16 (6))**.

The secretary of a public company must be suitably qualified for the post (e.g., a qualified lawyer, or accountant from one of the Chartered bodies or a chartered secretary) and the directors must ensure that he has the requisite knowledge and experience **(s.273)**. A person not so qualified can be appointed as secretary of a public company only if he held the post of secretary of a public company for at least three years of the last five years. No formal qualifications are required for secretaries of private companies where such companies decide to have a secretary. Particulars of the secretary of every company must be included in a register of secretary (the register must be kept at the company's registered office); and the register must be open for inspection. Where the secretary is a natural person the register must state his Christian name or forename and his surname and his service address **(s.277)**; and where the secretary is a company or a partnership firm which is a legal person (i.e., LLP), the register must state the company or firm name and its registered or principal address **(s.278)**. Any change of secretary, notice must be notified to the Registrar within 14 days **(s.276)**.

If having appointed a company secretary, the office of secretary of a company (including a private company which has not taken advantage of the exemption under section 270 (1)) becomes vacant or any reason the secretary is unable to act (e.g., because of death or illness) then if the company has an assistant or deputy secretary, he may fill the position of secretary. Failing this, the directors may authorise any other person to act as secretary **(s.274)**.

Duties

The secretary is an officer of the company **(s.1261)**; so many of the duties imposed by company legislation on 'officers' also affect him. Thus he must service meetings of the board of directors and general meetings of the members, assist the directors to comply with their personal obligations under company law and stock exchange requirements such as the Combined Code of Corporate Governance, and communicate with members. He has to sign the annual return and accompanying documents and deliver them to Companies Registry; he must keep and make available registers such as the registers of directors and secretary; and in the event of the company's liquidation he may be liable if he is guilty of misfeasance **(s.212 IA).**

Powers

In the initial stage the office of the secretary did not carry much importance and the company secretary was considered as a mere clerk or servant who had to do what he was told by the directors **(Barnett Hoares v South London Tramways Co. (1887))**. As the size of companies expanded and their administration became more complicated, the secretary's function grew in importance. In **Panorama Development Ltd. v Fidles Ltd. (1971)**, the Court of Appeal held the secretary to   be the company's chief administrative officer and as such has ostensible authority to enter into contracts concerned with the administrative side of the company's affairs (such as the hiring of cars).

In the **Panorama** case Lord Denning MR had this to say about modern company secretaries:

'Times have changed. A company secretary is a much more important person nowadays. He is an officer of the company with extensive duties and responsibilities. He is certainly entitled to sign contracts connected with the administrative side of the company's affairs, such as employing staff, ordering cars and so forth'.

This case leaves open the extent of the secretary's ostensible authority to bind the company. It could be that previous judicial pronouncements that a secretary has no ostensible authority to enter into contracts relating to the company's ordinary commercial transactions **(Houghton v Nothard, Lowe & Wills Ltd. (1927)** or to borrow money on the company's behalf **(Re Keadib Trust (1939)** would no longer hold good.

The company secretary does not have authority to make entries in the register of members **(Re Indo-China Steam Navigation Co. (1917)**. Such entries can only be made by him with the approval of the directors or all of the members **(Re Zinotty Properties Ltd. (1984))**.

Chapter 13

The Auditor

The development of the limited company has made possible the complete separation of ownership and management and the need for accountability of the managers to the owners of the concern. Hence with the passing of the Joint Stock Companies Act 1944, companies were for the first time required to have their accounts audited.

The purpose of this chapter is to deal with the most important provisions of the Companies Act directly affecting auditors, and to discuss the case history which formulated the present position of the auditor so far as negligence is concerned.

Qualification of Auditors

A person can only be appointed as auditor of a company if he is a member of a recognised body of accountants established in the UK (e.g., the Institute of Chartered Accountants for England and Wales, and the Association of Chartered Certified Accountants) or if he has been approved by an EEA competent authority outside the UK or if the Professional Oversight Board, acting on behalf of BIS, recognises him as suitably qualified as a result of reciprocal arrangements with the country in which he is qualified. An employee or officer of the company cannot be appointed as auditor **(s.1214)**; but a firm ('firm' in this context means partnership firm or body corporate) providing auditing services can be the auditor of another company as long as the service provider is controlled by qualified persons and the individuals carrying out the audit on behalf of the service provider are qualified to be appointed statutory auditors.

Where the company appoints a firm which is not a legal person as its auditors, the appointment is of the firm, rather than of the individual partners of the firm. The auditors' report has to state the name of the senior statutory auditor, the name of the firm and be signed by the senior statutory auditor in his own name for, and on behalf of the firm **(s.503)**. The firm will decide who is its senior statutory auditor (see the Guidelines issued on this matter by the Auditing Practices Board which is part of the Financial Reporting Council).

Appointment of Auditors

Every company except a *dormant* company (i.e., a company which has not had any significant accounting transaction since incorporation or since the end of its previous financial year) and *small* companies which are audit-exempt (see Chapter 14) must appoint an auditor **(s. 485 – private companies; s. 489 – public companies)**. Certain non-commercial companies in the public sector that are audited by a public sector auditor (the National Audit Office) are not subject to an audit under the Companies Act **(s.482)**. The person appointed as auditor of the company under sections 485 or 489 is called the 'statutory auditor'. Where a company is audit exempt its balance sheet must include a statement by the directors that the company is audit exempt, that the members have not required the company to obtain an audit of its accounts and that the directors take responsibility for producing the compliant accounts. Members of a company which would otherwise be audit exempt have a right to demand an audit of their company's accounts as long as they hold at least 10% in nominal value of the company's issued share capital (or if the company does not have a share capital, they constitute 10% in number of the company's members) and they give the company notice not later than one month before the relevant financial year that they want an audit of the accounts **(s. 476)**. Certain companies engaged in financial services business such as insurance and banking are not entitled to audit exemption even if they are dormant.

Section 485 gives members of a private company general power to appoint the auditor by ordinary resolution during the period for appointing auditors. Except for the first financial year of the company, the period for appointing the auditor for the next financial year is 28 days beginning either with the end of the period for sending out copies of the accounts and reports to the members for the previous financial year or if the accounts and reports are sent out earlier, the day on which they are sent out. The directors usually appoint the first auditor and can fill casual vacancies. Once appointed, the auditor of a private company is deemed to be re-appointed unless the company decides otherwise or the auditor was appointed by the directors **(s. 487)**. Members holding 5% of the voting rights in a private company (or a lesser percentage if so specified for this purpose by the articles) can prevent the auditor being re-appointed automatically by giving notice to the company before the end of the financial year for the accounts which the auditor was auditing. Where the auditor of a private company is not reappointed automatically, then for any financial year other than the first, an appointment must be made within the period of appointing auditors **(s.485 (2))**.

Section 489 gives members of a public company general power to appoint the auditor by ordinary resolution; and apart from the first auditor of the company who is invariably appointed by the directors and an auditor appointed by the directors to fill a casual vacancy, the appointment is done usually at the meeting at which the accounts are laid. Once the auditor is appointed, he holds the office until the conclusion of the following accounts meeting which is usually the annual general meeting. If, however, he wishes to continue in office then he must seek specific re-election by the company in annual general meeting.

If a company fails to appoint an auditor within 28 days of circulation of the accounts (for private companies), or at the general meeting that considers the previous year's accounts (for public companies) the directors must inform **BIS** which has default power to appoint one **(s.486 - private companies; s. 490 - public companies)**.

Removal of Auditors

The members of a company may remove an auditor before the expiration of his term of office by ordinary resolution, notwithstanding any agreement to the contrary **(s. 510)**. However a certain procedure under section 511, designed mainly to protect the independence of auditors, has to be followed. Special notice to move the resolution must be given to the company, which must send a copy forthwith to the auditor. Where the auditor wishes to contest his removal, he has a right to prepare representations for circulation to the members; and should he make such representations, they should not exceed a reasonable length and must not be used as a vehicle for defamatory matter. The representations need not be circulated if they are received by the company too late for circulation; but in such a case the auditor may require them to be read out at the meeting. If the resolution is passed the company must notify the Registrar within fourteen days **(s.512)**.

A removed auditor is entitled to attend the annual general meeting at which, had it not been for his removal, his term of office would have expired. He also has a right to attend any

annual general meeting at which it is proposed to fill the
vacancy, to receive all notices relating to the meeting, and to
be heard at any such meeting on any matter which concerns
him as former auditor of the company.

Section 994 (1A) provides that if an auditor is removed from
office for an improper ground, such as divergence of opinions
on accounting treatments or audit procedures, this would be
unfair prejudicial conduct to the interests of some of the
company's members; so that such members can petition for
relief under section 994 for unfair prejudicial conduct in the
way the company is run (see Chapter 15).

Resignation of Auditors

An auditor may resign his position by depositing a notice of
resignation at the company's registered office **(s. 516)**. This
notice must include either a statement that there are no
circumstances connected with the resignation which he
considers should be brought to notice of the members or
creditors of the company, or a statement of any such
circumstances **(s. 519)**. Where such circumstances exist the
statement must be sent within 14 days to every member or
creditor, even if they are not entitled to receive notice of the
annual general meeting. The company or any aggrieved
person may apply for a court order to restrain the circulation
where the auditor is abusing his rights to secure needless
publicity for defamatory matter. The auditor may deposit
with the statement a signed requisition for an extraordinary
general meeting to receive and consider the circumstances of
his resignation **(s. 518)**. Further, he is entitled to attend the
annual general meeting at which his term of office would
have otherwise expired, to receive all notices of, and other
communications relating to the general meeting, and be heard

on any part of the business which concerns him as former auditor **(s.502 (2))**.

Where in the case of a major audit, the auditor ceases to hold office (or in the case of an audit which is not a major audit the auditor leaves office before or his tenure of office expires) both the auditor and the company must inform the appropriate auditing authority that the auditor has ceased to hold office and of the circumstances or reasons if any **(s.522-525)**.

Remuneration for Auditors

The general rule is that remuneration shall be fixed by the members of the company by ordinary resolution, or in such way as the company in annual general meeting may determine. In cases where the directors or **BIS** appointed the statutory auditor, they will fix his pay or remuneration **(s. 492)**. 'Remuneration' includes sums paid in respect of expenses, and it must be shown in a note to the annual accounts, in the directors' report, or in the auditor's report as specified by the Secretary of State. Remuneration for the auditor must be disclosed in a note to the annual accounts.

The Status of Auditors

The auditor's status under company legislation cannot be generalised since section 1173 does not include in its definition of the term 'officer' an auditor of the company. However, for the following provisions, the auditor is very clearly regarded as an officer of the company:

(a) **Statutory Liability – Civil Law**. For the purpose of misfeasance under section 212 of the Insolvency Act 1986 the auditor will be regarded as an officer and may be ordered by the courts to compensate the company for any loss arising from such offences. In addition, section 532 of the Companies Act states that any provision in the company's articles to exempt an auditor for negligence, default, breach of duty or breach of trust or by which the company directly or indirectly provides an indemnity for negligence or other default shall be void. However, section 533 permits the company's articles to make provision for the company to indemnify the auditor against the legal costs incurred by him in any proceedings (whether civil or criminal) against him for breach of his duties as long as he successfully defends the action or is granted relief by the courts under section 1157 (power of the courts to grant relief in case of honest and reasonable conduct). Moreover, the auditor may rely on the benefit of any *liability limitation agreement* which he has with the company limiting the amount of his liability to the company in respect of any negligence, default, breach of duty or breach of trust occurring in the course of the audit of accounts for a specified financial year as long as the agreement complies with section 535 (terms of liability limitation agreement), and it is authorised by members of the company in accordance with section 536.

Members of a company can pass a resolution before the agreement is made approving the agreement's principal's terms, or can approve the agreement by resolution after the agreement is made. A private company may pass a resolution before the agreement is made to waive the need for members to approve the agreement. A liability limitation agreement can only last for one financial year **(s.535 (1))**; and it is effective only if it is fair and reasonable under section 537 (factors such as the auditors responsibility under the Act, the nature and purpose of the auditor's contractual obligations to the company and the professional standards expected from him are relevant to determine what is 'fair and reasonable').

A liability limitation agreement has to be disclosed in a note to the annual accounts.

(b) **Statutory Liability –Criminal Law**. For the purpose of sections 206 – 211 and section 218 of the Insolvency Act (officers' offences in liquidation) the auditor is treated as an officer of the company.

Duties of Auditors

The primary duty of an auditor is to report to the members of the company on the accounts and on every balance sheet, profit and loss account, and all group accounts laid before the company in annual general meeting during his tenure of office, and to set out the way he has approached the audit **(s. 495)**. The audit report must specifically state (a) whether the accounts have been properly prepared in accordance with the relevant financial framework (b) whether they have been prepared in accordance with the requirements of the Companies Act (and where applicable, Article 4 of the IAS Regulation) and (c) whether in his opinion a true and fair view is given of them. Such opinion is a personal one; the auditor does not guarantee the accuracy of financial statements. The report must also state whether in the auditor's opinion the information given in the directors' report is consistent with the accounts. The auditor's report must be either unqualified or qualified; and it must include a reference to any matters which the auditor wishes specifically to bring to the members' attention without qualifying his report. The auditor's report must state the name of the auditor and be signed and dated by him. Section 499 gives the auditor a general right to information from a wide range of persons such as directors, employees, subsidiary undertakings and persons holding or accountable for any of the company's books, accounts or vouchers, to ensure that the auditor is able to carry out a successful audit. Section 507 makes it an offence for anyone to knowingly or recklessly cause the auditors' report to include false information. It is also the auditor's duty to carry out such investigation as will enable him to form an opinion on the following matters: whether proper books of account have been kept (see later); whether adequate returns for the purposes of the audit have been received from branches not visited by him; whether he has received all the information and explanation which he considered necessary for the purpose of the audit **(s.498)**. These matters are referred to in the report only if the auditor is not satisfied.

The Companies Act indirectly places additional duties on the auditor. Section 1150 which refers to 'valuation by a qualified independent person', requires the auditor under section 593 to provide valuation reports on non-cash assets taken as the consideration for shares to be issued by a public company; section 837 (4), which is concerned with distribution of profits based on qualified accounts, requires the auditor to state in writing whether the distribution is in contravention of the provisions of sections 830 (restrictions on distributions of profits) and 831 (restrictions on distributions of assets). Section 92 requires the documents submitted to the Registrar for re-registration of a private company as a public company to include a statement by the auditor as to whether, in his opinion, the amount of the net assets at the latest balance sheet date was not less than the company's called-up share capital and its undistributable reserves. However, if the accompanying balance sheet has been qualified by the auditor, he must decide whether the qualification is material in relation to the company's net assets.

The auditor, as a professional involved directly or indirectly in financial transactions in the regulated sector, is under a duty to report any knowledge or suspicion of persons engaged in money laundering to the appropriate authority; otherwise he will incur criminal liability under the Proceeds of Crime Act 2002 and the Money Laundering Regulations 2003. Money laundering is the process whereby the proceeds of a criminal activity, such as drugs trafficking, terrorism and tax evasion, are converted into assets which appear to originate from a legitimate source. This activity is conducted by criminals to provide a lawful cover for their sources of income. Both the Proceeds of Crime Act and the Regulations require financial institutions and non-financial businesses which are regulated to take measures to prevent money laundering such as by appointing a Money Laundering Reporting Officer **(MLRO)** and by implementing other procedures as part of their internal control to comply with the legislation. The legislation also creates three main money laundering offences, namely, (a) **laundering** (including assisting in the laundering); (b) **failing to report** to the relevant authority (the relevant authority is either the Money Laundering Reporting Officer or the Government's National Criminal Intelligence Service) persons known or suspected to be involved in money laundering activities; and (c) **tipping off** or **disclosing** information which is likely to prejudice an investigation by a **MLRO** or an individual. General defences to the money laundering offences include intention to make a report to the relevant authority but there was a reasonable excuse for not doing so; buying or using property in good faith and for value; and duress (e.g., fear of physical violence).

Negligent Liability and Auditors

As was stated earlier, no person can be appointed as an auditor unless he is a member of a recognised body of accountants. Hence, his report renders credibility to the financial statements of a company, and is relied on by others. The auditor is under a legal duty 'to bring to bear on the work he has to perform that skill, care and caution which a reasonably competent, careful and cautious auditor would use', (per Lopes L.J. in **Re Kingston Cotton Mill Co. (1896)).**

In general, an auditor has a legal duty to take care, whether imposed by specific contract or otherwise; and failure to show care, skill and reasonable competence could make the auditor liable for damages. It is important to distinguish negligence from carelessness. Negligence exists only where a legal duty exists to take care. Such a legal duty may exist where the relationship of one person to another could cause loss or injury by an act or omission to act, under the terms of a contract or at law.

The problem of negligent liability of auditors is manifold and dynamic. There are two main areas of difficulty:

(a) **Reasonable standard**. This is not easily defined mainly because of the dynamic nature of the business world. 'What is reasonable skill, care and caution must depend on the particular circumstances of each case' **(Re Kingston Cotton Mill Co.)**. For example, in that case the auditor was not required to attend and observe the stocktaking procedure. Today it is standard practice for auditors to attend stocktaking. Scant guidance is given by case law as to what constitutes reasonable care. An auditor will be negligent for not verifying cash-in-hand **(London Oil Storage v Sear Husluck & Co. (1904)** and work-in-progress **(Re Westminster Road Construction & Engineering Co.**

(1932). In **Re City Equitable Fire Insurance Co. Ltd.**, it was held that an auditor can accept certificates only from a person who is in the habit of dealing with and holding securities and whom the auditor considers to be trustworthy. In **Re Thomas Gerrard & Son Ltd. (1968)**, insufficient time was given to the auditors for completing the audit. They noted the alterations of invoices which were falsified and accepted the explanation of the director; but failed to probe the matter in sufficient detail. In arriving at his decision the judge noted two important points: (i) in the absence of adequate time to complete the audit, the auditors should have issued either a qualified report or none at all (ii) the auditors having been put on guard by the falsification of the invoices, and their suspicion aroused, should have investigated the matter further. The auditor can be sued by the company for failing to detect that the company was committing a fraud, as long as the controllers of the company who were the cause of the fraud would not benefit from the action. Thus, in an insolvent liquidation of "a one-man company", if the controllers of the company are the cause of the fraud, the liquidator cannot take action on behalf of the company to recover damages for a negligent audit which causes the company loss **(Moore Stephens (a firm) v Stone & Rolls Ltd. (2009)**.

The auditor may use any limitation liability agreement which he makes with the company to limit his liability to the company for negligence, default, breach of duty or breach of trust arising during the course of an audit.

(b) **Legal duty to third parties**. It is not generally difficult to show that a duty of care by the auditor to his client exists since this is based on contract as evidenced by the letter of engagement. The problem is whether the auditor owes a duty to third parties. Accounts could be relied upon by investors, creditors, banks, and government authorities; and the auditor's report gives credibility to those accounts. If such a duty of care can exist, then what are the limits? In **Caparo Industries plc v Dickman (1990)**, the House of Lords decided that in general the auditor owes a duty of care only to the company and to the shareholders as a body; and not to individual shareholders either as shareholders or as potential investors of the company. The only time when a duty of care can exist to third parties would be if the accounts were prepared for their benefit or if they commissioned the accounts **(Smith v Eric Bush (1989))**. In **ADT Ltd. v BDO Binder Hamlyn (1996)**, the defendant auditors prepared the accounts of a targeted company which the claimants wanted to take over. At a formal business meeting between the targeted company and the claimants which the auditors attended, the auditors informed the claimants that the accounts were accurate, when in fact they were not. The claimants took over the targeted company and suffered loss. The High Court held the auditors liable for professional negligence because they had assured the claimants that the accounts were accurate, knowing that the claimants would rely on them without further inquiry. In **Commissioners of Customs and Excise v Barclays Bank plc (2006)**, the House of Lords said that the auditor will be liable to third parties for his statements only if the circumstances clearly show that he was assuming responsibility to them for what he said.

Chapter 14

Accounts

Introduction

Part 15 of the Companies Act 2006 requires all registered companies, apart from private companies subject to the small companies regime, to prepare full accounts for each financial year for their members. The purpose of the accounts is to enable the members to review the past management of the company by the directors and to use their votes to influence future policy and management. Also, subject to exemption given to unlimited companies under section 448, copies of the annual accounts and relevant reports (e.g., Directors' Report and Auditors' Report) have to be filed with the Registrar of Companies. This ensures public disclosure of a company's financial affairs especially for persons who want to do business with it; and it is the trade off for the limited liability protection given to the company's members for the company's debts. Normally, the accounts prepared for the members and those for filing will be identical; but if the company is a private company it may wish to make use of the exemptions given to small and medium sized companies in which case separate accounts will be prepared for the members and for filing. Directors of a company have specific statutory duties to see that the accounting requirements are observed (**ss. 387** and **389** – keeping adequate accounting records; **s.394** – preparing annual accounts; **s. 415** –preparing directors' report; **s. 423** – circulating copies of accounts and reports to members; and **ss. 444** to **447** – filing obligations of accounts and reports at Companies Registry).

Part 15 has been redrafted to make it easier for different types of companies to know the accounting requirements which apply to them. Thus, companies are classified as small companies, quoted companies and unquoted companies.

Small Companies. Sections 382 - 384 state that a company qualifies as a small company if it is a private company (but it must not be involved in financial services business such as banking, investment or insurance, and it should not be a member of a group which includes a public company) and it satisfies two of the following three criteria in the relevant financial year: **turnover figure** (not exceeding £6.5 million net); **balance sheet total** i.e., its total assets (not exceeding £3.26 million); and **number of employees** (not more than 50).

Small companies file less financial information with the Registrar than other companies would have to file. They do not have to file a copy of their profit and loss account or a directors' report; and they need only file an abbreviated version of their balance sheet (but they still have to prepare accounts, whether full accounts or a simplified version of the accounts, and reports for their members). In addition, most small companies which have subsidiary undertakings are exempted from preparing group accounts **(398)**.

Small companies are also exempt from having to have their annual accounts audited as long as they satisfy the two conditions for small companies' audit exemption, namely, turnover (not more than £6.5 million) and balance sheet total (not more than £3.26 million) in the financial year in question **(s. 477)**. However, even in such cases, a member(s) holding 10% of the share capital can insist on a statutory audit by serving written notice on the company at its registered office during the financial year to which it relates and not later than one month before the end of that year **(s.476)**.

If a private company does not satisfy the requirements to qualify for small company exemptions, it may still get some accounting exemptions if it qualifies as a **medium-sized company**. Sections 465 - 467 provide that a company is a medium-sized company if it is a private company (but it must not be involved in financial services business or be a member of a group which includes a public company) and it satisfies two of the following three criteria in the relevant financial year: **turnover figure** (not more than £25.9 million); **balance sheet total** (not more than £12.9 million); and **number of employees** (not more than 250). A medium-sized company need only file a modified profit and loss account where certain items such as cost of sale, gross profit or loss and other operating costs can be combined to give one heading 'gross profit or loss' (but full accounts must be filed if it is preparing IAS accounts); and if it is preparing Companies Act accounts, it can omit disclosure with respect to compliance with accounting standards and its directors' report does not have to include non-financial key indicators such as information relating to environmental and employee matters. Unlike, the exemption given to small companies, a medium-sized company which is a parent company has to prepare group accounts unless it is exempted under sections 400 to 402 (see post).

Quoted Companies. Section 385 (2) provides that a quoted company is a company whose equity share capital has been included on the official list of a regulated UK Exchange or is officially listed in an EEA State or is admitted to dealing on either the New York Stock Exchange or the exchange known as Nasdaq.

A quoted company must prepare and file full accounts and reports including a directors' remuneration report. A quoted parent company has to prepare consolidated accounts in accordance with International Accounting Standards **(IAS)**. Moreover, in addition tosending full accounts and reports to its members, a quoted company has to publish preliminary announcements of annual results and full annual accounts and reports on a website. Access to its websites must be made available to members of the public without a charge.

Unquoted Companies. Section 385 (3) provides that an 'unquoted company' means a company which is not a quoted company. An unquoted company has the option of preparing either Companies Act accounts or IAS accounts; and the amount of information relating to directors' remuneration which must be included in the accounts is not as extensive as is required of quoted companies.

Accounting Records. The expression 'accounting records' is not statutorily defined; but it would contain the day-to-day entries of monies received and expended by the company, record of assets and liabilities and statements of stocktaking. The accounting records may vary with the type of business. For a small business, the records may include items such as bank statements, purchase orders and invoices; but a more complex business may have integrated records held in electronic form. The principal purpose of the accounting records is to enable the company to prepare annual accounts complying with the Companies Act and, where applicable, with International Accounting Standards.

Section 386 requires every company to keep adequate accounting records sufficient to show and explain the company's transactions and to disclose with reasonable accuracy, at any given time, the financial position at that time. The accounting records can be kept at the company's registered office or any other place as the directors see fit;

and they must be open at all times to inspection by the company's officers **(s.388)**. If the directors decide to keep the records outside the United Kingdom then accounts and returns with respect to the business dealt with in the records must be sent to and kept at a place in the United Kingdom and open to inspection to the company's officers. The accounting records must be kept for three years (six years for a public company) from the date on which they are made up.

Section 389 imposes criminal liability on every officer of the company who is in default where the company fails to keep adequate accounting records.

Annual Accounts. The directors of a company are under a duty to prepare annual accounts that report on the performance and activities of the company for each of its financial years **(s. 394)**. The annual accounts are the individual accounts of the company **(s. 394)** and, where applicable, group accounts **(s. 399)**. The annual accounts consist mainly of two documents: a profit and loss account, also known as *income statement*, (this account shows how the company is performing during the financial year) and a balance sheet, also known as *statement of financial position*, (this account shows the wealth or net worth of the company as at the end of the financial year). The annual accounts must give a true and fair view of the company's financial position for the financial year **(s. 396** – CA 'individual accounts'; **s. 404** – CA 'group accounts)**. A company's financial year is the same as its accounting reference period.

A company's 'accounting reference period' is the period, usually twelve months, for which the accounts are made up. The accounting reference period begins on the day after the date to which the last accounts were prepared and ends on the date on which the accounting reference period ends (called 'the accounting reference date') or a date seven days earlier or later than the reference date, if the directors find it more convenient. For new companies, the accounting reference date must be the last day of the month in which the anniversary of the company's incorporation falls **(s. 391)** unless the company changes its accounting reference date in accordance with section 392. Thus, if the company was incorporated on 2nd November 2011, its first accounting reference date will be on 30th November 2012 and 30th November for every year after that. A company's first accounting reference period must be for a period of more than six months, but not more than 18 months, beginning with the date of its incorporation and ending with its accounting reference date, again subject to any change in the reference date. A company can change (shorten or extend) its current or immediately previous accounting reference date by notice to the Registrar **(s. 392)**. A change of reference date will not be allowed, however, if the filing deadline of the accounts and reports for the period which the directors wish to change has already passed **(s. 392 (2))**. There are also restrictions on extending an accounting reference date such as that the reference date cannot be extended to a point where the accounting reference period lasts for more than 18 months from the start date of the accounting period (unless the company is in administration) and that the reference period cannot be extended more than once in five years (unless the company is in administration or it is bringing its accounting reference date in line with that of its parent company or subsidiary in the UK or other EEA state).

The provisions concerning the form and content of annual accounts are found in legislation, both national and European, and in accounting standards (guidelines) developed by the British accountancy profession through the Accounting Standards Board (ASB) and the International Accounting

Standards Board (IASB). The Boards have written a number of guidelines (a recent one issued by ASB for small entities being the 'Financial Reporting Standard for Smaller Entities') to deal with problems normally encountered by companies when they are preparing their accounts.

Companies can choose to prepare their accounts using the financial reporting framework provided for by the Companies Act 2006 and national standards (Schedule 1 format of the 2008 Regulations for 'Companies Act individual accounts' and Schedule 6 format for 'Companies Act group accounts'), or in accordance with the International Accounting Standards Board standards ('IAS individual accounts' and 'IAS group accounts). The latter have been adopted by the European Commission. However, the Companies Act provides for a particular financial reporting framework to be used in certain cases, namely, that group accounts of a parent company whose securities are admitted to trading on a regulated market must be IAS group accounts **(s.403 (1))**; and the accounts (individual or group) of a company which is a charity must be Companies Act accounts **(s. 395; s. 403)**. Accounts prepared in accordance with IASB Standards must include a statement to this effect in the notes to the accounts (notes to the accounts are required in certain cases to expand or clarify numerical information given in the accounts in order to produce a 'true and fair view' of the accounts). Companies which choose the IAS framework for their accounts must continue to use that framework for subsequent accounts and can only change to Companies Act framework if there is a relevant change in circumstances. A 'relevant change in circumstances' arises (a) where the company ceases to be a company whose securities are admitted for trading on a regulated market; (b) in relation to individual accounts, where the company has become a subsidiary of another company which uses Companies Act accounts; and

(c) where the parent undertaking of the company ceases to be an undertaking with securities admitted to trading on a regulated market **(ss. 395, 403)**. The ASB has proposed that as from 1 January 2012, all companies whose securities are publicly traded must prepare IAS accounts.

At the end of each financial year of the company its accounts have to be approved by the board of directors. The board should only approve the accounts if it is satisfied that they give a true and fair view of the financial position of the company and, in the case of group accounts, the group **(s.393)**. The phrase 'true and fair view' has not been statutorily defined; but it may be that it means the view that the accounts have been prepared according to the correct accounting standards and legal requirements. The auditors, in giving their opinion on the accounts, have a duty to consider whether the board could be satisfied that the accounts give a true and fair view of the company's financial position **(s. 393 (2))**. The accounts must then be signed by a director on behalf of the board as a whole. The signature must be on the balance sheet; and, if the accounts are prepared in accordance with the provisions applicable to companies subject to the small companies' regime, the balance sheet must contain a statement to this effect in a prominent position above the signature.

Every director who is knowingly a party to signed accounts commits an offence if the accounts do not comply with the requirements of the Companies Act and, where applicable, of Article 4 of the IAS Regulation **(s. 414)**.

Group Accounts. Section 399 provides that if, at the end of its financial year, a company is a parent company (i.e., it has subsidiary undertakings such as having another company or a partnership to carry on business on its behalf) its directors must prepare group accounts, as well as individual accounts for the year unless the company is exempted from preparing group accounts under sections 400 to 402. A company which is subject to the small companies' regime and is a parent company has an *option* to prepare group accounts.

Section 400 exempts a parent company from preparing group accounts if (a) its securities are not publicly traded on a regulated market and (b) the parent company is itself a subsidiary undertaking (a "sub-parent company") of an immediate parent undertaking (the "main parent company") which is established under the law of an EEA state and (c) its own individual accounts are included in an EEA group accounts of the larger group. Section 401 provides similar exemption for a sub-parent company included in non-EEA group accounts of a larger group. The sub-parent company has to disclose in its individual accounts that it is exempted from preparing group accounts; and it must disclose also the name of the main parent undertaking (and the country in which it is incorporated, if the main parent company is non-UK incorporated, or the address of its principal place of business, if the main parent undertaking is unincorporated). A sub-parent company is only exempted from preparing group accounts if it is wholly owned by the immediate main parent company; or, if it is not wholly owned by the immediate main parent company, the immediate parent company holds more than 50% of the shares in the sub-parent company and the holders of the remaining shares in the sub-parent company do not insist on the company preparing its own group accounts. Shareholders with minority shares in the sub-parent company can insist on the sub-parent company preparing its own group accounts if such shareholders hold more than half of the remaining shares in the sub-parent company or 5% of the total shares in the company and they give the company notice not later than six months after the end of the financial year before that to which the accounts relate. Also, section 402 exempts a parent company from preparing group accounts, whether CA group accounts or IAS group accounts, if *all* its subsidiaries could be excluded from consolidation in Companies Act group accounts under section 405.

Companies Act group accounts normally take the form of a consolidated balance sheet and a consolidated profit and loss account. In general, these accounts combine the information contained in the separate balance sheet and profit and loss account of the parent company and the subsidiaries, but with any adjustments which the parent company thinks necessary (e.g., writing off inter-undertakings debts). A parent company whose securities are publicly traded on a regulated market must prepare group accounts in accordance with international accounting standards (IAS group accounts).

A parent company preparing Companies Act group accounts must state in notes to its consolidated accounts the identity of each of its subsidiary undertakings, as well as information about the shareholdings in the subsidiary; and if any of its subsidiaries is excluded in the consolidation, the reasons for excluding such subsidiaries. Section 405 allows a subsidiary undertaking to be excluded from consolidation in Company Act group accounts in certain circumstances such as if its inclusion is not material for the purpose of giving a true and fair view of the group's financial position (but two or more undertakings may be excluded if they are not material taken altogether); or if severe long-term restrictions substantially hinder the exercise of the rights of the parent company over the assets or management of that subsidiary; or if the information necessary for the preparation of group accounts would involve disproportionate expense or delay to the members; or if the interest of the parent company in the subsidiary undertaking is held exclusively with a view to subsequent resale.

Companies within the same group enterprise are treated as a single unit for accounting purposes if they are within the control test as laid down in sections 1159 and 1162. In essence, the test is three-fold. First, if Company 'A' has the majority of voting rights in Company 'B', or, if it is only a member but in addition has the right of voting control (either actual or by virtue of a shareholder agreement) or the right to appoint or remove the majority of the board of directors of Company 'B', then Company 'B' is deemed in law to be a subsidiary of Company 'A'. Secondly, if Company 'A' has a right to direct the operating and financial policies of Company 'B' by virtue of some provision in Company 'B's constitution or by a control contract, or Company A has a participating interest (i.e., an interest in the shares in Company 'B' held by or on behalf of Company 'A') in Company 'B' and either exercises a dominant influence over it, or Company 'A' and Company 'B' are managed on a unified basis, then Company 'B' will be a subsidiary of Company 'A'. A participating interest is presumed where Company 'A' holds 20% of Company 'B's shares. Thirdly, if Company 'B' has a subsidiary, Company 'T', the latter will also be a subsidiary of Company 'A'.

Directors' Report. The directors of a company are required to prepare for each financial year of the company a directors' report and, where the company is a parent company and it prepares group accounts, a group directors' report **(s.415)**. The directors' report must disclose the matters specified in section 416 of the Companies Act and Schedule 5 of the 2008 Regulations such as the names of the directors and the principal activities of the company; political donations and expenditure exceeding £2000 and, unless the company is exempted under the small companies regime, the amount that the directors recommend should be paid as dividend and a business review of the company. The purpose of the business review is to inform the members of the company and help them assess how the directors have performed their duty under section 172 (duty to promote the success of the company). The business review must give a fair review of the company and it should deal with the principal risks and uncertainties facing the company. A quoted company's business review has to cover such things as environmental matters (including the impact of the company's activities on the environment), the company's employees and social and community issues, and information about persons who have contractual and other arrangements with the company which are essential to its operations – unless the disclosure of such information will be seriously prejudicial to those persons or to the public interest. The directors' review need not disclose information about impending developments or matters in the course of negotiation if, in the directors' opinion, disclosure would seriously prejudice the company's interest. Where the directors have nothing to report on environmental issues, employees, social and community matters etc, the review must say so. A quoted company must also include a corporate governance statement in the directors' report (or else attach the statement to the report or publish it on its website). This statement must identify the corporate governance code which applies to it, and state whether it has not followed it and why; give certain other information such as the main features of the company's or group's internal control and risk management systems in relation to the financial reporting process, give details about capital structure which may be a barrier to takeovers; and describe the composition and operation of its administrative, management and supervisory bodies and their committees.

Unless the company is exempted from audit under section 477 (small companies) or section 480 (dormant companies), the directors' report must include a statement that the directors have taken all reasonable steps to ensure that all relevant audit information have been provided to the company's auditors.

The directors' report must be approved by the board of directors and signed on its behalf by a director or the secretary of the company. If the report is prepared in accordance with the small companies' regime, it must contain a statement to this effect in a prominent position above the signature. As with the accounts, it is an offence triable either way to knowingly be a party to a signed inaccurate directors' report **(s. 419)**.

Directors' Remuneration Report. Only quoted companies have to prepare and file a directors' remuneration report. In addition to the aggregate remuneration of directors, this report has to include details of individual directors' remuneration packages, the company's policy on directors' remuneration, and the role of the board and remuneration committee on remuneration for the directors.

The directors' remuneration report for each financial year of the company must be approved by the board and signed on behalf of the board by a director or the secretary of the company. Directors' remuneration report for the preceding financial year has to be approved by the members prior to their annual general meeting; but the vote by members will not have any legal effect on the rights of the directors to get their remuneration.

Publication of Accounts and Reports. Section 423 requires every company to send a copy of its annual accounts and reports (including any relevant auditors' report) to every member and debenture holder of the company, and to every other person entitled to receive notice of general meetings (e.g., the company's auditor) as long as the company has a current address of that person. For a private company, members must receive a copy of the accounts and reports not later than the end of the period for filing the accounts and reports at Companies Registry (which is 9 months from the end of its financial year) or if the accounts and reports were filed earlier, the actual date of filing them. For a public company, a copy of the accounts and reports must be sent to members at least 21 days before the date of the relevant accounts meeting at which the members are to consider the accounts and reports, which is usually the annual general meeting **(s.424)**. Section 437 requires a public company, but not a private company, to lay a copy of its annual accounts and reports before its members in general meeting (called the 'relevant accounts meeting) and this meeting must be held within 6 months (4 months for quoted companies) beginning with the day following the end of company's financial year (i.e., its accounting reference date). It is common practice for a resolution to be proposed at the meeting for members to adopt or approve the accounts and reports; but if the resolution rejects them, it has no legal effect on their validity since the law does not require members' approval of the accounts and reports. A public company must file a copy of its annual accounts and reports at Companies Registry within 6 months after the end of its financial year. Accounts and reports filed at Companies Registry are public documents.

Instead of sending out full accounts and reports, a company may provide its members and other persons entitled to receive them with summary financial statements which comply with the requirements of section 427 (form and contents of summary financial statements: unquoted companies) or section 428 (form and contents of summary financial statements: quoted companies). However, summary financial statements can only be issued if the accounts and reports are audited and the person entitled to receive the accounts and reports agree to accept summary financial statements instead of full accounts and reports.

Revision of Defective Accounts and Reports. If the annual accounts or reports (directors' report or directors' remuneration report) or a summary financial statement of the company are inaccurate in that they did not comply with the requirements of the Companies Act (or, where applicable, of Article 4 of the IAS Regulation), the directors may prepare voluntarily revised accounts or a revised report or statement **(s. 454)** so that they give a true and fair view as at the relevant reference date of the accounts in question. An auditors' report on the revision must be given in the same way as the auditors reported on the original accounts and reports (and if relevant, summary financial statement).

The Secretary of State also has power to require the directors to prepare revised accounts and reports and statements if it appears to him these documents were defective **(s.455)**. If the directors refuse to comply, the Secretary of State can apply to the courts under section 456 for an order that they so comply.

Chapter 15

The Principle of Majority Rule

The Rule

It is a cardinal principle of company law that individual shareholders cannot sue for wrongs done to their company by its directors (including former directors) or by third parties, or to complain of irregularities in the conduct of the company's internal affairs. Any action on behalf of the company has to be brought by the board of directors since the board is vested with the powers of management of the company including the power to litigate on the company's behalf **(Art.3)**. If the directors refuse to act (e.g., because they themselves are the wrongdoers or because they feel that it is not in the interest of the company to take legal action against the wrongdoer), then the action has to be brought in the company's name by the members in general meeting after they pass a special resolution to start legal proceedings. The liquidator or administrator can also sue when the company is subject to a formal insolvency procedure such as where the company is in liquidation or administration (but not in a voluntary arrangement). This principle which prevents individual shareholders from suing on behalf of their company is known as the *Rule in Foss v Harbottle*.

There are two branches of the rule in **Foss v Harbottle**. First, if a wrong is done to the company, then the company being a corporate person in its own right is the proper claimant to bring the action; not individual members. The second branch of the rule is that if there is some irregularity in the internal management of the company which can be excused by a simple majority of members, no individual member can bring an action in respect of that irregularity. Where the irregularity relates to the conduct of a meeting, only if it would not invalidate the meeting or affect decisions taken at the meeting would the rule in **Foss v Harbottle** apply. Thus, if there is no quorum for the meeting **(Re The Cambrian Peat, Fuel & Charcoal Co. Ltd. (1908)** or if notice is not given to every member entitled to notice **(Musselwhite v C.H. Musselwhite & Son Ltd.)** the rule will not apply. In **Mc Dougall v Gardiner (1875)**, the articles empowered the chairman with the consent of the meeting, to adjourn a meeting and also provided for taking a poll if demanded by five members. The adjournment was moved and, on a show of hands, was declared by the chairman to be carried. A poll was then demanded but was refused by the chairman. The courts said that any action on the irregularity should have been brought by the company and not by an individual member because no harm was done to any member. However, in **Siemens Bros. & Co. Ltd. v Burns (1918),** where the chairman refused a demand for a poll by a member who held most of the voting shares after a special resolution was passed on a show of hands to alter the articles, the courts allowed an action by that member since the irregularity had clearly affected the passing of the resolution.

The rule has the obvious advantage of preventing multiplicity of actions. If each member was permitted to sue, the company could be harassed by many actions started and discontinued by several claimants. Also, with irregularities which could be cured by the company in general meetings, it would be a waste of the courts' time to entertain proceedings on them.

Exceptions to the Rule

The rule in **Foss v Harbottle** is subject to at least three common law exceptions, namely:

(a) **Illegal acts**. The courts will allow a member to bring an action to restrain the company and its directors from doing an illegal act. However, if the act has already been completed, the action has to be brought by the company itself and it may take the form of a derivative action (see post).

(b) **Personal rights**. A member whose personal rights as a shareholder are infringed or are about to be infringed by the company, while other members' rights are not affected, can bring an action to enforce those rights (as in **Pender v Lushington**, where a member was prevented wrongly from exercising voting rights on shares transferred to him). Similarly, acts which can be performed only by a special resolution that has not been properly passed cannot be validated by an ordinary resolution; so any member can bring an action to restrain the company from acting on the wrong decision taken on the basis that his personal rights as a member in relation to the internal management of the company are affected. In **Baillie v Oriental Telephone Co. (1915)**, directors wished to increase their fees, and called a meeting at which a special resolution was required. Although the correct majority was obtained the notice of the meeting was insufficient. A member successfully brought an action to restrain the directors from acting on the resolution

(c) **Fraud on the minority**. Acts by the majority who control the company are not ratifiable and, at common law, legal proceedings may be brought by individual members, if those acts amount to fraud on the minority. 'Fraud' means improper motive and not just 'deceit'; and it may be fraud done to the company or to a member himself. 'Control' normally means voting control; but in **Prudential Assurance Co. Ltd. v Newman Industries Ltd. (1982)** Vinelott J. extended it to include control by directors who do not exercise actual voting control but exercise control in practice. The following have been held to constitute fraud on the minority:

(i) *Expropriation of the company's property or the minority's property*. In **Menier v Hooper's Telegraph Works (1874)**, the controlling shareholders passed a special resolution at a members meeting to put the company into voluntary liquidation so that they could obtain possession of the company's assets to the exclusion of the minority. In an action by the minority, the courts held that the majority action amounted to fraud on the minority. In **Dafen Tinplate Co. v Llanelly Steel Co. (1920)**, the majority included an expropriation clause in the articles to enable them to expel a member because he had stopped purchasing steel from the company. The court held that it was fraud on the minority.

(ii) *An issue of shares to harm the minority*. In **Clemens v Clemens (1976)**, the claimant held 40 per cent of the shares while the defendant held 55 per cent. The defendant was also a director, and in order to decrease the claimant's voting strength, the defendant and his fellow directors proposed to issue new shares to themselves and as trustees for long-serving employees. The necessary resolutions were passed at the members meeting with the help of the defendant's votes. The effect was to reduce the claimant's voting strength to less than 25 per cent, thus depriving her of the right to block any special or extraordinary resolution that might be put before the meeting. The courts held that this constituted fraud on the minority.

(iii) *A negligent act by the directors*. In **Daniels v Daniels (1978)**, the controlling shareholders (husband and wife) who were also the directors bought land for the company for £4,250 and later resold it at the same price to the lady director. She resold the land for £120,000 five years later. In an action by a minority member against the directors for gross negligence, the company argued that since the minority was not alleging fraud no action could be brought on behalf of the company to recover the loss because of the rule in **Foss v Harbottle**. Templeman J. held that the action should be allowed since negligence by the majority had resulted in one of them obtaining a benefit from it and this was fraud in the wider sense. As a result of changes introduced by the Companies Act 2006, a claim may now be brought for a negligent act of the directors even if no director benefited from that act.

Framing an action under the exceptions

The action may be framed in one of three ways. It may be a *derivative action*, where the action is brought by a member of the company for a wrong done to the company, the cause of action is vested in the company, and the relief is sought on behalf of the company **(s.260 (1))**. This allows a member or a person to whom shares have been transferred (i.e., an unregistered transferee) or transmitted by operation of law (i.e., a personal representative of a deceased member, or a trustee in bankruptcy of a bankrupt member) to sue on behalf of the company to enforce rights derived from it.

A derivative action can only be brought under section 260 or in pursuance of an order of the court in proceedings under section 994 for unfair prejudice (proceedings for protection of members against unfair prejudice are discussed in Chapter 16). Section 260 permits a derivative claim only in respect of "a cause of action arising from an actual or proposed act or omission involving negligence, default, breach of duty or breach of trust by a director of the company". Wrongs involving a breach of the directors' general statutory duties to the company can therefore be the subject of a derivative claim; and it is quite clear that instances of the fraud on the minority exception where the wrong is done to the company would be as a result of a breach of duty by the directors. However, there is no need for the member ('the applicant') to show that the wrongdoers controlled the company. Thus, the wrongdoers could be the company's directors (including former directors and shadow directors) or third parties or both **(s.260 (3))**; but a derivative action against a third party would only be allowed if the cause of action arose out of a breach of duty by the directors such as where the third party knowingly received company assets transferred in breach of trust or was a party to the breach of duty or where the directors refuse to sue the third party for a wrong done to the company because the directors are motivated by loyalty to the third party rather than to the company. The wrong could have been committed before the applicant became a member of the company; but it must not have been ratified by the shareholders.

A derivative action under section 260 is not very popular because the applicant has to obtain permission from the courts in order to continue the proceedings. The procedural steps to be complied with before the courts will hear the substantial claim are as follows:

 (a) The applicant who institutes derivative proceedings against the wrongdoers must apply to the courts for permission to continue the action. This requires him to show in his application and the evidence filed in support of his application for permission, a *prima facie* case that the wrong arises from an actual or proposed act or omission involved negligence (even if the director in question did not benefit from his wrongdoing), default, breach of duty or breach of trust **(s.261)**. The company does not have to provide any evidence at this stage. If, on the basis of the evidence filed, the applicant cannot make a *prima face* case for the grant of permission, the courts must dismiss the application and make any consequential order as is appropriate (e.g., order as to legal costs).

(b) If the applicant establishes a *prima facie* case, the courts may require the company to provide exculpatory evidence, and on hearing the application for permission, the courts may grant the application to proceed to the substantive action, or refuse permission and dismiss the claim, or adjourn the proceedings on the application and give directions on such terms as they see fit.

The courts have to take account of certain matters set out in section 263 when deciding whether to grant the applicant permission to continue a derivative claim, such as (a) the views of disinterested members; (b) whether the applicant is acting in good faith in seeking to continue the claim. In **Nurcombe v Nurcombe (1985)**, a husband and wife were directors and only shareholders of the company. The husband diverted a valuable property development contract which he had negotiated for the company to another company which he had owned. The couple later divorced and the divorce settlement of the husband's wealth took account of the benefit he had received from the diverted contract, through his own company, when assessing the lump sum payment to be made to his ex-wife. After receiving his payment, the wife started a derivative action on behalf of their company to recover the lost benefit of the contract diverted by him. The Court of Appeal prevented her from suing on behalf of the company in a common law derivative action. In **Barrett v**

Duckett & Ors. (1995), the court refused to grant permission to a member to bring a derivative action because the purpose of the action was not to benefit the company but rather to harass an ex son-in-law; (c) where the cause of action results from an act or omission that has yet to occur, whether the act or omission could in the circumstances be likely to be authorised by the company before it occurs or ratified by the company after it occurs. Whether a wrong committed by the directors can be ratified by the members in general meeting is for the courts to decide. Section 239 (7) requires the courts to look for guidance from case law prior to the commencement of the Companies Act 2006. Under case law certain wrongs done to the company could not be ratified, such as an illegal act, a negligent act by the directors which benefits them **(Daniels v Daniels (1978)**; and an issue of shares to harm the minority **(Clemens v Clemens (1976))**. While a negligent act by the directors which did not result in a benefit to them was ratifiable by the general meeting passing an ordinary resolution and so could not be the subject of a common law derivative action **(Pavlides v Jensen (1956)**, section 260 (3) now permits a derivative claim for ordinary negligence by the directors. Where breaches are ratifiable, the directors in question (if members of the company) and any members connected with them (e.g., their spouse) are not allowed to vote on the resolution **(s.239 (2)**; and (d) whether the cause of action is of such a nature that the applicant could pursue it in his own right as a personal action rather than on behalf of the company **(s.263 (3))**. In **Franbar Holdings Ltd. v Patel (2008)**, the courts refused permission to a member to bring a derivative action against the directors for alleged breach of their duties to the company because, on the facts of the case, the member had alternative actions under a shareholder agreement action and a petition under section 994 of the Companies Act for unfair prejudice which he could pursue.

The courts have to refuse permission for the applicant to continue the proceedings as a derivative action in three situations. First, if a person acting in accordance with the general duty of directors under section 172 (duty to promote the success of the company for the benefit of its members) would not seek to continue the claim, such as where it would not be in the company's interest to enforce its legal rights. Here, the courts would consider how a hypothetical director would act in the circumstances **(Mission Capital plc v Sinclair (2008))**. Second, if the act or omission giving rise to the cause of action is yet to occur, and it was authorised by the members, permission to continue the derivative action must be refused. Third, if the act or omission giving rise to the cause of action has already occurred and it was authorised by the company before it occurred or was ratified by the members since it occurred permission must also be refused **(s.263 (2))**.

A claim brought by a company can also be continued as a derivative claim if the cause of action on which the claim is based is such that it could be brought originally as a derivative claim (because it involves a breach of duty etc by the directors). The member seeking permission to continue the company's claim as a derivative claim has to rely on the grounds specified by section 262, namely, that the manner in which the company commenced or continued the claim amounted to an abuse of the process of the court; or that the company had failed to prosecute the claim diligently, and that it is appropriate for the claimant to continue the claim as a derivative claim. The procedure for permission to continue the claim as a derivative claim is similar as the procedure under section 261 (application for permission to continue a derivative claim) and the criteria to be taken into account by the courts in deciding whether to grant permission are identical.

Section 264 makes provision for the possibility of another member (applicant) applying to the courts for permission to take over an existing derivative claim from a member where the manner in which the member commenced the claim amounted to an abuse of the court; or where he failed prosecute the claim diligently or where it is appropriate for applicant to continue the claim (e.g., because the member lacked the financial resources to pursue the claim).

The action may be a purely ***personal action*** brought by a minority shareholder to assert his own rights against the company (as in **Pender v Lushington** where the controllers of the company deprived a member of his voting rights). Strictly speaking, this is not a wrong done to the company but a wrong done by the company (or by its directors) and so does not fall within the exceptions to **Foss v Harbottle**. However, on occasions, the same facts can give rise to both possibilities. In **Johnson v Gore Wood & Co. (2000)**, the House of Lords stated where a loss is suffered by both the company and a shareholder as a result of a breach of duty by the directors, the shareholder will only be allowed to bring a personal claim if his loss is separate and distinct from the loss suffered by the company. If the shareholder's loss is simply just reflective of the company's general loss (such as where the loss suffered by the company results in a diminution in value of a shareholder's shares), a personal action by the shareholder for that loss will not be allowed. In practice, where a shareholder brings an action for personal loss, the action will not be brought under the common law fraud on the minority exception, but rather under section 994 of the Companies Act for unfair conduct prejudicial to minorities or under section 122 (1)(g) of the Insolvency Act to wind up the company compulsorily on grounds that it is just and equitable for the courts to do so (see Chapter 16).

Finally, the action may take the form of a ***representative action*** (i.e., a class action) where the wrong is done to the shareholders and others by those controlling the company, in addition to injury to the company. No damages can be awarded here; only an injunction or a declaration is given. However, where a declaration is given it will in effect assert a right which, if breached, will result in damages being awarded to each member. Where the minority shareholder abandons a representative action, any other member whom he represents can continue the action by applying to the courts to be substituted as claimant **(Moon v Atherton (1972))**.

Chapter 16

Statutory Protection for Minorities

Minority shareholders are also given statutory protection against abuses by their company and its controlling shareholders. They can initiate a **BIS** investigation, or apply to the courts for relief on grounds of 'conduct unfairly prejudicial' to them, or petition for the compulsory winding up of the company on the 'just and equitable' ground under section 122(1)(g) of the Insolvency Act 1986.

The Department for Business, Innovation and Skills.
BIS has statutory powers under the Companies Act 1985 to investigate both the affairs of the company and the ownership of the company. **BIS** must investigate the company's affairs **(s.431)** and the ownership of shares in, or debentures of, the company **(s.442)**, if minorities holding at least ten per cent of the company's capital (or 200 members) request it and justify their application. The applicants may have to deposit a security for costs. **BIS** can investigate the company's affairs on its own initiative if it suspects that the company's affairs are being carried on in a manner which is likely to be prejudicial to members or fraudulent to the creditors or that the board of directors is in breach of its duty or has been withholding information to members **(s.432)**. It can also investigate the ownership in shares and debentures of the company if it has good reasons to do so **(s.442)**.

The investigation is carried out by inspectors who have wide powers. They can call for the production of books and documents by past or present officers and agents, and examine documents by past or present officers and agents, and examine on oath. On the inspectors' findings, **BIS** may institute civil proceedings in the company's name; or petition for a winding up order on the 'just and equitable' ground; or for some other remedy for unfair prejudicial conduct to the interest of some of or the members generally; or for a disqualification order against the directors.

Unfair Prejudice

As an alternative to the much more restrictive conditions imposed by section 260 on 'derivative actions' under the exceptions to the rule in **Foss v Harbottle**, section 994 of the Companies Act 2006 gives a member or a person to whom shares have been transferred (an unregistered transferee) or transmitted (a personal representative or trustee in bankruptcy who is not on the register of members) the right to petition the courts (**BIS** may also petition following an investigation of the company) for relief on grounds that there is unfairness in the way the affairs of the company are being, have been or will be conducted by the persons in control of the company and this 'unfairness' is prejudicing or will prejudice the interests of the members generally or some of them (including the petitioner). This section is intended for minority use; but it does not preclude the possibility of a majority shareholder using it as well, unless the member could have used his voting control to get rid easily of the conduct complained of **(Re Baltic Real Estate Ltd (1992))**. The petition for unfair prejudice may be brought against the individual wrongdoers as well as the company.

The courts will scrutinise the conduct of the board of directors when considering how the affairs of the company are being conducted, since it is the board which is vested with the powers to manage the company; and where a holding/ subsidiary relationship exists the courts may examine the conduct of the holding company rather than that of the directors of the subsidiary company, should the holding company be responsible for conducting the affairs of the subsidiary **(Nicholas v Soundcraft Electronics Ltd (1993)).** However, 'control' is wide enough to include members' voting control; so the courts may even examine the manner in which the controlling majority is exercising its votes.

According to Lord Hoffman in **O'Neill v Phillips (1999)**, 'unfairness' will arise if either (a) there is a breach of the legal rules on which the petitioner had agreed that the business should be conducted (e.g., a breach of members' rights in the memorandum, articles or companies legislation) or where the directors are in breach of their duties, or (b) the rules are being used by the majority in a way which is contrary to the equitable principle of good faith (relevant to small private companies which are in effect quasi-partnerships). In **O'Neill v Phillips**, the owner of a one-man company (**P**) transferred some of his share to his key employee (**O**) and made him a director. **P** also told **O** that he hoped **O** would take over the day to day running of the business when **P** retired and that when that happened they would share the profits equally. **P** eventually retired and **O** ran the business on his own; and the profits were shared equally between them. There were suggestions that **O** would be given half the shareholding in the company; but no formal agreement was made to this effect. As a result of losses made by the company, **P** was forced to come out of retirement and took charge of the management from **O**. **P** stopped sharing the profits equally and only paid **O** a salary and dividends on his existing shares. **O** petitioned under section 994 for relief on the basis that his legitimate expectation of acquiring half the shareholding and of continuing to receive half the company's profits had been unfairly prejudiced. However, the House of Lords dismissed the petition on grounds that **P**'s informal promise to **O** was given on the basis that **O** would manage the business so that **P** did not have to be involved in the day-to-day business and that **P** had reserved the right to withdraw **O**'s responsibilities. There was nothing unfair or inequitable in what **P** did.

A minor infringement will not be sufficiently 'unfair' to merit relief under section 459 (per Hoffmann LJ in **Re Saul D. Harrision and Sons plc (1995)**. Similarly, conduct will not be 'unfair' (in the case of a small private company) if the majority had made a fair offer to buy the shares of the complaining minority before the matter came to the courts **(West v Blanchet and Another (2000))**.

The unfair conduct which is the subject of litigation must be prejudicial to the membership interests of the petitioner. Conduct will be 'prejudicial' if it causes financial harm to the petitioner's interest, such as where the value of his shareholding is seriously diminished or jeopardised by reason of the conduct. 'Membership interest' is the interest of the petitioner in his capacity as a member of the company. Thus, where personal matters of the member (such as the right to be employed by the company or for the company to purchase the member's land) are affected by the conduct of the persons in control of the company, the member will not be able to obtain relief under the section. While some judges, in the past, have given a narrow interpretation of 'membership interest' restricting it to membership rights protected by company legislation, such as membership rights in the articles, modern judges, notably Lord Hoffman, have been prepared to give the phrase a broader interpretation by extending it to cover legitimate expectations as to the conduct of the company's affairs which may arise from private agreements and understandings between the parties as would normally occur in the case of small domestic companies called quasi partnerships. Such understandings could relate to the right to participate in the long term management of the company, in the absence of any wrongdoing by a member (see Hoffman J in **Re a Company (No.008699 of 1985) (1986)**. In the case of a public company, there could be no legitimate expectation that a member will be involved in the permanent management of the company (per Parker J in **Re Astec (BSR) plc (1999)**; so that any petition under section 994 for relief on the basis that the petitioner has been removed as a director of a public company by the persons in control of the company will not succeed **(Re Tottenham Hotspur plc (1994)**.

Petitions have been granted under section 994 where the directors are the majority shareholders of a small domestic private company and they pay themselves excessive salaries leaving no profits for payment of dividend to the other shareholders or for the company reasonably to carry on its business **(Re a Company (No. 004415 of 1996) (1997)**; where the directors urge shareholders to accept an offer of a take-over bid by another company in which the directors had a financial interest while ignoring a much more favourable alternative offer **(Re a Company (No. 008699 of 1985) (1986)**; where, in the case of a small domestic private company, the members had formed the company on the understanding that each member would be involved in the permanent management of company and one was later removed from the board (without just cause) without a fair offer to buy his shares **(Brownlow v G.H. Marshall Ltd. (2000))**; and where the directors sell the company's assets to another company (in which they had a major holding) on unfavourable terms **(Parkinson v Eurofinance Group Ltd.**

(2001). A petition based on poor management by the board is unlikely to succeed **(Re Elgindata Ltd (1991)**, unless the conduct amounts to serious mismanagement which is prejudicial in a financial sense to the company **(Re Macro (Ipswich) Lt. (1993)**.

In considering whether the alleged conduct is unfairly prejudicial to the petitioner, the petitioner's own bad conduct in relation to the company is ignored. This is in contrast to a petition under section 122(1)(g) of the Insolvency Act to wind up the company on the 'just and equitable' ground (see post). In **Re London School of Electronics Ltd (1986)**, the petitioner was removed from his directorship after he had alleged that the majority shareholders had diverted business from the company to themselves. The petitioner then set up a rival college and took with him a number of students who were enrolled with the company. He claimed that the company's conduct was unfairly prejudicial to him. His claim succeeded.

In granting relief on a section 994 petition, the courts can make any order except an order to wind up the company. An order may include, under section 996, an order allowing the petitioner to commence civil proceedings in the company's name (a derivative action) such as where the directors' breach of duty indirectly prejudices the interests of the petitioner, thus dispensing with the **Rule in Foss v Harbottle**; an order regulating the future conduct of the company; an order requiring the company to refrain from doing or continuing the act complained of by the petitioner; and an order requiring the purchase of the shares of any member of the company or by the company itself. In **Re H.R. Harmer (1959)**, the court granted an order under a similar minority section to prevent the controlling shareholder who had ignored board resolutions and ran the company as if it was his own, from interfering in the affairs of the company. Where an order is made for the purchase of a member's shares, the valuation of the shares should be based on principles of 'fairness'. According to the House of Lords in **Scottish Co-operative Wholesale Society v Meyer (1959)**, the valuation procedure should be the price of the shares before the prejudicial conduct had diminished their value. If the company's articles contain a mechanism for valuation and it is fair, the courts will use it **(Re Castkeburn (1989))** unless the valuation procedure will lead to an unjust result **(Re Abbey Leisure (1990))**. Moreover, if the company is a small domestic private company the courts will not allow the shares to be purchased on a discounted-basis (i.e., to allow for the fact that the shares to be bought are only a minority holding and do not give control **(Strahan v Wilcock (2006)** (*unreported*). However, if the company is a large company with a body of shareholders quite distinct from those managing the company, the courts must allow the shares to be purchased on a discounted-basis to reflect their minority holding. On the occasions where the courts have made a purchase order against another member, it is usually the minority's shares which are required to be purchased at a fair price. However, if the circumstances require it, the courts may require the minority to purchase the shares of the majority (i.e. the respondent), as in **Re Nuneaton Borough AFC No.2 (1991)**. According to the Privy Council in **Gamlestaden Fastigheter v Baltic Partners Ltd. and Others (Jersey) 2007**, an unfair prejudicial conduct remedy may be granted to the petitioner even though the remedy does not benefit him in his capacity as a member, but in some other capacity such as a creditor.

Just and Equitable Winding up
Under section 122 (I)(g) of the Insolvency Act 1986 a company may be wound up by the courts if the courts are of

the opinion that it is just and equitable that the company should be wound up, such as where there is fraud and oppression, or deadlock in the management of the company and this deadlock cannot be resolved in any other way. This is a course available to minorities if they wish to terminate the company's existence and is considered more fully in Chapter 17. Nevertheless it should be pointed out that the courts' have a discretion under section 125(2) of the Insolvency Act to strike out the petition if the petitioner acted unreasonably in not pursuing an alternative remedy (e.g., a section 994 remedy). In practice, aggrieved shareholders will bring joint petitions for a just and equitable winding up and for unfair prejudice, since conduct which is insufficient to found an unfair prejudice petition may still be sufficient to found a winding up petition on the "just and equitable" ground **(Hawkes v Cuddy (2009)**. In **Re A Company (1983)**, the courts dismissed a winding up petition under the just and equitable ground, because the petitioner had refused an improved offer by the members to buy his shares. However in **Re Abbey Leisure (1990)**, the courts allowed a petition to wind up a company after the company's main business (a night club) had been sold and the company was trading under ancillary objects.

Chapter 17

Insider Dealing

The 1977 White Paper on 'The Conduct of Company Directors' described Insider Dealing (or insider trading) as 'where a person buys or sells securities when he, but not the other party to the transaction, is in possession of confidential information which affects the valve of those securities. Furthermore the confidential information in question will generally be in his possession because of some connection which he has with the company whose securities are to be dealt in (e.g., he may be a director, employee or professional adviser of that company)'.

Criminal Liability

Insider dealing is a criminal offence and is now governed by Part V, ss.52 – 64 of the Criminal Justice Act 1993. In order for the Act to apply a number of pre-requisites have to be satisfied.

First, the offence of insider dealing can only be committed by an 'individual' (i.e., a natural person), and not a company.

Second, the individual must have dealt in relevant securities of a company while in possession of price-sensitive information. Under section 55 a person 'deals' in relevant securities if he buys or sells (or agrees to do so) whether directly or through agents. 'Relevant securities' includes shares, debentures, warrants, and options **(Schedule2)**.

Third, the information possessed by the insider must be inside information. Section 56(1) states that the information has to be 'unpublished price-sensitive' information. This means that the information must relate to particular securities or to a particular company, be specific or precise, must not have been made public, and would have a significant effect on the market price of the securities if it was made public. Non-exhaustive guidance is given by section 58 as to when information is already in the public domain. This includes where the information is published in accordance with rules of a regulated market; it is already contained in public records; it can be readily acquired by those likely to deal in the securities; or it is derived from public information. The fact that the information can only be acquired by persons exercising diligence or expertise, by observation, on payment of a fee, or is only published outside the United Kingdom will not exclude it from being already in the public domain.

Fourth, the individual dealing in the securities with the benefit of price-sensitive information must be an insider within section **57(1)**. A person will be an insider if he *knows* that the information is inside information, and is in possession of that information, and *knows* that it is from an inside source by acquiring it through: (a) being a director, employee or shareholder of a company; or (b) having access to the information by virtue of his employment, office or profession (e.g., professional such as bankers and lawyers); or (c) the direct or indirect source of the information comes from a person in category (a) or (b). Individuals who come within category (a) and (b) are called *primary insiders*; and individuals within category (c) are called *secondary insiders* or *tippees*. In relation to (a) it is not necessary to show that employees were in a position giving them access to the inside information. Thus the office cleaner who obtains information by unauthorised means (e.g., secretly reading the minute book of the directors meeting) will be a primary insider. In the case of (b) there is no need for there to be a connection between the individual and the company when he had access to the information. Thus public servants such as officers of regulatory agencies will be primary insiders. In the case of (c), the offence is only committed if the secondary insider knows both that the information is inside information and that it came from an inside source.

Fifth, the dealing must take place on a 'regulated market' such as **the Stock Exchange**, or through a 'professional intermediary' (in an off-market transaction). A regulated market will necessarily involve the securities of a public company. However, since an 'off-market transaction' can include market makers in over the counter transactions, this can also bring the securities of a private company within the scope of the Criminal Justice Act where a professional intermediary is involved. Private **face-to-face** transactions (not involving a professional intermediary) fall outside the scope of the Act.

The Three Offences

There are three ways in which the offence of insider dealing can be committed under the Criminal Justice Act. These situations are set out in section 52 and are where the insider (whether primary or secondary insider):

(a) **deals** in the price-affected securities in relation to the information; or

(b) **encourages** another person (without disclosing the information) to deal in the price-affected securities while knowing or having reasonable cause to believe that the dealing encouraged would occur on a regulated market or by a professional intermediary; or

(c) **discloses** inside information to another person other than in the proper performance of the functions of his employment, office, or profession.

Section 52 covers the situation where inside information is acquired passively.

Defences

Various defences can be relied on to a charge of insider dealing under the Act. There are *general* defences contained in section 53 and *special* defences in Schedule 1.

Under section 53 it is a defence in relation to the dealing and encouraging offences that the individual: did not expect the dealing to result in a profit or avoidance of loss; had reasonable grounds to believe that the information had been disclosed widely enough that those dealing without the benefit of it would not be prejudiced; or would have done what he did whether or not he had the information. It is a defence to the disclosure offence that the individual did not expect anyone to deal upon disclosure of the price-sensitive information.

The special defences in Schedule 1 only apply to the dealing and encouraging offences. It is a defence that an individual acted in accordance with price-stabilisation rules; that market-makers and their employees have acted in good faith; or where the individual is in possession of market information it was reasonable in view of his position to have acted as he did. The burden of proof rests with the defendant to prove on a balance of probabilities that a defence applies.

Penalties
Section 61 states that an offence of insider dealing is triable either way. On conviction on indictment, the offence is punishable by an unlimited fine and/or up to seven years imprisonment. On summary conviction the penalty is a maximum fine and /or six months imprisonment. A contract entered in breach of the Act will not be void or voidable; although the courts may refuse to enforce it on grounds of public policy **(Chase Manhattan Equities Ltd v Goodman (1990))**.

Civil Liability
The Criminal Justice Act does not contain any civil remedies. Any such liability will arise under existing common law. Directors owe a fiduciary duty to their company, and not to individual shareholders **(Percival v Wright)**. So if they trade on inside information they will have breached their fiduciary position and will be liable to the company for any unauthorised profits **(Industrial Development Consultants Ltd. v Cooley; Regal (Hastings) Ltd. Gulliver)**. The position of an insider other than a director (e.g., a secondary insider) is less clear. It might be argued that a person who receives information from a fiduciary in confidence – namely, a director – is 'impressed' by that person's fiduciary duties, in the same way as a person who knowingly meddles with trust property and may become constructive trustee **(Belmont Finance Corp Ltd. v Williams Furniture Ltd. (No.2) (1980)**. This view seems to be gaining ground among the English judges, especially where the third party has actual

knowledge of the directors' breach of duty (see Slade LJ in **Rolled Steel Products Ltd. v British Steel Corpn)**.

Prosecutions

A prosecution for insider dealing can only be commenced by or with the consent of the Secretary of State or the Director of Public Prosecutions **(s.61 (2))**. Consent can also be given to the Stock Exchange to institute proceedings.

Investigations

Under section 168(3) of the Financial Services and Markets Act 2000 the Secretary of State or the Financial Services Authority can appoint inspectors to investigate suspected insider dealing.

Financial Services and Markets Act 2000

In addition to the 1993 Act, insider dealing is also regulated by the FSMA. Section 118 of the Act introduces a new 'market abuse' offence, controlling the behaviour of persons involved in relevant securities on designated markets. It makes unlawful two types of behaviour, namely, misusing information which a regular market user would consider as relevant when deciding on what terms transactions in investments should be effected; and manipulating markets. It is also an offence to require or encourage market abuse.

Unlike the CJA, where the offence of insider dealing can only be committed on proof of 'knowledge' by the insider that the information which he is using to effect the transaction is inside information, liability for the market abuse offence is strict in the sense that the offence is committed if the behaviour in question falls below the standards expected from the regular user of the market. The Financial Services and Markets Tribunal, set up under the Act to hear appeals against administrative fines imposed by the Financial Services Authority for market abuse or for requiring or encouraging such abuse, will set the standards of the regular market user. Section 118 also allows the Financial Services Authority to apply to the courts for a whole range of civil remedies for market abuse.

Chapter 18

Liquidation

This is the process of terminating a company's life. Its assets will be realised to pay its debts, surpluses (if any) will be distributed to shareholders, and the company's name will be removed from the register by the Registrar of Companies. Another name for liquidation is 'winding up'. The Insolvency Act 1986 identifies two types of winding up: (i) a compulsory winding up by petition to the courts and (ii) a voluntary winding up by resolution of shareholders.

Compulsory Winding up

The High Court has jurisdiction to wind up any company (including a building society and a provident society) in England; but if the company's paid up capital does not exceed a statutory limit (at present £120,000), then the County Court of the district where the registered office of the company is situated usually has jurisdiction to order winding up concurrent with that of the High Court.

By section 122(1) of the Insolvency Act a company may be wound up by the courts on any of the following seven grounds, although in practice, most of the compulsory petitions to wind up are made under one of the last two grounds:

(a) **Where a company has passed a special resolution that it be wound up by the courts**. This ground is available to the company itself or to all of the directors but it is rarely used since shareholders would normally prefer a voluntary winding up to reduce court costs.

(b) **Where a company incorporated as a public company has failed within a year to obtain a trading certificate under section 117 of the Companies Act 1985**. This ground is only available to the Secretary of State for the Department for Business, Innovation and Skills (**BIS**)

(c) **Where an 'old public company' within the meaning of the Companies Consolidation (Consequential Provisions) Act 1985 has failed to re-register within the period for 'old public companies'**. This ground is obsolete since there are no old public companies today.

(d) **Where a company has not commenced business within a year from its incorporation or has suspended business for at least a year**. This ground is available only to contributories (i.e., shareholders (past and present) who are liable to contribute towards the assets of the company in the event of a winding up where the shares are partly paid). Contributories can only apply for a winding up in these circumstances if they have taken their shares directly from the company by allotment (even if they have never been entered on the register of members) or by transmission from deceased or bankrupt shareholders (though with bankrupt shareholders the trustee in bankruptcy must be on the register). Otherwise they must have held their shares for six out of the last 18 months preceding the presentation of the petition and for those six months must have been on the register (**s.124(2)**).

A petition based on this ground is granted at the discretion of the courts. If there is good reason for the suspension of business or if the winding up is opposed by the majority of shareholders, or if the company proves that it intends to recommence business and has the financial resources to do so, the courts will refuse to grant a winding up order. In **Re Middlesborough Assembly Rooms Co. (1880)**, a company was formed for the purpose of erecting, using and letting assembly rooms. It began certain building work and then a trade recession caused the shareholders to proceed no further until conditions improved. A shareholder petitioned a year later to wind up the company but the courts dismissed the petition because it was opposed by most of the shareholders and the company was still financially able to proceed with the work and to make a profit.

(e) **Where the number of members of a company falls below two (unless the company converts itself into a single member company in accordance with the Companies (Single Member Private Limited Companies) Regulations 1992)**. This ground is available only to a contributory and he need to have held his shares for six of the last 18 months preceding the presentation of the petition to wind up the company.

(f) **Where a company is unable to pay its debts**. This ground is available to creditors and, in the case of an insolvent private company where repayment of capital was made under section 171 of the Companies Act within one year preceding the commencement of winding up, the directors and the recipient of the capital payment. A shareholder cannot use this ground to base a petition (unless the company was unlimited) since he would have no interest in the winding up of an insolvent company, there being no surplus assets for distribution.

By section 123, a creditor may base a petition on this ground if he shows that (i) he is owed a sum exceeding £750 (this sum may be increased by statutory instrument) and has served on the company at its registered office a written demand for payment in the prescribed form (see **Form 1 Insolvency Rules 1986**) and the company has for three weeks thereafter neglected to pay the sum due or to secure or compound for it to the reasonable satisfaction of the creditor; or (ii) in England and Wales, execution or other process on a judgement in favour of him against the company has been returned unsatisfied wholly or in part; or (iii) it can be proved to the courts' satisfaction that the company is unable to pay its debts as they fall due; or (iv) it can be proved to the courts' satisfaction that the amount of the company's assets is less than the amount of its liabilities.

Under (i) personal service of the statutory demand is required; postal service and demand by telex will not do **(Re A Company (1985))**. Moreover the three-week period of grace does not include the day of service and the day the petition is filed in the courts. A petition based on a disputed debt will be dismissed by the courts if there are substantial grounds by the company for disputing it **(Re Laceward Ltd. (1981)**. Even if the debt is undisputed, the courts may still dismiss the petition if the creditors holding a majority of the debts oppose it; but the courts will also consider the reason for the differences between the creditors. In **Re Southard & Co. (1979)**, the court refused to grant a petition by a creditor holding a majority in value of the company's debts, which was opposed by creditors holding smaller sums, since the company was already in voluntary winding up and the object of the petition was to oust the original liquidator.

Under (ii) and (iii) the requirement that the value of the petitioner's debt should exceed £750 does not apply; but in practice the courts usually insist on this. Inability to pay debts can be established where a company without any valid reason refused to pay a debt when it falls due **(Taylor's Industrial Flooring Ltd. v M.H. Plant Hire Manchester Ltd. (1990))**.

(g) **Where it is just and equitable to wind up the company**. This ground is available to contributories, **BIS** and, in the case of an insolvent private company, the directors and the recipient of a capital payment under section 709; and it enables the courts to subject the exercise of legal rights to equitable considerations **(Ebrahimi v Westbourne Galleries Ltd.)**. For convenience, the cases decided so far under (g) will be considered under five broad categories but these categories are not exhaustive and may be extended by the courts at any time.

(i) *Failure of substratum*. A distinction is made between physical and financial substratum. With the former, if the main purpose of company is impossible to achieve, the courts will grant a winding up order. In **Re German Date Coffee Co. (1882)**, a company was formed with a view to obtaining a German patent in order to make coffee with dates. The German patent was never granted, but the company did acquire a Swedish patent. Nevertheless the company was put into compulsory winding up under ground (g). Suspension of the main purpose of the company is not, however, a failure of substratum **(Re Kitson & Co. Ltd. (1946))**. With the latter, it must be established that the company is continuously making a loss, and is unlikely to be able to carry on business for much longer, before the courts will be prepared to wind it up **(Re Suburban Hotel Co. (1867)**.

(ii) *Illegality of objects and fraud*. If the company is formed for an illegal or fraudulent purpose, the courts will grand a petition under (g). In **Re T. Brinsmead & Sons Ltd. (1897)**,

TB and his sons were employed by JB & Sons as piano manufacturers. They left JB & Sons and formed their own company to finch as much trade as possible from them. The courts held that it was just and equitable to wind up the company since it was initiated to carry out a fraud.

(iii) *Deadlock.* Whether or not the courts will grant a petition on the ground that there is deadlock in the management of the company will depend on the nature or character of the company. If it is a public company, or a private company with a body of shareholders quite distinct from those managing it and capable of constituting a general meeting, the courts will not normally intervene; since the general meeting may resolve the deadlock by the due process of majority decision, such as by removing the directors or by appointing additional directors where the articles permit it. In this way, the deadlock could be resolved. It is only when the general meeting cannot act (e.g., because members show so little interest in the company's affairs that a quorum could never be achieved for a general meeting) that the courts will intervene.

If the company is a small company with no body of shareholders separate from those managing it, then the courts are more ready to intervene. In **Re Yenidje Tobacco Co. Ltd. (1916)**, the only two shareholders and directors with equal management and voting rights became so hostile as to refuse to speak to each other. Despite this, the company still made high profits. The courts held that as there was complete deadlock, a winding up order would be granted.

(iv) *Oppression.* If the persons who control the company are guilty of serious oppression towards the minority members, whether in their capacity as members or directors, the courts may wind up the company on just and equitable principles. In

Loch v John Blackwood Ltd. (1924), the managing director, who held the majority of voting shares together with his co-directors, refused to hold general meetings or to submit accounts to the petitioners or to recommend a dividend. The suspicion was that his conduct was deliberate in order to enable them to acquire the minority's shares at undervalue. A winding up order was order as granted.

(v) *Grounds analogous to dissolution of firms.* If the company is a small domestic company in the form of a quasi-partnership, that is to say, it is everything like an unlimited liability partnership except that it is incorporated, the courts will apply the principles analogous to those which govern the dissolution of partnerships upon the 'just and equitable' ground. In **Re Fildes Bros. Ltd. (1970)**, Megarry J. said: 'In deciding whether a quasi-partnership exists, the courts must consider the contractual rights between the parties as is shown in the articles; and where the articles don't have much bearing on the matter, recourse has to be had to what the parties were shown to have agreed in any other manner'. Thus, it is likely that the courts will consider a company to be a quasi-partnership if it has only a few members, all or most of whom are directors and with equal voting shares.

In **Ebrahimi v Westbourne Galleries Ltd.**, **E** and **N** had been in partnership as carpet dealers; later they formed a company with themselves as directors and only shareholders to take over and carry on the business, and subsequently appointed **N's** son third director and shareholder. The company made good profits, all of which were distributed as directors' pay. Subsequently, disputes having arisen concerning the running of the business, **N** and his son *bona fide* exercised their statutory power to remove E from his directorship by ordinary resolution in accordance with section 303. **E** petitioned to wind up the company on the just and equitable principle because the company was a quasi-partnership, and there was an underlining agreement that they should form the company on the basis that each would be a director. The House of Lords held that there may be circumstances in which the rights of the members have not been exhaustively defined in the company's constitution, such as where they became members on the basis of an understanding that each of them would be entitled to participate fully in its management. The termination of the relationship in which **E**, who was now entirely excluded from the management and from remuneration as a director, was entitled to have the company wound up on the 'just and equitable' ground.

Apart from the seven specific grounds already dealt with for a compulsory winding up of a company, section 124(5) of the Insolvency Act allows the official receiver to present a winding up petition where a company is being wound up voluntarily, and the courts are satisfied that the liquidation cannot be continued with due regard to the interests of the creditors or members (e.g., because of the liquidator's misconduct). An administrative receiver or an administrator has power to petition for a winding up; but if it is an administrator who petitions, the petition must be coupled with an application to discharge the administration order since a winding up order cannot be made while an administration order is in force **(s.140 IA)**.

Procedure for Winding Up Order

The winding up petition has to be in the form prescribed by the Insolvency Rules, lodged at the office of the Registrar of the Companies Court and verified by affidavit. A copy of the petition is required to be served on the company at its registered office. It must also be published in the Gazette and an appropriate local newspaper at least seven days before the day fixed for the hearing.

After the presentation of the petition but before the actual hearing, the courts may appoint the Official Receiver (an officer of the Insolvency Services, an Executive Agency of **BIS**, attached to each court having insolvency jurisdiction) or other fit person to act as 'provisional' liquidator to preserve the company's assets. Once he is appointed the directors' powers of management automatically terminate as with the making of a winding up order. In addition, no legal proceedings can be commenced or continued against the company without leave of the courts **(s.130 (2))**. Even without the appointment of a provisional liquidator the courts may, on application, grant a stay of legal proceedings against the company **(s.126)**. At the hearing of the petition, the courts may dismiss it, or make any order that they think fit. A winding up petition presented by a creditor cannot be dismissed simply because the company has no assets **(s.125)**; but in such a case the creditor must still prove that it would enable him to obtain some payment, such as by setting aside a preference **(Re Crigglestone Coal Co. (1906)** or by enabling him to receive his wages from the company through the Redundancy Fund **(Re Eloc Electro-Optieck and Communicate BV (1982))**. A winding up by the courts commences at the time the petition is filed; but if it was filed after a resolution had been passed for voluntary winding up, winding up is treated as commencing at the time of the passing of the resolution **(s.86 IA)**.

Procedure after the Winding Up Order

Once a winding up order is made, the courts will give a copy of the order to the Official Receiver who will send a copy to the Registrar of Companies. The Registrar will then publish notice of this fact in the Gazette. The Official Receiver becomes liquidator of the company. He obtains custody and control of the company's assets (but the legal ownership of the assets does not vest in him unless the courts so order), replaces the directors and may re-engage the company's employees.

The Official Receiver may require a statement of affairs from the directors (or secretary). If he finds that the assets are not sufficient to meet liquidation expenses and the company's affairs do not require investigation he may apply to the courts for a dissolution order, after serving notice on contributories and creditors. If he does not serve notice of his intention to apply for a dissolution order, a quarter in value of the creditors can require him to summon a first meeting of members and creditors to appoint someone else to replace him as liquidator. The person to be appointed must be a qualified insolvency practitioner. The Official Receiver himself may decide to call a first meeting of members (contributories) and creditors within 12 weeks of the winding up order if there is a prospect of a professional liquidator being appointed. In such a case he must advertise the meeting in the appropriate media and send to the creditors a notice of the meeting, together with the forms of proxy and proof of debts. Creditors wishing to vote must lodge a proof of debt with the Official Receiver before the meeting, and a proxy must be lodged if a creditor wishes to appoint someone else to vote for him or if the creditor is a limited company. Where each meeting nominates its own liquidator, the creditors' nominee will prevail. The first meeting will also decide whether a liquidation committee should be appointed from among the creditors. The function of such a committee is to assist and supervise the work of the meeting's own liquidator and to consent to the exercise of those powers of the liquidator which can only be exercised with consent of the courts, the liquidation committee or **BIS**.

Effect of Compulsory Winding Up

(a) **Disposal of assets**. Any disposition of the company's property, transfer of shares, or alteration of the status of its members after the commencement of winding up is void unless the courts otherwise order **(s.127)**. The courts will normally sanction transactions entered into in good faith and in the ordinary course of business. In **Re Park Ward & Co. Ltd. (1926)**, the courts sanctioned the issue of secured debentures made by the company in return for a loan to enable it to pay wages due to staff, even though the lender knew at the time that a winding up petition had been filed in the court. However, in **Re Leslie Engineers Co. Ltd. (1976)**, where the directors of a company paid £250 in postal orders to a creditor after the commencement of winding up, the courts refused to sanction the transaction, notwithstanding that the disposition was made indirectly through a third party (i.e., the Post Office) since the payment was not in the interest of the company.

(b) **Stay of legal proceedings**. Legal proceedings which have already commenced against the company are halted unless the courts give leave to proceed **(s.126)**.

(c) **Seizure of company property**. Any seizure of the company's assets after the commencement of a winding up is void **(s.128)**. Execution levied against the company before the commencement of winding up will also be set aside unless it was completed **(s.183)**. Execution is completed when assets are seized and sold. Even so the sheriff is required to retain the proceeds of sale in his hands for 14 days if they exceed £500, and if during this period he learns of the liquidation proceedings he has to hand over the money to the liquidator though not before deducting the costs of execution **(s.184)**. This provision equally applies to a voluntary winding up.

Powers of a Compulsory Liquidator

The powers of a liquidator appointed by the first meeting of members and creditors to replace the Official Receiver fall into two categories: those which he may exercise without sanction and those which require sanction by the liquidation committee, the courts or **BIS**. The liquidator may exercise the following powers without consent: power to sell and transfer the company's property; power to issue negotiable instruments, raising loans on the security of the company's assets, and executing documents in the company's name; power to prove in the bankruptcy of any contributory; and power to do other things necessary to wind up the company's affairs and distribute assets. The liquidator may exercise the following powers only with consent: power to bring or defend any legal proceedings on behalf of the company; power to carry on the company's business so far as is necessary for its beneficial winding up; power to appoint a solicitor; power to make compromises with creditors and contributories.

In addition to the above powers the liquidator can institute a **private examination** of individuals, with the courts' consent, in order to facilitate his examination of the company's affairs.

Liability of a Liquidator

Where a liquidator breaches any of his duties he may be liable in damages in misfeasance proceedings under section 212 of the Insolvency Act.

Calls on Contributories

A contributory is a present or past member of the company who is liable to contribute to the assets of the company to an amount sufficient for the payments of the company's debts in full in the event of a winding up **(s.74)**. In the case of a company limited by shares, a contributory is only liable to the extent that the shares are partly paid. No Liability attaches to him on fully paid shares.

Where it is necessary to make call on contributories, the liquidator is required to up two lists: an 'A' List of contributories who were members at the commencement of winding up, and a 'B' List who were members during the year preceding the commencement of winding up. The liability of contributories on the 'B' List is limited. First, they are liable to pay what is due on the shares which they previously held, and then only so much of the amount due on the shares as the present holder are unable to pay. Second, they can be required to contribute only to debts incurred while they were members, and which are still outstanding.

Voluntary Winding Up

This commences by resolution of the shareholders. The type of resolution required will depend on the reason for the winding up **(s.84)**. If the company was formed for a fixed duration or purpose as specified by its articles, and this has now been achieved, an ordinary resolution will suffice. A special resolution is required if the company is being wound up because it cannot pay its debts, and in all other cases. A copy of the resolution to wind up voluntarily must be sent to the Registrar of Companies within 15 days **(s.89(3))**; and the resolution must be advertised in the Gazette within 14 days after it is passed otherwise criminal sanction may be imposed on the company's officers including its liquidator **(s.86)**.

Once the resolution to wind up is passed, the company must cease trading unless it is for the purpose for its beneficial winding up; and, unless the liquidator agrees, no transfer of shares can be made during this period.

A voluntary winding up may take two forms. It may be a members' voluntary winding up, or a creditors' voluntary winding up. The first is possible only if the directors (either unanimously or by majority decision) make a declaration of solvency within five weeks immediately preceding the date of the passing of the resolution to wind up. The declaration can be made at the meeting for wind up as long as it is done before the resolution is passed. The declaration should contain a statement of the company's assets and liabilities at the latest practicable date, and should state that it is the directors' opinion that the company will be able to pay its debts (including interest) in full within a period not exceeding 12 months from the commencement of the winding up **(s.89)**. It is a criminal offence to make a false declaration without reasonable grounds. The directors must, under penalty, file the declaration with the Registrar of Companies within 15 days after the resolution to wind up.

A members' voluntary winding up is controlled by the members. Thus, there is no legal obligation for a liquidation committee; the liquidator is appointed by the members but he must be a licensed insolvency practitioner; and although the directors do not lose office their powers cease as soon as the liquidator is appointed unless the members in general meeting or the liquidator agrees for their powers to continue. In the absence of consent for the directors to continue to exercise their powers, the liquidator will have to apply to the courts for a special manager to be appointed if he considers that the nature of the business or the members' or creditors' interests require some other person to manage the business in order to wind it up **(s.177)**. The employees are not dismissed automatically on the commencement of the winding up **(Fowler v Commercial Timber Co. Ltd. (1930))**. If no declaration of solvency is made, then the winding up must necessarily be a creditors voluntary winding up. The directors are required to call a creditors' meeting within 14 days after the members meeting to wind up the company **(s.98)**. Creditors must be given at least 7 days notice of their meeting and notice must be sent by post. The notice must also be advertised in the Gazette and in two local newspapers and the advertisement must state the name and address of the insolvency practitioner (if the members in general meeting had nominated one to act as liquidator) who will provide the creditors with any information which they may reasonably request prior to their meeting, or a place in the locality where a list of creditors can be obtained free of charge.

If a liquidator is nominated by the company before the creditors meeting, he cannot exercise any of his powers under section 165 without the courts' consent (e.g., power to dispose of the company's assets) until the creditors, at their meeting, approve his appointment **(s.166)**. However, he may take control of the company's assets, dispose of perishables and do anything necessary to protect the assets; but he must disclose all such matters at the creditors meeting. He is also obliged to ensure that the company and its directors comply with their duties regarding the calling of creditors meetings and bring the matter to the courts' attention if they fail to do so. The liquidator's appointment will result in the automatic termination of directors' powers (unless the creditors later decide otherwise) and employees' contracts. In the event of a liquidator not being nominated before the creditors meeting, the directors' powers, during this period, are subject to the courts' control.

The creditors' meeting is presided over by a director nominated by the board of directors and it will receive a full statement by the directors as to the company's financial affairs, a list of creditors with details of securities and other matters specified by the Insolvency Rules. The meeting may also replace the company's liquidator with its own liquidator and may appoint a liquidation committee which cannot exceed five creditors and a similar number of members with the creditors having the final say over the members' representation on the committee. Votes at the creditors meeting are determined by value of debts.

A creditors' voluntary winding up can also arise where the winding up starts as a members winding up and the liquidator subsequently forms the opinion that the company will be unable to pay its debts. Section 95 requires him, in such a case, to summon a creditors meeting within 28 days. Creditors must be notified of the meeting by personal notice and newspaper advertisements and should be provided with all such information as they may reasonably require. A statement of the company's assets and liabilities must be laid before the meeting which will then take control of the winding up.

Regardless of the type of winding up, the liquidator of a voluntary winding up is under a duty to contact creditors individually, as they appear from the company's records and ask them to submit claims. Failure to contact a creditor will be a breach of duty for which the liquidator will be liable **(James Smith & Sons (Norwood) Ltd. v Goodman (1936))**. A voluntary liquidator is not liable for contracts made by him on behalf of the company during the course of the winding up. The courts have power under section 112 to determine any question arising in the winding up and to make any order (such as to stop the winding up) as it would have been able to make had the company gone into compulsory liquidation.

The fact that a company is under a voluntary winding up and that a liquidator has already been appointed does not prevent a secured creditor from exercising a power in the debenture to appoint a receiver to protect his security, even if the liquidator can adequately realise that security **(Re Potters Oil Ltd. (No. 2) (1986))**.

Assets in a Winding Up

The liquidator's main function is to see that the assets are got in, realised and distributed to the creditors, and if there are surpluses, to the members. Assets available for distribution include not only those assets which exist at the date of the liquidator's appointment but also assets which the company owned at the date of commencement of winding up although it no longer owns them. Thus in a compulsory winding up, any disposal of a company's assets after its commencement (unless otherwise directed by the courts) may be recovered **(s.127)**. Even pre-liquidation transactions can be set aside under various provisions of the Insolvency Act where the company is insolvent such as transactions at undervalue and voidable preferences; and these go towards the general pool for the company's creditors. The relevant provisions are outlined below and apply to both compulsory and voluntary liquidation, unless otherwise indicated.

(a) **Section 183**: **Incomplete executions**. Any incomplete execution against the company's goods or land immediately before winding up commences is void (see ante).

(b) **Section 239**: **Fraudulent preference**. Any disposal of company property and any charge (fixed or floating) created within six months before the commencement of winding up is void as a fraudulent preference, if done voluntarily at a time when the company was insolvent and with the intention of preferring one creditor over another. If the person preferred was connected with the company (e.g., a director or shadow director, or his associate such as his relatives, or a person whom the company employs) the period is extended from six months to two years **(s.240)** In **Re Kushler Ltd. (1943)**, the directors of an insolvent company arranged for the company to repay a bank loan which was guaranteed by one of them. The bank was ordered to repay the loan to the liquidator as it was a fraudulent preference. Similarly, in **Re Matthews Ltd. (1982)**, two cheques amounting to £17,000 were paid within two months before winding up to clear an overdraft which was guaranteed by the directors. The courts held that the payments were made with the intention of preferring the bank at the expense of the other creditors.

If there was no desire to confer an advantage on a creditor, but rather to benefit the company, the disposal or charge will not be invalid. In **Re F.I.E. Holdings Ltd. (1967)**, a company executed a legal charge on its factory in favour of a bank; the evidence showed that its intention was to keep on good terms with the bank, in the hope of future banking facilities. The courts held that the charge was not a fraudulent preference.

Where proceeds are recovered by the liquidator on the ground that the payments were a fraudulent preference, the proceeds are to be used for the benefit of the general creditors of the company and do not go to the debenture holder even though he has a floating charge on all the company's assets (Millett J. in **Re Mc Bacon Ltd. (1920))**.

(c) **Section 245: Floating charges to secure existing debts**. Any floating charge on the company's property created within 12 months before the commencement of winding up to secure an existing unsecured debt is invalid if the company was insolvent at the time the charge was created. If the charge was given to a person connected with the company the period is extended from 12 months to two years regardless of the company's financial position at the time the charge was created.

The charge cannot be invalidated under this section if consideration was given for it **(s.245(a))**. If the charge was created to secure a loan of 'new money', subsection (a) requires the new money to be given to the company 'at the same time as, or after, the creation of the charge'. Thus if the money is given to the company before the charge is executed, the charge will be invalid, unless the interval is so short that it can be regarded as *de minimis*, for example, a 'coffee break' (per Slade J in **Power v Sharp Investments Ltd. (1993)**. In **Power v Sharp Investment Ltd.**, the defendant company agreed to lend money to Shoe Lace Ltd. on the security of a fixed and floating charge on the latter's property. The money was lent but the charge was not executed until one month before Shoe Lace Ltd. went into liquidation. The Court of Appeal, ruling on the validity of the floating charge, declared the charge invalid under section 245. The Court stated that the words 'at the same time as, or after, the creation of the charge' was intended to exclude from the exemption for new money any money paid in consideration of the charge even though the money was paid in consideration of the charge unless the interval was so *de minimis*. If the loan was made after the charge was created and was used (as was intended) to pay off an existing unsecured debt owed to the same creditor or in which the creditor had an interest (e.g., as guarantor), the loan will not be money paid 'to the company' for the purpose of the exemption since the company would not have any control over the money **(Re Fairway Magazines Ltd. (1992))**.

A bank which is given a floating charge by an insolvent company as continuing security for an existing overdraft and future loans can rely on further advances made to the company after the charge is given as 'new money' for the floating charge and will be secured to that extent. Moreover, it will be able to rely on the **Rule in Clayton's Case (1816)** where credits were later paid in by the company. This rule presumes that the payments were intended to reduce the existing overdraft, thus leaving the new money to be utilised by the charge. In **Re Yeovil Glove Co. Ltd. (1965)**, a floating charge was given to a bank to secure an existing overdraft of £68,000 at a time when the company was insolvent. The bank allowed the company to draw on its account further sums amounting to £110,000. Within twelve months of the creation of the charge the company went into liquidation, the debit balance on this account being £67,000. The courts held that the loan of £68,000 had been repaid by the subsequent credits of £110,000 to the account. The balance (£67,000) owing at the commencement of liquidation was 'new money' lent after the charge was created; so the charge was valid for the loan of £67,000.

Section 245 cannot invalidate a floating charge created by an insolvent company within the prescribed period if the charge crystallised before the commencement of winding up and the creditor sold the security to pay off his unsecured debt. In **Mac Builders (Glasgow) Ltd. v Lunn (1986)**, a company which owed a creditor £54,500 gave him a floating charge for that loan and in consideration and in consideration for a further advance. Subsequently, the creditor appointed himself receiver under the terms of the debenture after the company defaulted with its payments; and in that capacity sold the company's assets and applied the money in repaying the debt owed to him. Shortly afterwards the company went into liquidation and the liquidator attempted to recover the money on grounds that the floating charge was created within 12 months of the commencement of winding up at a time when the company was insolvent. The Court of Appeal held that the liquidator could not recover the money because the section invalidated a floating charge only on a winding up and therefore did not invalidate the repayment of a secured debt made by a company prior to the commencement of winding up.

(d) **Section 238: Transactions at undervalue**. Transactions entered into by an insolvent company within two years preceding the commencement of winding up can be set aside by the courts unless they were entered into in good faith for the purpose of carrying on business and there were reasonable grounds to believe that they would benefit the company. A transaction at undervalue occurs where the company makes a gift, or enters into a transaction for no consideration, or for consideration which on the face of it is worth significantly less than the value of the benefit received by the company. There is a presumption that the company was insolvent (unless the contrary is proved) if the transaction was made by the company with a person connected with it.

In addition, the assets of the company can be swelled by taking recourse to the following sections:

(e) **Section 178: Onerous property**. The liquidator may disclaim onerous company property such as land burdened by onerous covenants, stocks and shares, unprofitable contracts and property which is unsaleable or not readily saleable because it binds the possessor to the performance of an onerous act or to the payment of money. The liquidator does not have to obtain the courts' permission before he can disclaim such property, and he may disclaim it at any time. However if a person interested in the property makes a written request asking the liquidator to decide whether he will disclaim, but the liquidator does not inform him in writing within 28 days that he will disclaim, then he will not be able to do so at a later date.

For a disclaimer to be valid it must be in writing and in the prescribed form as set out in the Insolvency Rules. Any person injured by the disclaimer is treated as a creditor of the company to the amount of his injury, and may prove for that amount.

(f) **Section 212: Misfeasance action**. The courts have power to require any officer of the company who has misapplied, or become liable or accountable for, the company's money or property or been guilty of any misfeasance or breach of any fiduciary or other duty to the company to repay or restore or contribute to the assets of the company by way of compensation for the wrong. An auditor, director, promoter, liquidator and manager are officers for the purpose of this section; but a receiver, being only a representative of secured creditors, is not **(Re B. Johnson & Co. (Builders) Ltd. (1955))**. However an administrative receiver is. Misfeasance proceedings can be commenced by the liquidator, official receiver, or contributory (with the courts' consent). In **Re Thomas Gerrard & Son Ltd. (1968)**, auditors were held liable in misfeasance proceedings when they failed to detect that the directors had falsified the accounts to conceal a payment of dividends out of capital.

(g) **Section 213: Fraudulent trading**. If during the course of an insolvent winding up, it appears that the company was carrying on business with intent to defraud creditors or for any fraudulent purpose, the courts may make any culpable person personally liable for all or any of the company's debts. A company is 'carrying on business' even if it has stopped trading and is only collecting assets and paying creditors **(Re**

Sarflax Ltd. (1979)). The most common form of fraudulent trading is where the directors order goods knowing that the company will not have the money to pay for them **(R v Grantham (1985))**. A creditor who receives money in payment of his debt and knows that it was obtained by fraud of the directors is a culpable person even if he took no actual part in the fraudulent trading itself **(Morris v Banque Arabe et Internationale D'Investissement SA (No. 2) (2000))**. Paying one creditor at the expense of another is not 'fraudulent' for the purpose of the section. In **Re Sarflax Ltd.**, a company stopped trading, and one of its directors used its assets to pay off trading debts owned to its parent company. This was done at the expense of another creditor to whom the company owed a substantial sum. The court held that merely preferring a creditor at the expense of another did not amount to an 'intention to defraud' under the section.

Civil liability can only arise where the company is in a winding up. However criminal liability for fraudulent trading can attach whether or not the company is in winding up and this is governed by section 993 of the Companies Act.

(h) **Section 214: Wrongful trading**. If a company continues to trade when it is insolvent and later goes into insolvent liquidation, the liquidator may apply to the courts for an order that a director or shadow director of that company should contribute to the company's assets. The liquidator must however establish that the director was trading on behalf of the company when he knew or ought to have concluded that the company had no reasonable prospect of avoiding insolvent liquidation. Whether a director (or shadow director) knew or ought to have concluded that insolvent liquidation was unavoidable will depend not only on what a reasonably diligent person should have known or concluded on the basis of his own subjective knowledge, skill and experience, but also by the general knowledge, skill and experience that might reasonably be expected of a person carrying out the same functions as were carried out by that director **(s.214(4))**. Thus a director is judged by the higher of two standards measured either subjectively according to the person or objectively according to the job. In **Re Produce Marketing Consortium Ltd. (No.2) (1989)**, Knox J. stated that in applying the objective standard the qualities expected from the director will depend on the type of company and its business. The qualities will be 'much less extensive in a small company in a modest way of business with simple accounting procedures and equipment, than it will be in a large company with sophisticated procedures'. The company's accounts will contain the necessary information to enable a director to make an informed judgement as to whether or not a company which is making a loss will be able to avoid insolvent liquidation; and while the courts do not expect a director to have the technical accounting expertise of a professional accountant (unless his position is that of finance director), he is expected to act as a reasonably prudent businessman. Thus if he displays unrealistic optimism with no factual basis for it, this behaviour will not be excused by the courts in proceedings for wrongful trading. In **Re DKG Contractors Ltd. (1990)**, the company was a family-run business which went into insolvent liquidation. No proper accounts were maintained, all income and expenses were kept in a black book updated by the director's wife, and all monies received from the company's customers were paid over to the director. In proceedings for wrongful trading, the director argued that he had little knowledge of what was involved in being a director. It was held that he ought to have realised that there was no reasonable prospect of avoiding liquidation, since the simple record of receipts and payments was capable of providing the company's cash flow status.

A director is judged not just on facts known to him but also on facts which he would have known had the company complied with its obligations under the Companies Act (e.g., to keep proper accounting records). In **Re Produce Marketing Consortium Ltd.**, the directors did not receive the accounts which showed disastrous results because the accounts were two years late and not available. Nevertheless, the directors were deemed to have had knowledge that the company was in financial difficulty because, with reasonable diligence and the appropriate level of skill, they could have obtained this information from the accounting records which would have disclosed with reasonable accuracy the company's financial position at any time. As they failed to make changes in the business to minimise the loss to creditors, they were held liable for wrongful trading and were ordered to pay £75,000 contribution (the amount by which the company's assets had been depleted from the time the accounting figures should have become available to the directors indicating that the company was certain to fail).

It is necessary when trying to establish a wrongful trading claim for liquidators to identify a particular date at which a conclusion should have been reached by the directors that there was no reasonable prospect of the company avoiding insolvent liquidation. This is because the courts, in ordering any contribution payable by a director, will normally calculate the extent of the contribution on the basis of losses incurred by the creditors from the period commencing with the specified date (this date being the date from which the director's conduct caused the company's assets to be depleted). In **Re Brian D Pierson (2000)**, the liquidator relied on the June 1994 accounts which showed that the company was making increasing losses as the relevant date, even though the company did not go into insolvent liquidation until January 1996. Establishing the probable date at which the company ought to have liquidated can also be problematic. This is because it is not the intention of the section to prevent a company from trading while it is insolvent; but only to prevent the directors from engaging in wrongful trading. Thus, if the date specified by the liquidator does not accurately prescribe the period of wrongful trading it will be fatal to the liquidator's case. In **Re Sherbourne Associates Ltd. (1995)**, the court dismissed an action under section 214 on the basis that although it was probable that the date chosen by the liquidator was indicative of a period in which the company had been trading whilst insolvent, the date was not conclusive that wrongful trading took place. The court concluded that on the date specified by the liquidator there had been reasonable prospect to which the directors thought the company could avoid liquidation. In this instance the liquidator was refused permission to substitute a new date for the one which had been pleaded as it would have prejudiced the defence. A wrongful trading claim survives the director and can be pursued against his estate **(Re Sherborne Associates Ltd.)**.

It is a defence to a section 214 claim for directors to show that they took every step they ought to have taken to minimise the potential loss to the company's creditors. This may require the directors to take immediate professional advice or else stop trading. In **Re Continental Assurance Co. of London plc (No.4) (2007)**, an insurance company suffered huge unexpected losses and subsequently went into insolvent liquidation. In an application by the liquidator for a contribution order against the directors for wrongful trading, the court refused the application because, during the period specified by the liquidator as the period when the directors were involved in wrongful trading, the directors had taken professional advice as to the company's solvency and had continued to trade on the basis of that advice until they realised that the company was in fact insolvent, It is no defence for a director to argue that he was an inactive director and had left the running of the business to his fellow directors **(Re Brian D Pierson)**. Moreover, section 1157 of the Companies Act 2006 which provides that a director who acts honestly and reasonably may be excused from liability for negligence or breach of duty, does not apply to an action for wrongful trading **(Re Produce Marketing Consortium Ltd.)**.

If the courts make an order for contribution, then like section 213 (liability for fraudulent trading), they may at the same time disqualify the directors from holding office for between two and fifteen years from being involved directly or indirectly in the promotion, formation or management of a company. Section 214 is wider than section 213 in that it does not require the liquidator to prove 'fraud' before a contribution order can be made against a director. On the other hand the section applies only to directors (including former directors and shadow directors) whilst section 213 applies to any culpable person trading on behalf of an insolvent company.

A liquidator's application under section 214 will ordinarily be financed from the company's assets which have been realised under the liquidation process. If the assets are not sufficient; the liquidator can recoup the cost from the contribution.

Proof of Debts

Before a claim can be admitted, a creditor must give the liquidator evidence of his debt. This is done by affidavit verifying the debt; and it must state whether the creditor is or is not a secured creditor. Failure to indicate this may result in the security being forfeited. To prove his debt the creditor must attach to the affidavit particulars thereof and specify all vouchers by which the particulars may be substantiated. If the company is solvent all debts and liabilities existing at the date of commencement of winding up are provable. However, if the company is insolvent unliquidated claims for damages in tort are not admissible although the courts may permit the injured party to pursue his action in tort so that his claim can be converted into a liquidated sum. Statute-barred debts are not payable.

Types of Creditors
In the main, there are four types of creditors: secured; unsecured; preferential; and deferred.

(a) **Secured creditor**. This is any person holding a mortgage, charge or lien on the property of the company for the debt due to him. He may rely on the security and not prove at all; the liquidator may then redeem it by payment in full. Or he may realise the security and prove for the deficiency where he is not fully secured. Or he may value the security and prove the deficiency; in which case the liquidator may buy the security off him at its estimated value. Or he may surrender the security and prove for the whole debt. He is deemed to surrender the security where he fails to inform the liquidator of his security.

(b) **Unsecured creditor**. Also known as an ordinary creditor, he is in that category which can be divided into those who are entitled to preferential payments and those who are not. The term 'unsecured' is in contrast to the category legally defined as 'secured' creditors. The general rule is that all debts provable in insolvency are to be paid *pari passu*; but this rule is subordinate to the provisions of the Insolvency Act 1986 which set out the order of priority of payment whereby preferential creditors rank after secured creditors with fixed charges, but before creditors secured by floating charges and unsecured (or ordinary) creditors. The last being creditors who are not preferred in any way nor are deferred or postponed by any relevant legislation, and having no security which they can realise in order to claim some prior payment of their debt, will rank equally together after secured and preferential creditors.

(c) **Preferential creditor**. This is a creditor who by section 175 of the Insolvency Act is given preference in respect of some types of debts. These debts rank equally among themselves, but rank after debts secured by a fixed charge. The list of preferred debts under section 175 includes wages or salaries of employees for four months prior to the relevant date, to a statutory maximum (at present £800) per employee and all accrued holiday remuneration. Advances made for the payment of wages which are preferential are also preferred debts; so that the persons who lent money to pay the wages will be subrogated to the rights of the employees. Crown debts such as taxes and national insurance are not preferential but are treated as ordinary unsecured debts.

(d) **Deferred creditors**. This is a postponed creditor who is not, by reason of special circumstances, able to claim payment of his debt until after the discharge of debts owing to secured, preferential and ordinary creditors. This debt usually relates to unpaid dividend.

Distress for Rent by Landlord
A landlord is in a special position, because he has the power to distress for rent owing by the company by taking

possession of its assets. However in a compulsory winding up if he seizes the company's assets by way of distress within three months before the making of the winding up order he has to return the assets or their proceeds (if the assets were sold) to the liquidator for payment of the preferential debts **(s.176)** The distrainor can keep the assets only if the distrain was made outside the three-month period **(Re Memco Engineering Ltd. (1986))**.

Order of Payment in a Winding Up

After creditors with the benefit of a 'Romalpa' clause recover their property and creditors secured by a fixed charge realise their security, the order of payment of debts by the liquidator will be as follows:

(i) The costs of winding up, charges and expenses including remuneration for the liquidator.

(ii) Preferential debts under section 175

(iii) Debts secured by a floating charge. However, a proportion of the net realisation proceeds (i.e., after deduction of the cost of realisation and preferential debts) of the floating charge assets must be set aside for the benefit of unsecured debts. This proportion is 50% of the first £10,000 and 20% of the balance (subject to a maximum limit of £600,000 to be set aside for the payment of the unsecured debts). The floating charge creditor is not entitled to a share in the statutory proceeds set aside for unsecured creditors for the part of his debt which remains unpaid **(Re Airbase (UK) Ltd. (2008))**. Unsecured creditors are not entitled to a share of the proceeds of the realisation proceeds of floating chare assets if the net assets are less than £10,000 or if the cost of distribution to the unsecured debts is disproportionate to the benefits.

Where there are several floating charges which are valid, priority is given to the first in time; and the debts secured by the later floating charges will bear the full impact of the proportion which must be set aside for unsecured debts.

(iv) Ordinary unsecured debts.

(v) Interest accrued since the company went into liquidation

(vi) Deferred debts.

Use of Insolvent Company's Name

When an insolvent company goes into liquidation its name becomes a prohibited name and its directors or shadow directors cannot within the next five years use another company to trade under that name or a name which is so similar as to suggest a connection with the insolvent company without the courts' consent **(s.216)**. For breach of this provision the directors will be personally liable for the debts of the second company while they managed it **(s.217)**.

Dissolution of the Company

This ends the company's corporate existence. In a compulsory winding up, if the liquidator is not the Official Receiver, then on completion of the winding up he will summon a final meeting of creditors and then notify the Registrar of Companies. The Registrar will note this fact on the company's file and three months later the company is dissolved **(s.146)**. If the Official Receiver is the liquidator the procedure is the same except that there is no final meeting of creditors. In a voluntary winding up, after final accounts are approved by the company in general meeting (and by the creditors in a creditors winding up) and filed with the Registrar, the company is dissolved three months thereafter unless the courts order otherwise **(s.201)**.

The Registrar also has power to dissolve a company without a winding up if he has reasonable cause to believe that the company is not carrying on business and it does not reply to his inquiries and notices **(s.652)**. He has to send two letters to the company; the second between four to six weeks after the company fails to reply to the first letter as to whether or not it is carrying on business. If a month passes and the company still does not reply to the second letter, the Registrar will advertise by notice in the Gazette that the company will be struck off the register within three months of publication date unless cause is shown to the contrary. When the company is struck off the register, the Registrar must publish this fact in the Gazette; the publication date is deemed to be the date of dissolution. Section 653 provides that the liability, if any, of every director, managing officer and member shall continue as if the company had not been dissolved. A dissolved company may be resuscitated by the courts within twelve years after a winding up **(s.651)**, and within twenty years if struck off the register under section 652.

Chapter 19

Reconstruction and Amalgamation

The words 'reconstruction' and 'amalgamation' have no precise meanings; but distinguish (i) internal reconstruction; (ii) external reconstruction and (iii) amalgamations (merger, take-over).

Internal reconstruction occurs where there is an internal reorganisation of a company's share or loan capital. It may involve an alteration of capital under section 618 (subdivision or consolidation of shares), section 622 (redenomination of share capital), section 641(reduction of share capital); section 630 (a variation of class rights); or sections 895, 896 and 899 (arrangements/reconstructions). An internal reconstruction can affect only one company.

External reconstruction occurs where a company forms a new company, which purchases the undertaking of the original company and then carries on business with the same shareholders. An external reconstruction may seem pointless; but until 1948 a company was unable to alter its objects clause, hence an external reconstruction was one means of getting round the *ultra vires* rule. Today it is rare because all new companies have unrestricted objects unless they choose in their articles to restrict their objects. Nevertheless, an external reconstruction may still occur under section 895 through a scheme of arrangement, and under section 110 of the Insolvency Act 1986 (see below).

Amalgamation by its very nature involves separate companies. It occurs where two or more companies or their businesses are combined into one company, or into the control of one company. Amalgamation may occur under a power in the articles of each company; by a sale under section 110; under a scheme of arrangement; and by sale of one company's shares to another (the take-over).

Internal Reconstruction

Apart from the alteration of capital and variation of rights attached to shares, a company may be able to make a compromise or arrangement with its creditors or its members under section 895, and such an arrangement (subject to established procedures being followed under sections 896 and 899) may bind those members or creditors who disapprove of it. The procedure for a compromise (arrangement) of this nature is called a 'scheme of arrangement'. The procedure requires an application to be made to the courts by the company, or any creditor or member (or if the company is being wound up or is in administration, by the liquidator or administrator) for an order to summon persons affected by the scheme to attend a company meeting to consider it **(s.896)**. At the meeting the scheme must be approved by a simple majority representing three quarters in value of the debts of the creditors or class of creditors or members or class of members (as the case may be) present and voting either in person or by proxy. A second application is then made to the courts by the persons who asked for the meeting for the courts to sanction the scheme. The scheme will then bind all the persons affected by it once approved by the courts **(s.899)**.

The courts cannot sanction a scheme unless it involves the company either through the board of directors or by a majority of members in general meeting or otherwise. In **Re Savoy Hotel Ltd. (1981)**, a shareholder who had a majority holding of a class of shares proposed a scheme to purchase the shares of another class. The court held that, although not supported by the company, the scheme was in fact between the company and its members since the company would be obliged to register the name of the proposer of the scheme in its register of members in the event of it being accepted. In **Re Alabama New Orleans, Texas and Pacific Junction Rly Co. (1891)**, Fry L.J. said that in deciding whether to sanction the scheme 'The court is bound to ascertain that all the conditions required by the statute have been complied with; it is bound to be satisfied that the proposal was at least so reasonable that an intelligent and honest man, who is a member of that class (of persons affected by it), and acting alone in respect of his interests as such a member, might approve of it'. The courts have no power to confirm a compromise or arrangement which is illegal or *ultra vires*. Thus, for example, the requirements of section 641 still have to be satisfied if there is a reduction of capital.

An arrangement under section 895 may involve debenture holders giving up their security in whole or in part in exchange for shares in the company; and preference shareholders giving up their rights to arrears of dividend, and converting their shares into debentures. A compromise or arrangement under section 895 can be made without the company going into liquidation; but if the company is being wound up, or is about to be wound up voluntarily, compromises or arrangements with creditors may be made under other sections, namely, (a) a scheme of arrangement under section 895 itself, (b) a compromise or arrangement made by the liquidator in exercise of his statutory powers under sections 165 and 167 of the Insolvency Act, (c) voluntary arrangements with creditors under sections 1 and 7 of the Insolvency Act.

External Reconstructions and Amalgamations

External reconstructions and amalgamations (other than take-overs) may be effected where the courts sanction a scheme of arrangement under section 899. Section 900 provides that where a scheme is proposed for the purpose of, or in connection with, the construction of the company or the amalgamation of the company with another company (e.g., members agree to surrender their own shares and have them cancelled in return for shares in another company) and under the scheme the whole or any part of the company's undertaking is to be transferred to another company, the courts may, either by the order sanctioning the scheme or by a subsequent order, make any provision including the transfer of property and liabilities of the transferor company to the transferee company and the dissolution, without winding up, of the transferor company. Where an order made by the courts under section 899 (order sanctioning compromise or arrangement) and under section 900 (order facilitating reconstruction or amalgamation) alters the company's constitution, the order and a copy of the company's amended articles must be delivered to the Registrar unless the order has been incorporated into the articles **(s.901)**. Alternatively, section 110 of the Insolvency Act may be used to allow a company to sell or transfer the whole or any part of its undertaking to another company on the terms that the consideration be divided among members of the transferor company. The consideration may take the form of cash, shares or other interest in the transferee company.

A transaction under section 110 involves three stages: (i) the transferor company has to be put into voluntary winding up; this will invariably be a members voluntary winding up (ii) a special resolution is required to vest the necessary authority upon the liquidator of the transferor company (iii) the whole, or part, of the transferor company's undertaking is sold or transferred to another company (the transferee company). Where the consideration for the transfer or sale is shares in the transferee company, the arrangement for the transfer or sale will normally provide that the liquidator shall give the members notice of the shares for which they are entitled, and the time within which they must apply. Failure to apply within the time stipulated will forfeit a member's right to the shares. In **Postlethwaite v Port Phillips Mining Co. (1889)**, the agreement provided that all the shareholders in the transferor company should apply to the liquidator for the shares in the transferee company within ten days after notice requiring them to apply, and that failure to do so would entitle the liquidator to dispose of any shares not applied for. A shareholder failed to apply for the shares within the stipulated time. The courts refused to give him any relief. Where shares not taken up are sold, the liquidator must give the proceeds to the members for whom they were intended **(Re Lake View Extended Gold Mine Co. (1900))**.

A transfer or sale under section 110 is binding on all the members of the transferor company, whether or not they agree to it **(s.110 (5))**; but a member who did not vote in favour of the special resolution and who informed the liquidator of his dissent in writing within seven days of the resolution being passed may demand either that the special resolution be disregarded, or that his shares be purchased at a price determined by agreement or by arbitration **(s.111)**. This limited protection given to a dissentient member cannot be excluded by a provision in the articles **(Bisgood v Henderson's Transvaal Estates Ltd. (1908)**.

Under a section 110 reconstruction or amalgamation, creditors of the transferor company must be paid by the liquidator in the usual way; and if they feel that they would be prejudiced by the transfer of the company's assets to the transferee company, they can petition for a compulsory winding up or for a supervision order. A special resolution for reconstruction or amalgamation is invalid if within a year, an order is made by the courts for a winding up of the company (unless the courts sanction the resolution). The section 110 procedure can also be used in a creditors voluntary winding up, in which case the liquidator's authority will come from the courts or the liquidation committee rather than from the members by special resolution. In addition, members would not be entitled to any shares in the transferee company unless there were surplus assets.

The main disadvantages of a section 110 amalgamation are that the transferor company has to go into liquidation before the merger can be achieved, and that the liquidator is required to keep cash of an uncertain amount in hand to pay off creditors and any dissenting members. The advantage of transferring a business from one company to another with the same shareholders in the end is that in this way the business may be diverted from a company with a tangled history to a new company with an untarnished image.

A section 895 external reconstruction involves more detailed rules of procedure (e.g., explanatory circulars have to be sent to creditors and members and directors' interests in the scheme must be disclosed, so that all parties are fully aware of what is being suggested). The main advantage of a section 895 amalgamation is the absence of any provision analogous to section 111 of the Insolvency Act for the protection of dissentient members. However, if a so-called scheme is really a sale under section 110, the requirements of section 110 cannot be evaded by calling the sale a 'scheme of arrangement' under section 895 **(Re Anglo Continental Supply Co. (1922))**. Section 895 also dispenses with the need for a company to go into liquidation first before the merger can be effected.

Mergers and Divisions of Public Companies

Where a scheme of arrangement is proposed between a public company and its creditors or members to facilitate a merger or divisions of the company such as where a public company proposes to transfer its entire undertaking, property and liabilities to another existing public company (or two public companies propose to transfer their undertaking etc. to a new company whether or not public) in return for shares in the transferee company to be held by members of the transferor company **(s.904)** or a public company proposes to divide all its undertakings etc. between two or more companies each of which is an existing public company or a new company (whether or not a public company) **(s.918)**, additional requirements to those under section 895 have to be met. The scheme has to be approved by the shareholders of the transferee company (unless the transferee company was set up specifically for the scheme), draft terms of the merger or divisions must be drawn up and adopted by the directors of the companies involved, a copy of the draft terms must be delivered to the Registrar who must publish notice of receipt in the Gazette at least one month before the date of any meeting of shareholders to consider the scheme, and experts reports on the draft terms must be drawn up for each company involved (except for any company formed specifically for the scheme).

Take-overs

A 'take-over' is amalgamation by purchase of shares, and normally occurs where one company makes an offer directly to the shareholders of another company for the purchase of their shares. The offer will state a price at which the shares can be purchased (usually at a slightly higher price than the market price); fix a time within which the offer may be accepted, and make it conditional that the holders of a certain precentage in value (usually 90%) accept the offer before the offeror company can be bound. If the holders of the agreed percentage of the shares accept the offer the offeror company will purchase the shares and may even be able to acquire compulsorily (i.e., squeeze-out) the shares of the remaining minority shareholders who did not accept the bid by invoking the provisions contained in sections 974 – 989 which implement Articles 15 and 16 of the EU Takeover Directive. Even the minority shareholders themselves may force the offeror company to purchase their shares (i.e., minority shareholders have statutory "sell-out" rights under the sections). For sections 974 - 989 to apply two conditions must be satisfied. First, the offer must be made to acquire all the shares (or all of a class of shares) in the offeree company on identical terms, except for shares already owned at the date of the offer by the offeror company and its nominees, subsidiaries or a company over which it has de facto control. The offer can be a joint offer by two or more companies providing they obtain the shares jointly and accept the obligations imposed by the sections **(s.987)**. Secondly, the offer must be approved by the holders of at least 90 per cent in value of the shares concerned within the time specified for accepting the bid. Where the offer relates to different classes of shares each class is the subject of a separate offer so that the holders of 90 per cent of each class of shares must accept for the 90 per cent threshold to be reached. Debentures carrying the right to convert into shares on a take-over constitute a class of their own. Shares acquired by the offeror company and its associates during the course of the offer otherwise than by acceptance of the offer (e.g., through a private or a market purchases) can be counted when determining whether the offeror company has reached the threshold as long as they were acquired for less than the offer price. So too can shares of shareholders who cannot be traced, but here the courts' consent must be obtained **(s.981 (6))**.

Once the two conditions are satisfied, the offeror company may, within three months (six months of the date of the offer in the case of a takeover of private companies) of acquiring the necessary percentage of the shares serve notice on the dissentients of its intention to acquire their shares. If the consideration in the offer bid was a choice of cash or shares in the offeror company, the dissentients must be given six weeks after receiving the compulsory acquisition notice to choose, and must be told what consideration they will receive if they do not choose **(s.981)**. The offeror company is then bound and entitled to acquire the dissentients' shares. It sends the consideration to the offeree company to hold on trust for the dissentients and also an instrument of transfer executed on behalf of the dissentients for registration in its favour **(s.981)**, unless the courts otherwise direct after an application to it by the dissentients **(s.986)**. Any dissentient who wishes to stop the acquisition of his shares can apply to the courts for relief within six weeks after receiving the acquisition notice and the offeror company must meet its own costs unless the application was unnecessary, improper or vexations, or there was unreasonable delay or conduct on the applicant's part **(s.986 (5))**. In general, the courts are reluctant to uphold objections by dissentients, because if an offer is approved by the holders of 90 per cent in value of the relevant shares, then *prima facie* it has to be fair **(Re Grierson, Oldham and Adams Ltd. (1967)**. Only if the sections are being abused, such as where the majority seek to expropriate the minority's interest when there is no genuine take-over **(Re Bugle Press Ltd.)** will the courts uphold the objection.

In addition to the above statutory provisions, public companies also have to comply with rules set out in the City Code on Takeovers and Mergers and administered by the Takeover Panel.

Chapter 20

Corporate Governance

A company limited by shares is an artificial person created by law. It has two organs: a board of directors which is vested with the powers to manage the business; and members who hold investments in the company. Although the members of the company have control over the composition of the board (e.g., they can refuse to reappoint members of the board and can remove them from the board) they do not have any control over the day to day exercise of the board's powers. It is therefore essential that an effective system of governance is in place to fill this gap. The system by which companies are directed and controlled is known as corporate governance.

Poor corporate governance can lead to corporate failure and corporate scandal, as happened with Enron in America and Marconi in Europe. Elements of poor corporate governance are the dominance of an individual or group of individuals at board level, an inactive board, lack of independent scrutiny of the board, lack of supervision by the board of subordinates to whom major tasks have been delegated, inadequate communication with members of the company, the obsession of the board for short-term profitability at any cost, and poor quality accounting systems which can result in misleading information about the company going undetected.

In the United Kingdom, the corporate governance framework operates at two levels – through legal regulations such as the Companies Acts; and through externally recognised codes of best practice such as the Revised Combined Code 2003 on corporate governance of listed companies, responsibility for which rests with the independent Financial Reporting Council. The Revised Combined Code 2003 which originated from the Cadbury and the Hampel Reports, has been updated at regular intervals of which the most recent update was June 2008, and it is mainly principles-based, that is to say, it sets out principles of best practice for good corporate governance. This is in contrast to the system which operates in the United States of America. The US system is rules-based requiring a lot of compliance work by companies to meet detailed rules laid down by US legislation for good corporate governance (see for example, the Sarbanes-Oxley Act 2002 which was passed by the US Congress following the collapse of Enron). In general, the Revised Combined Code deals with three matters:

(a) An effective board. The first main principle of the Code states that the company must have an effective board. The quality and effectiveness of the directors will determine the quality and effectiveness of the board. Thus, directors are required to have entrepreneurial skills and all new and existing directors must be given appropriate training to develop their skills. The composition of the board should consist of a balance between executive directors and non-executive directors (in particular independent non-executive executives) of which half the board, excluding the chairman, must be non-executive directors (unless the company is below the FTSE 350). This is to encourage balanced decisions-making (by non-executive directors contributing and questioning the direction of strategy). The role of the chairman of the board (the chairman is responsible for running the board and for ensuring that board members are supplied in a timely manner with accurate information to make decisions) and the role of the chief executive (the chief executive is responsible for running the company) should not be exercised by the same person. This is to ensure that no individual or group of individuals can dominate decisions taken by the board such as in determining non-executive directors' pay. The board should meet at regular intervals to discharge its duties on matters reserved for its decision (such as on mergers and takeovers, and on the acquisitions and disposals of company's assets); and it should be supplied promptly with enough information of sufficient quality to enable it to discharge its duties. The directors must submit themselves for reappointment regularly and at least every three years

There should be a *nomination committee* consisting of a majority of independent non-executive directors and chaired by the chairman of the board or by a non-executive director. The committee must use formal and transparent procedures to recommend appointments to the board of persons from a diversity of backgrounds. There should be a *remuneration committee* made up entirely of non-executive directors and it must use formal and transparent procedures to fix executives' pay (non-executives' pay is fixed by the board). The criteria for pay should be based on individual performance as well as company performance. The company should be able to terminate executives' service contracts by giving notice of a year or less.

(b) Communications with shareholders. The board must create a genuine dialogue with the shareholders (both private investors and institutional shareholders). The annual report must state how the company operates, and must disclose the identity of the chairman and other officials (e.g., the chairmen of the nomination, remuneration and audit committees), the company's policy on executive directors' pay and the pay of each director. Notice and working papers should be sent to shareholders at least 20 working days before the company's annual general meeting; and the chairmen of the nomination, remuneration and audit committees must attend the meeting to answer shareholders' queries.

(c) Accountability and audit. The board should present a balanced and clear assessment of the company's position and future prospects. There should be proper internal control system in place to safeguard shareholders' investments and the company's assets. There should be an *audit committee* consisting of non-executive directors the majority of whom must be independent, to review the audit and the independence and objectivity of the auditors. For listed companies outside the FTSE 350, the chairman of the board of directors can sit on the audit committee if he is considered independent on appointment.

Compliance with the Combined Code. The listing Rules require all listed companies to state in their annual accounts how they are complying with the Code or explain why they are not complying with the Code. Where a principle of the Code is breached, the board of directors is only required to explain the reason for the breach.

Chapter 21

Examination Technique

Introduction

We know from experience that most students work very hard, but that very many fail to do justice to themselves in the examination. We firmly believe that this is because many do not know what is expected of them, and are not familiar with the technique of writing specific answers in response to specific questions.

General

Students should bear the following general points in mind:

1. Read the instructions in the question paper carefully. Do not assume they are the same as last year's.

2. Read **all** the questions carefully before starting to write the answers. Do not worry if your mind goes completely blank when you first read them. You might even feel that you cannot answer a single question. Re-read the questions, and you will be pleasantly surprised to discover that there are some you can answer. Once you start writing you will recall things you learnt a long time ago, which were stored somewhere in the deep recesses of your memory.

3. Do the easiest question first, but not before you have read the others. To start by answering your easiest question calms your nerves, and gives you all-important confidence.

4. You **must** budget your time and allocate almost equal time to each question. However, it is not unusual to spend a little more time on your first answer. You will find that your writing speed improves with time. You should allow yourself ten to fifteen minutes to spare at the end for a final check-up on all answers.

5. Plan your answers in rough outline before you begin writing. Write down all the points you wish to discuss, and the names of relevant cases. As soon as you think of another point, write it down before it escapes your memory. It is perfectly reasonably to make rough notes on your examination script. You need not be anxious about the examiner noticing your sketch. In our experience, it creates a favourable impression on the examiner; it is a sign of an orderly mind.

6. Do not answer a question any part of which you do not understand.

7. Answer the question asked, and not the one you hoped to find. It is a mistake to assume that the mention of a topic in the question is an invitation for you to write everything you know about that and other related subjects. You must answer the question asked, and no other. Pages of irrelevant material are a waste of your valuable time, earn no marks and may annoy the examiner.

8. Remember that the examiner has prepared a marking scheme allocating marks to different parts of the question. It is essential that you answer all the questions you are required to answer. You must not spend a disproportionate amount of time on any question or part of it. You must answer all parts of the question even if it is in note form. Remember - no answer, no marks!

9. It is in your interest to get the examiner on your side. It should not come as a surprised to you that examination scripts are marked under pressure and in a hurry. Examiners have to meet the deadline set by the examination bodies. Try to help the examiner by writing neatly. Make use of headings and sub-headings and underline important parts of your answer. Examiners hate dull-looking unbroken long essays.

10. We know that it is far easier said than done, but if at all possible check over answers at the end. You may have missed out the important negative which is vital to your answer.

Use of Cases

Do not be over-anxious about the number of cases you will have to encounter and remember. They are intended to illustrate the legal principles stated, and are not meant to be committed to memory in their entirety. As a rule, it is sufficient to cite one case to support a legal point.

Of course, it looks better if you can remember the names of the cases, but it is not essential to remember all of them. You are expected to remember names of only important and well-known cases. If your memory is not good, don't despair. It is sufficient to say 'in a well-known case'; if you know it, it must be well-known. The examiner is interested in finding out whether you understand the principle established in a particular case, and does not expect you to relate the facts of the case in great detail. Resist the temptation to retell the 'story' in your own humorous and irresistible style, even if your tutor does so in class; the examiner has heard it before.

However, you must give sufficient facts to make sure of the decision.

It is permissible to invent hypothetical cases to illustrate your point as long as you make it clear that they are your own invention. Do not pretend that they are facts of some recent fictitious case.

Always underline case names and references to statute.

Answering Problem Questions

This type of question is meant to test your ability to apply basic legal principles to factual situations. Many candidates fail because they do not display their knowledge sufficiently and leave too much unsaid.

You should identify the legal points involved, explain the relevant principles, and apply them to a given set of acts and come to a conclusion. You must come to a conclusion; but it need not be a definite one. It is permissible to suggest alternatives, and make reasonable assumptions about additional facts or other information. Many problems are deliberately set with scope for agreement on both sides.

Remember it is the reasoning that earns marks, not a good guess at the right conclusion. The examiner wishes to see your reasoning set out in the script. You earn good marks even if you reach the 'wrong' conclusion i.e. different from that of the examiner.

If you are asked to advise one of the parties, there is no need to write a personal letter with all the unnecessary details. You should so it in the form of a note or memorandum concluding 'John Smith is advised ...' or 'It is submitted John Smith is likely to succeed...' Clever answers like 'John Smith is advised to consult his solicitors' should be avoided. Extra-legal advice regarding an individual's moral obligations etc.

should be avoided. Answers based on common sense are unlikely to earn many marks. The examiner expects legal advice, supported by legal authority.

Firm grip of the facts is essential. If the facts are complicated, you may draw diagrams (which you can cross out afterwards) to understand the problem exactly. Students must accept facts given. It is not very clever to criticise the examiner by suggesting or implying that the facts are insufficient, or that the question could have been better drafted. Similarly, it is not desirable to sound patronising by saying 'It is a good question' etc.

Chapter 22

Questions and Answers

Question 1

Ben who carried on a small but lucrative business as a motor vehicle repairer with a staff of eight, agreed together will all those employees to combine in a joint venture to carry on the business of second hand car sales and car hire with a company incorporated in the name of 'Rentacar'; each of the nine putting £6,000 into the undertaking. The company received its certificate of incorporation on 1 January. The following events have occurred and you are asked to consider each and advise accordingly.

(a) One month before incorporation, Ben representing himself as managing director of the company, agreed to purchase £1,000 worth of carpets and furniture for the directors' offices. These items were delivered but remain unpaid. The supplier wishes to know who, if anyone, can be made liable to pay.

(5 marks)

(b) The syndicate of nine were advised by the solicitor acting for it in the formation of the company that since it would in the ordinary course of its business, once incorporated, be giving credit advice and introducing those clients to customers who wished to purchase vehicles on credit terms to the various financial houses, there was a legal obligation to obtain a consumer credit licence under the 1974 Consumer

Credit Act from the Office of Fair Trading. Bill, one of the syndidate responsible for having the company's prospectus drafted, considered this obligation to be a mere formality; and he accordingly included in the prospectus a statement that the company had been granted a consumer credit licence. In fact at the time the company had merely made an application for such a licence. The Office of Fair Trading has since refused to grant the requisite licence, objecting to the antecedents of the company's financial director. You are consulted by those who subscribed for the company's shares, in reliance on the prospectus, as to their civil remedies.

(10 marks)

(c) In February Ben sold to the company through a friend (this was to conceal the fact that Ben was the true owner) some arc-welding equipment then several years old, at a price similar to that payable for new equipment. One of those who subscribed for the company's shares wishes to know what, if any, action may be taken.

(5 marks)

Answer
(a) As the company does not yet exist, the contract is not binding upon it **(Re English & Colonial Produce Ltd.)**. So the supplier of office furniture and carpets has no claim against the company itself. **Kelner v Baxter** decided that a company not yet in being, when an agent acts on its behalf, is unable to ratify the act. A valid ratification under agency law required the principal to be in existence when the agent's unauthorised contract is made. However, the agent is personally liable on the contract **(s.51 CA 2006)** unless there is an agreement to the contrary (see **Phonogram Ltd. Lane**). Ben is therefore liable to the supplier.

(b) Victims of untrue statements in a company's prospectus may have civil claims against the company itself, or its promoters, directors or experts.

(i) **As against the company**, from whom the shares were bought, the subscribers can claim rescission of the contract of allotment and also damages. These facts, however, would seen to exclude damages for fraudulent misrepresentation **(Derry v Peek)**, but would embrace a claim under section 2(1) of the Misrepresentation Act 1967, unless the company could establish that it had reasonable grounds to believe that the facts were true up to the time the contracts were made. Even if reasonable grounds were made out, damages could be awarded by the courts under section 2(2) of this Act instead of rescission. Damages may also be awarded under section 90(1) of the Financial Services and Markets Act 2000 for the misstatement.

(ii) **As against the directors and promoters**, liability is primarily dependent upon section 90 (1) of the FSMA 2000, which entitles any person who acquires the shares and suffers a loss as a result of the untrue statement to be compensated. Schedule 10 of the Act provides defences for directors and promoters; but the only one which might help them, but not Bill, is that they had reasonable grounds for believing the statement to be true, and did believe it to be true up to the time the shares were acquired. Liability may also exist against the directors for negligence at common law with **Hedley Byrne** principles, as redefined by **Howard Marine & Dredging Co. Ltd. v Ogden & Son Ltd.**

(c) Both promoters and directors owe fiduciary duties towards their company in relation to dealings with it. Any profit made can be retained only if it is fully disclosed to, and approved by the company. As a promoter, Ben would be liable to account to the company the profits he had made. The company can sue on this basis for the secret profits made **(Gluckstein v Barnes)**. On the facts, it may be that Ben is in breach of his fiduciary duty as a director. There are several aspects of this. A director is liable for secret profits made by reason of opportunities acquired as a result of his position, unless disclosed to and approved by the company **(Regal (Hastings) Ltd. v Gulliver)**. A director, directly or indirectly interested in a contract with the company, is under a duty to declare the nature and extent of his interest as soon as is reasonably practicable **(s.182)**. The disclosure could be at a board meeting, or by notice in writing to all the directors (in accordance with the provisions of section 184), or by general notice (in accordance in accordance with the provisions of section 185). He can declare his interest specifically or generally; but he cannot vote on the contract in which he is interested. Failure to disclose makes the contract voidable at the company's option. Section 190 applies strict safeguards to substantial transactions between the company and its directors, or to a person connected with the directors. Ben's friend may not be qualified as a connected person. He would if he was Ben's business partner. Section 190 applies to transactions which exceed £100,000 or 10 per cent of the company's net assets; but in this last case, it is subject to a statutory minimum value of £2,000. In the event, this may exclude arc-welding equipment. If section 190 is applicable, the transaction is voidable by the company unless first approved in general meeting. Thus Ben and his friend would be liable to account to the company for the profit.

The enforcement of claims rests with the company; and if it decides not to pursue them, a shareholder would be faced with overcoming the difficulties presented by the **Rule in Foss v Harbottle**, and seek to utilise either the fraud on the minority exception or section 122 (1) (g) of the Insolvency Act 1986 or section 994 of the Companies Act 2006 in order to enforce a claim against the defendants.

Question 2

Zed plc has an authorised share capital divided into 50,000 £1 preference shares, all of which are issued, and 100,000 £1 ordinary shares, of which 25,000 remain unissued. The rights attached to the preference shares include the right to have capital repaid before the ordinary shareholders, in the event of the company being wound up. The articles contain no provision for varying class rights, and the effect of any conversion of preference shares will be to cause the preference shareholders to lose their right to prior repayment of capital in a winding up. Zed plc has four directors all appointed last year who, in accordance with a provision in the articles of association which has been expressly incorporated into their service contracts, are entitled to hold office for a fixed period of five years from appointment.

Advise the company how it may implement the following proposals:

    (a) to convert its preference shares to ordinary shares;

                                          (10 marks)

    (b) to allot the 250,000 unissued shares to a merchant bank

                                          (5 marks)

    (c) to give new service contracts to the directors, whereby they will hold office for only three years from their appointment.

(5 marks)

Answer

The rights attached to preference shares are class rights; and they can be varied only if established procedures, principally for the protection of the affected class, are followed. Class rights can exist where there are, as in the question, more than one class of shares. The protection given to class rights are of two types. The first relates to the procedure which is necessary to vary the rights; and the second is for any dissentient shareholder to apply to the courts for the cancellation of the variation.

Class rights can be varied only if the holders of at least seventy five percent in nominal value of the issued shares of the class whose rights are affected (excluding any shares held as treasury shares) give their consent in writing informally, or a special resolution is passed at a separate meeting of the members of the affected class to sanction the variation, in addition to any other requirement necessary for the change **(s. 630)**. The statutory procedure is subject to any other restriction in the articles for variation of class rights **(s.630 (3))**. Therefore, if the articles provide a more onerous regime than the statutory procedure for varying class rights, for example, the articles require a higher percentage than the seventy five percent majority in nominal value of the issued shares of the affected class, the company must comply with the onerous regime. Similarly, if the class rights are stated to be entrenched rights, they cannot be varied by using the statutory procedure under section 630.

In the event of the appropriate procedure being followed, dissentient preference shareholders holding at least 15 per cent of the affected shares can apply to the courts within 21 days after the giving of the consent or the passing of the resolution to have the variation cancelled **(s.633)**. The courts may cancel the variation if they are satisfied that the variation would unfairly prejudice the preference shareholders. If the courts are not so satisfied they must confirm the variation and may make any ancillary order such as that the dissentients' shares should be purchased by the company. The company must send a copy of the court order to Companies Registry within 15 days.

(b) There are two basic problems to overcome before the 25,000 ordinary shares can be allotted to the merchant bank. First, Directors do not have implied powers to issue shares. They can allot shares only if they are authorised by the articles or if the members give them authority by ordinary resolution **(s. 551)**. They may be given general authority to issue shares or authority for a specific issue only. The authority has to state the maximum amount of shares that can be issued under it and the date when the authority is to expire, which must not be more than five years or such shorter time as the articles may provide without the authority being renewed. Secondly, since the shares which the directors propose to issue are 'equity securities', there is a statutory duty to offer the shares first to existing ordinary shareholders in proportion to their current holding **(s.561)**. This right of first refusal is known as a pre-emption right and it can be waived only by special resolution **(s.567)**.

Accordingly, it will be necessary for Zed plc to summon an extraordinary general meeting of its shareholders entitled to vote, to pass the necessary resolutions. Only the ordinary shareholders can vote on the special resolution to waive their statutory pre-emption rights; the preference shareholder can vote with the ordinary shareholders to grant authority to directors (where this is necessary to issue new shares), unless the preference shares carried restricted voting rights. Failure to follow the proper procedure will not invalidate the issue of the shares to the merchant bank but criminal liability **(s.579)** and civil liability **(s.563)** can be incurred by the company and its directors.

(c) Zed plc will have to summon a shareholders meeting to alter its article to reduce the period during which the directors may hold office. A special resolution is required to effect the change **(s.21)**. As the alteration will be in breach of the directors' service contracts Zed plc will be liable in damages to those directors **(Shindler v Norther Raincoat Co. Ltd.)**; but it cannot be prevented from altering its articles **(Punt v Symons Co. Ltd)**. A copy of the amended articles must be filed at Companies Registry.

Question 3

(a) A company's articles may empower the directors to issue shares to such persons on such terms and conditions as they may think fit.
What limitations have the courts placed on the exercise of such a power?

(10 marks)

(b) The share capital of Mark Ltd. was £2,000, all in ordinary shares held as follows:

Gwen	1,080 £1 shares
Arthur	900 £1 shares
Four other members	5 £1 shares each

Gwen and the four other members are the directors of Mark Ltd. Arthur was formerly a director, but was removed from office following a series of boardroom disputes. The articles provide that the company may from time to time by ordinary resolution increase the share capital by such sums as the resolution shall fix. A further provision in the articles gives each member a right of pre-emption, in proportion to his shareholding, if another member should die or wish to dispose of his shares.

The directors propose to put to Mark Ltd., at a properly called extraordinary general meeting, a resolution to increase the ordinary share capital to £3,750. The resolution will instruct the directors to offer 200 shares to each of those directors (the 'four other members' above) who have only a small holding in the company; and to allocate the remaining 950 shares to be held on trust for Mark Ltd.'s long-service employees. The purpose of the resolution is claimed to be to increase the involvement of the directors and employees in the company's fortunes.

Arthur claims that the effect of the resolution will be:

(i) to reduce the income he will receive from his shares.

(ii) to deprive him of the opportunity through his right of pre-emption, to acquire control of Mark Ltd. should Gwen die or wish to withdraw from the company.

(iii) to take away his veto over alterations to the company's articles.

Advise Arthur of any grounds on which he may seek to prevent the proposed increase in Mark Ltd.'s share capital.

(10 marks)

Answer

(a) Section 549 of the Companies Act 2006 provides that the directors may not allot shares unless they obtain prior consent from the shareholders to do so. Consent could be given either by an express provision in the company's articles or by ordinary resolution passed in a general meeting. The Act goes on to provide that the directors may be authorised to allot for a particular issue or generally, and that the authority may be granted conditionally or unconditionally. If the authority is given by resolution it must state the maximum amount of shares that can be allotted, and the date on which the authority to issue is to expire. The authority can exist only for five years at a time, while it can be renewed for a further five years by shareholders in general meeting. Although a breach of this provision is a criminal offence, the allottee's title to the shares is not at risk.

Directors also have a duty to act within their powers, and to exercise their powers for the purpose for which they were conferred **(s.171)**. The power to issue shares is exercised primarily to raise capital. Thus, an allotment which satisfies the procedural requirement may still be overruled on the ground that it was exercised for a collateral purpose. English cases where the directors' purpose had been questioned have concerned shares issued to prevent take-over by maintaining joint support in shareholder meetings. Such cases have gone against the directors, however genuine their belief that the take-over would be bad for the company, on the ground that the shares were issued for an improper purpose **(Hogg v Cramphorn, Bamford v Bamford)**. In both **Hogg v Cramphorn** and **Howard Smith Ltd. v Ampol Petroleum Ltd.**, the judges expressed the view that shares might be issued for some proper purpose other than to raise capital; but in the last case the issue was adjudged improper ever though, arguably, it was to secure working capital. It is to be noted that, as in the **Bamford** case, an improper issue can be validated by the vote of disinterested shareholders in general meeting.

(b) This problem is concerned with the position of a minority shareholder threatened with a substantial reduction in the possible 'enjoyment' of his shareholding rights by the proposed resolutions of the directors. The cases on both variation of class rights and alteration of the articles, such as **White v Bristol Aeroplane Co.**, **Sidebottom v Kershaw Leese &Co.**, and **Greenhalgh v Arderne Cinemas Ltd.**, make it clear that a shareholder cannot assume that there will be no alteration in the constitution of the company affecting his position as a shareholder. Whether he is seeking to utilise section 633 of the Companies Act to safeguard his interest in the shares or to invalidate a change in the articles, he must show that his rights and position as a shareholder are peculiarly under attack. A reduction in the enjoyment of those rights, failure to show that the majority are being given an advantage of which he as a minority is being deprived, will result only in defeat.

In the problem, Arthur appears to be peculiarly exposed to consequences which will affect no other member; and as **Clemens v Clemens Bros. Ltd.** suggests, the courts would subject the exercise of the directors' legal rights to equitable considerations and would invalidate their proposal by granting Arthur an injunction restraining the increase in capital, on the ground that the directors are not exercising their powers to issue shares bona fide in the interest of the company **(s.171)** knowing that their actions will have the effect of defeating Arthur's expectations and removing his power of veto in relation to the alterations in the articles.

Question 4

The articles of association of Clam Ltd. provide that:

(a) any prospective transferor of shares must first offer them to the other shareholders at a price to be fixed by the auditor. If no other shareholder accepts the offer within 28 days, he may sell them to whom he wishes.

(b) a shareholder is not entitled to appoint a proxy at any general meeting of the company, but must attend and vote in person.

Victor sold his shares in Clam Ltd. to Peter, who is not a member of the company, without first offering them to the other shareholders. He handed Peter a duly executed transfer of the shares form and the share certificate, but Peter took no steps to have himself registered as a member. Victor gave Peter an irrevocable proxy to attend and vote on his behalf at all general meetings of the company. The company has just declared a dividend on the shares.

(a) Advise Victor as to his rights in respect of the shares and the dividend and whether he is obliged to offer his shares to the other members.

(14 marks)

(b) Advise Peter whether he is entitled to attend, speak and vote at general meetings of Clan Ltd.

(6 marks)

(ACCA)

Answer

(a) Every member has a right to transfer his shares to whom he likes subject to any restriction imposed by the articles **(Weston's Case)** or unless the company is in insolvent liquidation **(s.127 IA)**. Where there is a contract to transfer the shares the vendor's duty is to hand over a valid instrument of transfer together with the share certificate, and to do nothing to hinder the purchaser's registration. There is no implied guarantee of registration **(London Founders' Assoc. Ltd. v Clarke)**. The transfer is effective only when it is registered by the company **(Powell v London Bank)**. Until registration, the transferee has a mere equitable interest in the shares transferred to him.

The transfer by Victor of his shares to Peter is complicated by the pre-emption clause in Clam's articles. By section 33, the articles constitute a statutory contract between each member and the company and the members among themselves. As part of this contract, Clam Ltd. or the other members may enforce the pre-emption clause against Victor if the transfer is in breach of the clause. No member can evade his obligation to make an offer of his shares to other members as required by the articles, by arranging for the sale of his shares to an outsider with the intention that the latter will not apply for registration **(Lyle and Scott v Scott's Trustees)**.

As Victor is still in the register of members the legal ownership in the shares still rests in him but he becomes trustee of the shares until the transfer is set aside. Notice of such trust cannot be entered in the register **(s.126)**; so Clam Ltd. will continue to treat Victor as the beneficial owner of the shares. Victor is entitled to receive notice of company meetings, and dividends declared on the shares; but he will have to hold them for Peter.

(b) Section 324 gives every member of a company with a share capital, if he is entitled to vote at a company meeting, a right to appoint an agent called a proxy to attend and vote for him. Such a person need not be a member of the company. This statutory right cannot be taken away by any contrary provision in the articles. Moreover every notice of a meeting must indicate that proxies can be appointed, and failure to do this will result in a fine on the officers in default although the irregularity will not invalidate the meeting **(s.325)**. A proxy can exercise all rights the member can exercise at the meeting such as to speak and vote at the meeting of the company.

The clause in the articles of Clam Ltd. prohibiting the appointment of proxies is therefore invalid. Peter as a proxy for Victor is entitled to attend and speak at the general meeting of Clam Ltd. Peter has the same right as Victor to demand a card vote; but usually, the articles require at least two persons to do so.

Question 5

Pipeweld Ltd. created a floating charge on its undertaking and assets 12 April to secure a loan of £90,000 from Lootend plc. This charge, which was duly registered, contained a clause prohibiting Pipeweld from creating any further charges ranking in priority to or *pari passu* with it. On 10 June Pipeweld Ltd. created a first fixed charge over its office premises in favour of the Crassey Banking Company. This charge also was duly registered. On 1 September Pipeweld purchased a workshop and stores building for £38,000. This building was purchased subject to an existing fixed charge in the sum of £20,000 in favour of Propser Bank, nut this charge was never registered by Pipeweld Ltd. In order to satisfy the pressing demands for payment from Influx Ltd., a major trade creditor, Pipeweld Ltd. on 19 November created a first floating charge over its book debts, bearing interest at 15% in the sum of £25,000. This was the amount then currently payable to Influx for goods already supplied. This charge too was duly registered.

The financial position of Pipeweld Ltd. deteriorated and it went into liquidation on 1 October the following year.

Advise the liquidator on the priorities to be accorded to the above charges.   **(ACCA)**

Answer

The basic rule as to priorities between secured creditors is that a legal charge takes priority over an equitable charge, whether fixed or floating **(English & Scottish Mercantile Investment Co. v Bruton (1892))**. An equitable fixed charge takes priority over a floating charge, even if created at a later date **(Re Castell & Brown Ltd. (1898))**. Floating charges rank according to the order in which they were created except that a later floating charge on a particular class of assets takes priority over an earlier general floating charge **(Re Automatic Bottlemakers (1926)**.

The principles outlined above, however, do not apply to a charge which is void for non-registration under section 860 of the Companies Act. This section, together with section 870, requires a registrable charge created by a company on its own assets to be registered at Companies Registry within 21 days of its creation otherwise it is void against the liquidator and subsequent creditors **(s.874)**.

Lootend plc will have priority over Grassey Banking Company only if Grassey had knowledge of the restriction on future charges before Grassey's fixed charge was created. It is common practice to register details of the restriction at the Registry so that potential creditors who make a search at the Registry before lending money to the company are deemed to have notice of the restriction even if they overlook the charge. But mere registration of the restriction is not enough to give them notice **(Wilson v Kelland (1919))**. So unless Lootend can prove knowledge by Grassey, Grassey's fixed charge will take priority.

Prosper Bank's charge will also take priority over Lootend's floating charge. In **Re Connolly Bros. Ltd. (1912)**, it was decided that where a company acquires land and at the same time creates a mortgage over the land in favour of the vendors or a third party, this charge will have priority over an earlier floating charge imposing restrictions on future charges. Lootlend may seek to invalidate Prosper Bank's charge on the ground of non-registration. However, although section 862 requires a company which acquires property already subject to an existing charge to register the charge within 21 days after the date on which the acquisition is completed, unlike section 874, non-compliance only results in a fine on the company and its directors in default. The charge is not rendered void against the liquidator and creditors **(Capital Finance Ltd. v Stokes (1969))** So, Lootlend's chance of success looks slim.

The floating charge given to Influx Ltd. is complicated by a number of factors. It is said to be a first floating charge but there is already an existing floating charge on the assets. In **Re Automatic Bottle Makers Ltd. (1926)**, it was stated that a general floating charge on the company's undertaking is postponed to a later floating charge on a particular class of assets. On this principle Influx's charge will prevail over Lootlends's charge. However as Influx's charge was created within one year before the commencement of insolvent liquidation proceedings against Pipeweld Ltd. the charge will be invalidated under section 245 of the Insolvency Act 1986 unless Influx proves that Pipeweld Ltd. was solvent on 19 November and ran into financial difficulties after that date.

Question 6: Linda and Susan have run a partnership business for several years. The major activity of the firm has been to operate a wine bar and restaurant. Business has been very good and the partners now wish to extend their business interests by acquiring new premises and opening a leisure complex. They have decided to form a private limited company with themselves as major shareholders and sole directors of the company. Linda and Susan seek your advice upon the issues listed below.

(a) The new company requires a long-term injection beyond the capital which Linda and Susan can subscribe.
What methods may the company use to invite investment and what types of capital may the company raise?

(b) The company is keen to minimise its expenditure in the early years of trading by keeping fixed, long-term, assets to the minimum.
What are the advantages and disadvantages for the company in raising mush of its capital requirement by debentures, particularly those secured by way of a floating charge?

(c) Assume that the company decides to issue ordinary shares to investors.
Discuss the position of minority shareholders and their power to dictate corporate policy to Linda and Susan or to challenge their right to be directors.

(d) Assume the business fails and the company proceeds into an insolvent liquidation.
What personal liability might Linda and Susan incur?

(e) What is the position if Linda or Susan should, during the lifetime of the company, decide to leave the business?
How might the departing shareholder realise her investment in the company?

(CIMA)

Answer: **(a)** As the company is a private company it is restricted in the ways in which it can raise capital. It cannot apply for a stock exchange listing of its shares or debentures or advertise such securities for sale **(s.170 Financial Services and Markets Act 2000).** However, the Secretary of State may exempt any advertisement offering securities if it is of a private nature (e.g., aimed at a few friends or a bank) or if it is aimed primarily at experts (e.g., those involved in the Eurobond market).

Investors may be invited to provide either share or loan capital. The former is raised by an issue of shares. The latter is raised by the issue of debentures. Both shares and debentures are long-term investments in the company but shares, unless issued as redeemable, are only realised when the company goes into solvent liquidation or on their resale. The provision of share capital by an investor makes him a member of the company and, unless such capital carries restricted voting rights, he has a say in the democratic process of the company. Loan capital makes the holder a creditor of the company and is repayable regardless of the company's assets so that failure to repay may result in foreclosure and resale of those assets.

 (b) A debenture is a document acknowledging a debt and it may be secured by a charge over property. A legal charge of land by a company is a debenture (**Kinghtbridge Estates Trust Ltd. v Byrne (1940)**).

A debenture is a safer investment than shares since interest is payable out of capital; and, if the company defaults with its payments, the investor has a right to appoint a receiver or liquidator. However, since the loan capital is not treated in law as part of the company's share capital, a debenture-holder is not a shareholder and so has no say in the management of the company. Debentures are usually secured by a floating charge which is a charge on general (as opposed to specific) assets which change from time to time.

The main advantage of issuing debentures secured by a floating charge is that the company can use the assets charged until the charge crystallises. As debentures carry a fixed rate of interest the company can calculate its liability early. The company is also able to avoid shareholders' pressure for a good dividend by issuing debentures rather than shares. Debenture interest is a charge on income for tax purposes, but dividend is not.

The main disadvantages of debentures are that as interest is payable regardless of the company's financial position the company is constantly under threat of receivership or liquidation. Also a floating charge may not be a good security for investors if the company's future prospects seem uncertain. So a higher level of interest may be required to attract investors.

(c) The rights attached to shares are usually found in the articles. Such rights include the right to vote, right to a dividend when one is declared, right to a return of capital if the company goes into liquidation. These rights are enforced by a shareholder against the company and against other shareholders in the same company by virtue of section 33 of the Companies Act 2006. But there are also membership obligations including the obligation to be bound by majority decisions taken at properly constituted members' meetings. The majority have the right to formulate company policy, and to remove the directors by ordinary resolution **(s.168)**, at such meetings. Only if the majority should act fraudulently can the minority challenge their act. Minority protection exists at common law in an action for fraud on the minority and under various statutory provisions (e.g., section 994 for unfair conduct prejudicial to members, 633 for variation of class rights; and section 122(g) of the Insolvency Act 1986 for oppression justifying a compulsory winding up of the company).

As long as Linda and Susan retain their controlling interest in the company the minority cannot influence company policy or remove them as directors.

(d) The liability of a member of a company limited by shares is limited to the amount unpaid on his shares in a winding up. So, as long as the shares held by Linda and Susan are fully paid up they do not have to contribute to the assets, unless they gave personal guarantees. Nevertheless, if it appears to the courts that the company's business was being carried on to defraud its creditors, the courts may make any person trading on behalf of the company liable for any or all of its debts **(s.213 IA)**. Linda and Susan may be liable on this basis. The courts also have power to make directors of the company liable for the company's debts if such officers were engaged in wrongful trading **(s.214 IA)**. To be liable for wrongful trading, it must be proved that the directors could have foreseen insolvent liquidation of their company and took no reasonable steps to minimise the company's liability (such as by ceasing to trade). Linda and Susan can also be liable on this basis.

(e) It is standard practice for a private company to include a pre-emption clause in its articles. Such a clause gives members a ready-made market for their shares when they wish to leave the company. This is particularly important for members since the shares of a private company cannot be offered to the public at large. Alternatively, the company itself may purchase the shares under section 709 out of capital provided that its articles authorise it and the directors make a statutory statement of solvency backed by an auditor's report **(s.713)**. Another solution is for the company to give financial assistance for the purchase of the shares.

Question 7: You are the financial adviser of Apeel plc. The board of directors is concerned at the low profits achieved in the current trading period, which will substantially affect the dividend received by shareholders. The board seeks your advice as to whether other funds might be utilised to give shareholders a satisfactory dividend return and how preference shareholders could be bought out, to achieve a uniform capital structure in future years. Write a report for the board, concentrating on the following specific issues:

(a) statutory restrictions upon the company's freedom to distribute funds as dividends;

(b) the feasibility of distributing to shareholders any surplus arising from a revaluation of the company's land and buildings;

(c) the possibility of using funds in the company's share premium account for the shareholders' benefit;

(d) the methods available to the company to carry out a restructuring of capital to repay the preference shareholders.

Answer: **(a)** Dividends can be declared only out of profits available for distribution **(s.830)**. 'Profits' means the amount by which the company's realised profits exceed its accumulated realised losses. Any provision in the accounts for depreciation or renewal of assets will be treated as a realised loss. A public company is further restricted from making a distribution if the effect would be to reduce the company's net assets to less than the aggregate of its called up capital and its undistributable reserves **(s.831).** Thus a public company will have to make good both its accumulated realised and unrealised losses.

Apeel plc will have to comply with the above provisions before it can distribute any of its funds by way of dividend.

(b) Since unrealised profits are treated as a statutory reserve, they cannot be distributed or applied in paying up debentures or amounts payable on issued shares; but if the articles permit it, fully paid bonus shares may be issued to members out of the revaluation reserve. Only if the surplus arising from the revaluation of Apeel's land and buildings is realised could it be distributed to members.

(c) The share premium account is treated as a capital account and is subject to the statutory rules regarding the reduction of capital **(s.641).** However, this account may be used to write off discounts and expenses on shares of the same issue and to pay for bonus shares issued to members **(s.610).**

(d) Section 641 allows a company to redeem its shares with the courts' consent; and section 684 allows it to do the same, but without resort to the courts, as long as certain conditions are satisfied. Under section 684 the shares must be issued as redeemable shares, there must be in existence non-redeemable shares, the shares must be fully paid up before they can be redeemed and the redemption must be effected on the terms set out in the articles. If the shares were not issued as redeemable, then they can be redeemed under section 690 but here the members' consent must be obtained. Such consent is given by resolution and it may be an ordinary resolution (for a market purchase) or a special resolution (for an off-market purchase).

A redemption of shares under sections 684 or 690 must be financed out of distributable profits or the proceeds of a fresh issue of replacement shares; and there are provisions to ensure that the capital of the company remains intact. A redemption of shares under section 641 will invariably result in a reduction of issued capital unless financed from the proceeds of replacement shares.

Question 8. Wonka's Chocolates plc was a company formed in 1962 by Mr. Wonka. The company's articles of association are in the form of Table A. Mr. Wonka still holds 5% of the company's 50,000 £1 shares, and his brother Billy holds a further 5%. The remainder are equally divided between Hazel, Toffo and Caramella who are also the company's directors.

The directors wished to change the company's name quickly in time for a new advertising campaign. Accordingly on 1 November they sent out notices calling an extraordinary general meeting of the company for 10 November the same year. The notice specified that the meeting would 'consider and, if it thought fit, pass with or without modification a special resolution to change the company's name'. This notice was sent to each of the shareholders, but because the directors had failed to keep a record of a letter from Billy advising the company of his change of address, he never received his copy of the notice.

On 10 November the directors and Mr. Wonka duly attended the meeting. The directors voted in favour of a resolution agreeing to the calling of the meeting with short notice, but Mr. Wonka voted against it. The directors then proposed a special resolution altering the name of the company to Chewy

Chocolate plc. Mr. Wonka then proposed an amendment to that resolution under which the company's new name would be Wonka's Chewy Chocolate plc. Hazel, who was the chairman of the meeting, ruled the amendment out of order, and the meeting then voted on the original resolution. The directors voted for it, but Mr. Wonka against. Hazel then declared the resolution passed by the necessary three-quarters majority.

Mr. Wonka and Billy now wish to challenge this alteration of the company's name.

Advise them.

(ACCA)

Answer

A company has power to change its name by special resolution **(s.77)**. A special resolution is one passed by a three quarters majority of the company's shareholders voting in person or by proxy at a general meeting, specifying the intention to propose the resolution as a special resolution **(s.283)**. To effect the change quickly the directors may summon an extraordinary general meeting rather than wait for the annual general meeting to act. Section 302 gives directors power to convene an extraordinary general meeting whenever they think fit.

While the directors of Wonka Chocolate plc have taken the course of action outlined above to expedite the change of name, the procedure followed to effect the change is flawed.

(a) **Advice to Billy**. Billy may seek to have the meeting and the resolution invalidated on the ground that he did not receive notice of the meeting. Section 310 provides that, subject to any contrary provision in the articles, every shareholder is required to be given notice of any general meeting. As **Young v Ladies Imperial Club (1920)** shows failure to provide notice even to a member who has no intention of attending the meeting will invalidate any resolution passed at the meeting. To mitigate the harshness of this rule section 313 states that accidental omission to give notice or the non-receipt of notice by, any person entitled to notice will not invalidate the meeting. Whether the failure by the directors to record Billy's letter amounts to accidental omission within section 313 is an arguable point. In **Re West Canadian Collieies Ltd. (1962)**, the removal of address plates from an envelope addressing machine which caused a few members not to receive notice of the company's meeting was held to be an accidental omission within an article like section 313. But in **Musslewhite v C.H. Musslewhite & Son Ltd. (1962)**, the omission to serve notice on some members because of a mistaken belief by the directors that they were not entitled to notice was held to be outside the scope of such an article.

(b) **Advice to Mr. Wonka**. Mr. Wonka may seek to have the meeting and the resolution invalidated on several grounds. First, he may argue that the notice for calling the meeting was too short. Normally, 14 days notice is required for an extraordinary general meeting. Shorter notice is only permissible if the holders of not less than 95% in nominal value of the voting shares agree to such notice. As the three directors have only 90% shareholding, they cannot validate the short notice. Secondly, as the notice did not give either the text or entire substance of the resolution, as is required for special resolutions (see **Re Moorgate Mercantile Holdings Ltd. (1980)**), the notice is also deficient in this respect. In **McConnell v E. Prill & Co. Ltd. (1916)**, a notice of a resolution 'to increase capital of the company' was declared invalid because it did not specify the amount of the increase.

Likewise in the present case, the notice that the company's name is to be changed is insufficient as the new name is not specified. Thirdly, Mr. Wonka can seek to render the special resolution void on the ground of the chairman's refusal to put his amendment to the vote **(Henderson v Bank of Australia (1890)**. Normally, notice of an amendment must be given unless the amendment does not cause a substantial change in the resolution. A change is substantial if it would cause a reasonable shareholder who had decided not to attend the meeting after receiving notice of the resolution, to change his mind and attend the meeting once he knew of the amendment. It may be that the reintroduction of the work "Wonka" in the name is a substantial change. Nevertheless, because the notice contains the phrase 'with or without modification' this will cover the possibility of an on-the-spot amendment. So Mr. Wonka can succeed also on this ground.

As the shareholders on the board together hold a majority of the shares in the company, Billy and Mr. Wonka, as minority shareholders, will have to overcome the procedural obstacle under the rule in **Foss v Harbottle** if they wish to invalidate the meeting and the resolution on the grounds specified. This may not be difficult. Billy may argue that his personal right as a shareholder to receive notice and attend the meeting has been infringed **(Pender v Lushington (1877))**. Mr. Wonka can circumvent the rule on the ground that the irregularities in the notice can be cured only by special resolution (see **Baillie v Oriental Telephone Co. (1915))**.

Question 9

The board of directors of Bubble Ltd. consists of three directors, only one of whom works full time for the company. They have decided that the company should enter into a contract of service with the full time working director for a term not less than five years, at a salary of £50,000 per annum, together with provisions for the reimbursement by the company of his travelling and other expenses. You have been asked to drawn up the agreement and to advise on the procedure necessary.

(a) What inquiries would you make in order to ensure that the contracts will be binding upon the company and the director, and what procedure would you advise the directors to follow in making the contract?

(b) What, if any, provisions are there in the Companies Act with regard to members' rights to inspect directors' contracts of service?

(c) Does the existence of a contract of service prevent the company from removing a director from office before the expiration of the term of the contract? If not, what provisions are there in the Companies Act with regard to payment of compensation?

Answer
(a) Directors are not servants of a company, so they have no claim to remuneration unless the articles provide therefor **(Hutton v West Cork Rly. Co. (1883))**. Nor can they appoint one of their numbers to a salaried position, unless authorised to do so by the articles. Article 4 of draft default model articles for both private and public companies makes it possible for the board of directors to appoint individual directors to executive positions in the company; and article 18 (private companies) and article 22 (public companies) permit the board to fix the remuneration of the directors for their service; though the directors are not allowed to have service contracts for more than two years without

shareholders' approval **(s.188)**. Therefore the articles of Bubbles Ltd. will have to be examined to see if they contain the necessary authority to allow the board to give a service contract to its full time director, and to provide him with a salary. If there is power in the articles, then a properly convened board meeting is required to carry out the transaction. The full time director may attend the meeting, but he must make a full disclosure of his interest and should not vote **(s.177)**. Since the service contract is likely to exceed two years, the agreement also has to be approved by the shareholders in general meeting before it can bind the company **(s.188)**.

The articles should also authorise the payment of travelling and other expenses. Statutory default articles (art.19 private companies) require the company to meet reasonable expenses (e.g., travelling and hotel expenses) properly incurred by directors in connection with the business of the company.

(b) Section 228 requires every company to keep copies of its director's service contracts at its registered office or at the place where its register of members is kept. It must also make available such contracts for inspection by its members without charge during business hours for at least two hours a day. In addition, where members' approval is required before service contracts are given to directors, the members must be allowed to inspect a written memorandum of the proposed contracts for at least 15 days prior to the date of the members' meeting.

(c) Section 168 gives members the ultimate control over the directors. The section allows the members to remove the directors from office at any time by ordinary resolution. Section 168 overrides any contract of service; but the directors' right to damages for breach of contract is not affected.

Non-contractual payment of compensation (including benefits otherwise than in cash) to directors for loss of office (e.g., when they cease to be directors on retirement or on removal from any office or employment in connection with the management of the company or any of its subsidiaries) is lawful only if it is approved by the members in general meeting, after proper disclosure has been made **(s.217)**. Small payments not exceeding £200 for loss of office do not require members' approval. Contractual payments made to directors for prematurely terminating their service contracts do not require the approval of a general meeting **(Taupo Totara Timber Co. v Rowe (1977))** but such payments must be disclosed to the general meeting in a note to the accounts laid before the meeting **(s.412)**.

Question 10

On 1 January this year the board of Webb Boutique Ltd. at a meeting made a declaration of solvency and this was filed at Companies Registry the next day. On 30 January a general meeting of the company, duly convened for the purpose, passed a special resolution winding up the company and appointed you as liquidator.

Your examination of the company's records discloses the following:

(a) £45,000 owing to the Uni Bank and secured by a floating charge on the assets created on 1 February last year, when the company's overdraft was £35,000. Since then £20,000 has been paid into the account in May, and items debited to the account totaled £30,000.

(b) £15,000 lent by Trupti Bartel and secured by a floating charge on the company's leasehold property last March, for payment of employees' wages at the rate of £3,000 per month for the last five months. Interest was set at 18 per cent per year.

(c) £10,000 lent by Yasmin, a director, on 1 October last year, and secured by a first fixed charge on the company's warehouse. £5,000 of the loan was used to reduce the company's overdraft at the Addington Loan Society, which was guaranteed by Yasmin; and the other £5,000 paid to Yasmin for arrears of her director's salary.

(d) £2,500 by way of default judgement suffered by the company at the suit of Lorraine during December last, and the sheriff has taken possession of the company's van in execution.

Assuming that liquidation expenses are £5,000, state any action that is called for on your part as liquidator of the company on the facts given. Your estimate of the assets is that the general body of creditors will be paid in full only with difficulty.

Answer
The company's life is in the process of being terminated by a members' voluntary winding up. Since the assets are insufficient to meeting the liabilities, it is my duty as liquidator to summon a creditors' meeting within 28 days to take charge of the winding up **(s.95 IA)**. Assuming that my appointment is confirmed by the meeting, I will have to examine the various claims to swell the assets and then to apply the proceeds for the payment of the debts according to the Insolvency Rules 1986.

My observation of the claims are as follows:

(a) The floating charge which secures the loan of £45,000 from the Uni Bank is caught by section 245 which invalidates any floating charge created within 12 months before commencement of liquidation when the company was insolvent unless the charge was created to secure a loan of new money. Only £30,000 of the loan is 'new money' to support the charge given to the Uni Bank. The bank is expected to take advantage of the rule in **Clayton's Case** to use the £20,000 paid into its running account by the company for the reduction of the overdraft of £35,000 to £15,000. This is quite proper under section 245 (see **Re Yeovil Glove Co. (1965)**). However if the £20,000 was paid into the bank within six months before the commencement of winding up, it could be recovered as a fraudulent preference under section 239 **(Re Matthews Ltd. (1982))**. Once the assets secured by the floating charge are sold, a proportion of the net realisation proceeds of sale must be set aside for the benefit of the unsecured creditors. This proportion is 50% of the first £10,000 and 20% of the balance (subject to a maximum limit of £600,000).

(b) The floating charge given to Trupti Bartel for the loan of £15,000 is not invalid under section 245 because consideration was given for the charge. However since the money was used partly to pay off a preferential debt (i.e. employees' wages for four months) and as preferential debts rank before floating charges, it is expected that Trupti Bartel will claim £12,000 as preferred and £3,000 with interest at the agreed rate as secured by the floating charge.

(c) The fixed charge given to Yasmin as security for a loan of £10,000 is void as a fraudulent preference **(s.239)**, since the loan was use partly to relieve her of the guarantee of the company's overdraft and partly for her salary as a director. In **Re Destone Fabrics Ltd. (1914)** where the facts were similar, the courts set aside a charge since the object of the loan was to benefit certain creditors and not the company.

(d) Since the execution on the company's van is incomplete, it may be set aside under section 183. The van may be recovered from the sheriff and Lorraine will be treated as an ordinary creditor for £2,500.

.

Question 11

(a) Examine, with examples from decided cases, two of the ways in which minority shareholders can seek relief from oppression by the majority.

(10 marks)

(b) Omnium Ltd. acts as agent for the holiday lettting of country homes. The shares are held by three directors: Lopez, Parker and Finn; and by Wharton, a minority shareholder who is not a director.

Lopez meets Lord Palliser, a landowner, in order to tell him about the services provided by Omnium Ltd. Palliser refuses to deal with Omnium Ltd because he doubts the business sense of Parker and Finn. Palliser however hears very good reports about Lopez, who he asks to act privately as consultant in the management of Palliser's estates. Part of this work will be to find for commission, suitable tenants for three large houses on the estates. Lopez agrees and starts to act for Palliser within a week. Lopez does not tell his fellow directors about the agreement with Palliser, but some months later, it becomes public knowledge. Parker and Finn are inclined to treat the whole matter lightly, and claim that in any case it will be good for Omnium's reputation even if the company dreives no material benefit from it. Wharton consides that honourable dealing would do much more for Omnium's reputation; he wishes the company to claim the commission Lopez earns on Palluser's holiday lettings.

Advise Wharton on the remedies he might seek in order to secure Lopez's commission for Omnium Ltd., and assess his chances of success.

(10 marks)
(ACCA)

Answer

(a) According to the rule in **Foss v Harbottle**, the wishes of the majority prevail even where a corporate irregularity is in issue, as long as it can be approved by the company acting in general meeting. The mere fact that the minority has been outvoted, and the company adopted policies it does not agree with, gives it no ground for complaint. However, in certain circumstances, the minority can initiate legal action either on the ground that **Foss v Harbottle** does not apply, or that a wrong has been inflicted on the company and requires redress. In addition, company legislation has provided safeguards for the minority of which the most well-known are, perhaps section 122(1)(g) of the Insolvency Act 1986 and section 994 of the Companies Act 2006.

On the face of it, perhaps the most appropriate exception is a statutory derivative action under the Companies Act 2006. Here, a minority shareholder is allowed to sue on the company's behalf for a wrong done by the directors to the company. This is possible if the directors have injured the company by expropriating its assets or causing other loss to the company as a result of their negligence and because they are in control of the company, thus preventing it from taking action. In **Daniels v Daniels (1978)**, the minority shareholder successfully argued that the defendant directors (man and wife) and majority shareholders had caused the company loss, by committing it to sell a house to the wife for £45,000. The house was then resold by the wife for £120,00 shortly after she purchased it from the company. A derivative action is not very popular because the minority shareholder must obtain the courts' permission to sue on behalf of the company. In effect, this means that he has to satisfy certain statutory requirements as a preliminary issue before the courts would hear the substantial complaint. Such requirements include establishing that the wrong involved a breach of duty by the directors, the action is not brought for an ulterior motive (**Barrett v Duckett & Ors. (1993)**, the importance that a person acting in accordance with s.172 (duty to promote the success of the company) would attach to continuing it, and whether the company would be likely to ratify the wrong alleged.

Section 122(1)(g) (a winding up on the just and equitable ground) enables a shareholder to obtain the admittedly rather drastic remedy of a winding up order if he can establish oppression. He need not show oppression to him as a member; oppression to him in some other capacity normally as a director, is enough; but he must be no way at fault (contrast **section 459 CA**). In **Ebrahimi v Westbourne Galleries Ltd. (1972)**, where partners converted their business into a company on the understanding that each would share in the management of the company, a winding up order was granted when one was removed as a director. The courts will also exercise its jurisdiction under this subsection when the substratum of the company has failed **(Re German Date Coffee Co. (1882)**, and where there is deadlock in the management of the company **(Re Yenidje Tobacco Co. Ltd. (1916)**.

(b) Lopez as a director owes general statutory duties to Omnium Ltd. and he seems to be in breach of one of these duties, namely, to avoid a conflict of interest. Section 175 provides that directors should not place themselves in a position where their personal interests or duties to others will (or are likely to) conflict with their duty to the company. This duty applies in particular to those cases where the company is not a party to the transaction or proposed transaction such as in the case of third party dealings by directors which may result in a conflict of interest (e.g., the exploitation by directors of the company's property, corporate information or opportunity for their own purposes without the company's knowledge and consent). Lopez did not pass on to the board detains of his offer from Palliser in a situation where his duty and interests conflicted. As **Regal (Hastings) Ltd. v Gulliver (1942)** emphasises, a director is in breach of duty where he makes a profit out of opportunities which come to him in the execution of his office. As **Industrial Development Consultants Ltd. v Cooley (1972)** makes it clear, it is no defence to argue that the company is not being deprived of a profit; the question always being whether a director is exploiting a corporate opportunity.

Wharton seems unlikely to succeed in a statutory derivative action against Lopez as it is an instance of an incidental profit rather than a misappropriation of corporate assets. This is a breach waivable by the company, as **Regal (Hastings) Ltd.** could have been, rather than a **Cook v Deek** expropriation. Hence the majority shareholders could waive or condone Lopez's breach, thus thwarting Wharton.

The statutory remedies offer little hope either. It is unlikely even if he wants to take such drastic action that Wharton could get a winding up order under section 122(1)(g) simply for this breach and its approval. This isolated incident is unlikely to constitute conduct sufficiently oppressive of

Wharton. Section 994 of the Companies Act, enabling the courts to make orders where the affairs of the company are or have been conducted in a manner unfairly prejudicial to the interests of some part of the members (including the petitioner) or of all the members is also unlikely to be successful. The section confines the unfairly prejudicial conduct to members as members to which Wharton's complaint confirms; but he will have difficulty establishing that the breach is so prejudicial and unfair as to justify judicial intervention. In **O'Neill v Phillips (1999)**, Lord Hoffman said that 'unfairness' under section 459 will arise if either (a) the directors have abused their powers such as where they have breached the terms of the articles or are in breach of their duties; or (b) the majority have used the legal rules in a way which is contrary to good faith. The attitude of the other directors may be sufficient to suggest that there is some benefit to the company resulting from Lopez's association with Palliser.

Table of Cases

Table of Cases

Table of Cases

Table of Cases

Table of Statutes

Index